Cordially Yours,

Ann Sothern

SEVEN STEPS FOREWORD...

IRIS ADRIAN: "I first saw Ann Sothern in the make-up room at Columbia Pictures. She was astoundingly beautiful and needed little in the way of make-up, with her large eyes being especially expressive. Of course, on this first occasion, she was seated and, to my surprise, when I saw her acting for the camera in a prison sequence, she was a tiny gal in very, very high heels."

AUDREY CHRISTIE: "I never knew her as Ann Sothern, but was well acquainted with her as Harriette Lake. She starred in George Gershwin's Pulitzer Prize-winning musical, *Of Thee I Sing*, and, as well as having a small role in this, I was her understudy. Harriette had this lovely puss and a lyric soprano that soared easily when she took the high notes. My singing voice was totally different, more comedic, and I dreaded having to go on for her."

JEFF DONNELL: "We worked together on three projects, all after her serious illness. She had a great sense of humor and never played the star with me, and I think she genuinely liked me. I know I liked her and admired her talent and beauty."

FRANCES GIFFORD: "Ann Sothern was a regular gal. We were both camera nuts, and I'd often spot her at MGM taking pictures of her fellow contract players. When I worked with her on *Cry Havoc*, she couldn't have been nicer, and I remember the affection she lavished on a little dog Robert Sterling had gifted her. When I had my car accident, she wasn't well herself but still found time to give me a cheery call."

MARSHA HUNT: "We did four films together and she was thoroughly professional, knew all her lines and marks. I thought of her as having one of the most beautiful faces in Hollywood, and also being gifted with a very lovely singing voice."

IRENE MANNING: "She always was a little on the chubby side, but very lovely looking. I first saw her at MGM, where I was contracted but never worked. They were grooming her as the new Jeanette MacDonald, but 'swing' came along and those Nelson Eddy-Jeanette MacDonald movies went out of fashion. Many years later I caught up with her again in San Francisco where she was given a tribute. Time had been kind. She still had that fabulous face and glowing complexion, though she was decidedly heavier. They showed clips of her films, and I realized all over again what a fine singer she was."

JAYNE MEADOWS: "What can I remember about dear Ann Sothern, whom I consider one of the most beautiful women ever to grace the screen? She was a cherished friend: talented, beautiful, brilliant and such great fun. My late husband, Steve Allen, helped create *The Tonight Show* over 51 years ago, and he is still considered the most influential star in the history of TV. Ann was on his various shows several times, and he always spoke highly of her, too, and thought her a brilliant performer."

Cordially Yours, Ann Sothern

Colin Briggs

BearManorMedia.com

Published by:

Bear Manor Media
PO Box 71426
Albany GA 31707

www.bearmanormedia.com

Cover Design by John Teehan
Book Design by Leila Joiner

Printed in the United States of America on acid-free paper

ISBN 978-59393-060-8
ISBN 1-59393-060-7

DEDICATION...

Another Ann—Rutherford—first caught my eye when my mother took me to the movies in 1945. The supporting feature was *Two O'Clock Courage* and, in those days of continuous sessions, we stayed on to see this film for a second time. Ann played a taxi driver, and her verve and engaging personality instantly attracted me. Soon afterwards, I saw her again in *Whistling in Brooklyn* with Red Skelton, the third in a popular series of *Whistling* films. In this one she was not only beautiful, but very intrepid, engaging in a hearty physical battle with the villains at the film's conclusion. So, to an eight-year-old kid, she was Wonder Woman.

Later, I caught up with some of her earlier work—*GWTW*, *A Christmas Carol*, *Pride and Prejudice*, etc.—and continued with my admiration by seeing her in *Murder in the Music Hall*, *The Madonna's Secret*, *The Secret Life of Walter Mitty* and *Adventures of Don Juan*. Many years went by, and occasionally I'd catch her on TV in *Perry Mason* segments and *Love, American Style*. When she made a movie comeback in *They Only Kill Their Masters*, I wrote

her and received a warm letter of response. This led to our first meeting in 1975, and we had reunions almost every year for the next nineteen years.

In person she proved to be as pretty as ever, confirming a statement Kathryn Grayson once made about her being "one of the prettiest girls at MGM." She was also intelligent, witty and a totally delightful person, whom I always looked forward most eagerly to seeing again.

Ann, I thank you for being my friend and also for all the generosity you've shown me, especially in regard to your willingness and aid in the preparation of this book, which I dedicate to you.

ACKNOWLEDGMENTS...

This book would be a non-event were it not for the computer skills of my longtime good friend, Gordon Hunter. A splendid photographer, many of the candid shots contained in this tome are his work. I must also thank Graham Window for his expertise in unraveling some technical problems which ultimately enabled the transfer of the manuscript to compact disc.

Thanks must be made also to the film studio photographers, whose stills and portraits beautifully illustrate its subject, Ann Sothern.

Most importantly, I thank the following actors and actresses whose remembrances of Ann were so willingly shared: Iris Adrian, Heather Angel, Lynn Bari, Marguerite Chapman, Jan Clayton, Jeff Corey, Myra de Groot, Olivia de Havilland, Jeff Donnell, Tom Drake, Frances Gifford, Rose Hobart, Kathleen Hughes, Marsha Hunt, Ruth Hussey, Marcia Mae Jones, Patsy Kelly, Patricia Knight, Irene Manning, Jayne Meadows, Dorothy Morris, Virginia O'Brien, Don Porter, Eleanor Powell, Jane Powell, Vincent Price, Ella Raines, Jean Rogers, Connie Russell, Ann Rutherford, Alfred Sandor, Elizabeth Welch and Jane Wyatt.

My gratitude is also extended to Ann Sothern's sister, Marion Tetley; the late columnist Lee Graham; Australian TV personality Hazel Phillips; impressionist Tracy Lee; Anabel Ford, daughter of actress Anabel Shaw; and Ann's hairdresser, Sally Veronski.

A special thank you to the late Allan Herzer, an Ann Sothern devotee, who invited me to his home, where I had the opportunity to view on video many of Ann's early works. These were mostly films made in the 1930s, which I'd never seen before, plus Ann's rare TV special of "Lady in the Dark."

Other fans and collectors of Ann Sothern material who were also very helpful: Kim Altana, Wayne Ellinger, Brian Matteo, Bev Montalbano, Alan Richards, Margie Schultz, Malcolm Smith, Ron Steward and Gary Zantos. Their sharing of articles, taken from various movie publications of the '30s, '40s and '50s, provided a lot of information contained in this book. As to the writers of these articles, most of their names are mentioned within. For those who are not, this is not an oversight. Unfortunately, in some cases, the source was unknown or the article incomplete with the author's name omitted.

To all of the above I express my heartfelt thanks, for you have made this labor of love so much easier to fulfill.

PREFACE...

From out of the blue I got a letter from BearManor Media publisher Ben Ohmart stating that he had read my articles in both *Classic Images* and *Films of the Golden Age*. He then asked if I'd be interested in penning a biography on Shirley Booth. Now, I've always had the greatest respect for Miss Booth; her work in *Come Back, Little Sheba* was a *tour de force* and her tender emoting in *About Mrs. Leslie* remains a favorite performance. As much as I liked and admired Miss Booth, I had to decline his offer. Booth's theatre roots started at an early age and, to do justice to this wonderful lady, I felt that someone who had access to the New York libraries would be best for the job.

Ben then asked if there was anyone else I might be interested in writing about. As his books had a leaning toward radio personalities (Shirley Booth had done *Duffy's Tavern*), I quickly and excitedly said, "How about Ann Sothern? She was radio's *Maisie* for many years." He said yes, and this book is the result.

Ann asked me on two occasions to think about writing a book about her and, "God willing," she's pleased with the result. Another wish she had was to have a street named after her in Ketchum, Idaho. She'd donated books and scripts to the Ketchum Community Library and paid for a room to be decorated at Moritz Hospital. Being a notable figure and very well-liked in the Ketchum community, let us hope that Ann's other wish will eventually be fulfilled.

My first meeting with Ann Sothern took place in her Beverly Hills home in 1973. After seeing *Nancy Goes to Rio* in 1950, I had written her, and she, though seriously ill with hepatitis at the time, had responded. From then until our meeting there had been Christmas gifts, including an advance copy of her LP, *Sothern Exposure*, and warm, friendly, written communications.

Walking up the steps of her lovely home on Angelo Circle, I caught a glimpse of Ann putting on her glasses and peeking through a window at us. (Gordon Hunter, a photographer friend, accompanied me.) Her maid Ruby answered the door, and we were duly introduced to Ann's sister, Marion, and the film producer, Sol Grosso. When these introductions were completed, the star entered the room. Ann was very polite and friendly but, initially, a little guarded. Petite at 5'1" she was instantly recognizable and, apart from a little lipstick, wore no makeup. Garbed in a simple emerald satin shift, which set off her large, blue-grey eyes and her flawless complexion, she looked an amazingly youthful 64 years.

As the meeting progressed, I asked for one of her latest portraits, and she left the room to retrieve a portfolio. Marion then informed me, "You are in; she likes you. If she didn't, you would have gotten the Sothern freeze and, believe me, she can turn it on just like *that*"—emphasizing her remark with a snap of the fingers. Upon her return Ann remarked, "You should know, Colin, that Marion was my secretary throughout the television series years, and she brought all your letters to my attention and sent the replies." Marion had married a war hero, Lieutenant Charles Tetley, and they had a son, who made her a grandmother. Bearing no physical resemblance to Ann, she did possess an abundance of personal charm and, as a writer, she later worked for Dear Abby. Bonnie, the younger sister, was also a singer and vocalized with both the Nat King Cole group and Artie Shaw's orchestra. There was also a period when she did an interpretive dance act, but finally settled on song composition. Her first marriage ended in divorce in 1956.

THE FIRST MEETING OF AS AND COLIN BRIGGS AT HER HOME IN 1973.

Sol Grosso was co-producer of *The Killing Kind*, a film Ann had just completed, and we were invited to the premiere. Unfortunately, we had to decline as we would be in New York at the time. Kissing me goodbye, Ann asked me to call her before leaving for the east coast, as she would provide me with a list of contacts in the various cities we planned to visit. Ann also asked Marion to drive us to the mansion she had owned and lived in during the MGM and TV star years.

When I called Ann later that week, she invited us over for the evening. Totally relaxed in a long white robe, she had a tape recorder on display. She had scored a tremendous success in *Mame*, and I asked if she had a recording of her songs from the show. Replying affirmatively, she then played these songs onto the ready tape recorder. Ann revealed how she kept tapes of all of her stage plays. "It makes it so much easier to relearn them if a repeat season of any of them comes up," she said. Listening to *Mame* was a revelation, and it was easy to understand why both the public and critics alike had taken this Auntie Mame to their hearts. Her heartfelt rendering of "If He Walked Into My Life," in particular, is second to none.

She then asked me to sing something for her. Sifting through her music, I spotted "The Impossible Dream," which I felt was more than appropriate for the occasion. As for me, having Ann Sothern as an accompanist was indeed a dream come true. Ann was very complimentary, as was Ruby, who appeared with snacks and coffee. Ann then played and sang very wistfully and with great feeling, a song she had written called "Are You a Good Boy?," which was to be the title song for her newest film, but the title *The Killing Kind* was considered to be more sellable. The combination of her lovely voice and wistful expression in her soulful eyes made the experience a very emotional one.

At Ann's home, on the occasion of the second visit, I had brought along some stills from her films. Being my first visit to Hollywood I went mad and bought hundreds of stills from favorite films. Ann asked who were the other stars I liked. Off the top of my head I mentioned Marsha Hunt, Olivia de Havilland, Ann Rutherford, Marjorie Reynolds and Julie Bishop. She said, "None of those girls work now," to which I replied, "Marsha does occasional TV and she had been in Australia for the play *The Little Hut*." Looking at the stills, she came across one from *Panama Hattie* and said a little acidly, "There's your friend, Marsha! Is she married?" I told Ann that she was indeed married, and also mentioned her recent fall and injured back. Ann then said a certain doctor at MGM was a wizard at fixing back ailments and to pass on his name to Marsha. This I did and Marsha's response was a bit of a surprise. "How odd, I knew him at MGM, too, but he's dead and has been for some time."

The warmer side of Ann's nature surfaced again as she marked our itinerary with places and restaurants which should not be missed; Brennans in New Orleans was a must for eggs benedict, and she said, "Please call Lila Lee and my sister Bonnie in New York City." As we left her home, she kissed us both and made us promise to call her when we returned to Los Angeles for our connecting flight home to Australia. The entire vacation was fabulous and meeting Ann, Marsha Hunt and Andrea King in Hollywood was an unbelievable experience to cherish forever.

Over the years there were many more memorable visits with this most gracious lady. Musical highlights included hearing the recordings of operatic arias that she sang at MGM in the early 1940s, accompanied by Earl Brent. The selections included "One Fine Day," "Love and Music," and "Oh, My Beloved Father"; her playing and singing of the songs she had written for *The Duchess of Pasadena*, a play in which she starred; and hearing the duets sung at the piano with her granddaughter Heidi.

During one of our visits, we were lunching at home with Ann, and we were treated to a vision of culinary splendor, showing Ann's sense of perfection as a decorator and gourmet. Our hostess was dressed in a white gown with a blue and salmon-pink pattern. The dining table was set with both salmon-pink cloth and napkins. After the main course, which featured salmon, Ann brought forth a low-calorie dessert she had prepared. Served in individual salmon-pink bowls, it turned out to be a nonfat mousse, strawberry-flavored but salmon pink in color. It was delicious and, with her daughter Tisha's arrival, Ann asked her to partake of the sweet. Although Ann assured her it had almost zero calories, Tisha declined, despite the fact that she was quite willowy and certainly not needing to be diet-conscious.

During one visit she drove us in her Rolls-Royce to a Marina Del Rey restaurant for lunch. Noticing I had contracted a heavy cold, she immediately made an appointment with her own doctor saying, "You must not fly home with a head cold."

There were generous invitations to fly us to Seattle, where she was starring in a play, to her granddaughter's wedding (at St. Paul the Apostle Church), and to an art exhibition in Los Angeles. Regretfully, we were committed elsewhere and were unable to accept, but were most certainly honored to be asked.

During a Chicago radio interview she mentioned me as "an Australian boy who knows more about me than anyone, including myself, and should write a book." My last contact with her was a telephone call two years before her death, when she requested that I do write the book.

Ann said in a 1989 interview with Leonard Maltin, "The public has been wonderful to me. I can't thank the public enough."

I thank you, Ann, for your wonderful screen persona and for the true friendship I found with the real you.

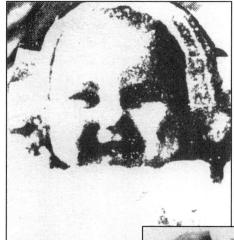

ANN (HARRIETTE LAKE), 1909

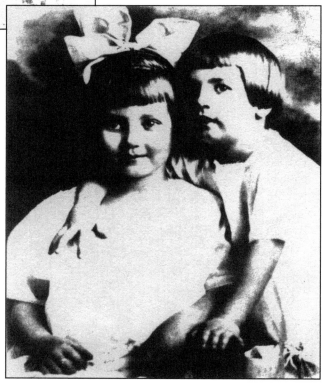

ANN AND SISTER MARION, 1914

Chapter One: "Harriette"

Ann Sothern was born Harriette Arlene Lake in Valley City, North Dakota, on January 22, 1909. Her parents were the Copenhagen-born concert singer, pianist and voice teacher, Annette (Yde) Lake and Walter J. Lake, a meat salesman and one-time frustrated actor. The family lineage included her maternal grandfather, Hans Nilson, a Dutch violinist, while her paternal grandfather was Simon Lake, inventor of The Argonaut (1897), the first successful submarine. "My mother had a beautiful dramatic soprano voice and both my sisters and I owe her musical knowledge for our tutelage in harmony and counterpoint," Ann said later.

Though Valley City is her birthplace she said, "My mother was on a singing tour and the only reason Valley City can claim to be my birthplace is that it had the closest hospital. You see, I arrived much earlier than expected." Her sisters, Marion, eighteen months younger, and Bonnie, seven years her junior, were tutored by their mother in singing, dancing and piano. She also arranged for Harriette to begin violin lessons at an early age. Their initial formal education took place in Waterloo, Iowa. She never liked the name Harriette and claimed, "It was inflicted on me because my father's very best friend was named Harry."

They moved to Minneapolis, Minnesota, where her father obtained work as a produce broker. Meanwhile, her mother continued with her concert engagements and, as a result, was traveling all over the country. When Harriette was old enough to join her, she did. Marion told me, "Ann and I were always very close and Mother had us do 'a sister act' when we were young kids. This was before I started school so I guess Ann was nearly six and I was four. I was

not in *The Show of Shows* with her. That was Marion Byron...just a coincidence that we had the same first name."

The two siblings attended Minneapolis public schools, as would their sister Bonnie. Soon after Bonnie's birth their parents separated. Walter Lake was
very much a practical and rather hard-headed businessman. Although he had
youthful acting aspirations, these were cast aside with maturity and the re-
sponsibility of supporting a family. His wife Annette, with her artistic family
background, was always concerned with music, singing and eventual fame, if
not for herself, then for her three daughters. Their father would continue to
pay for the girls' education and would support Harriette throughout her
teenage years. However, as youngsters, both Marion and Harriette would
miss the presence of their father. Their maternal grandmother, Mrs. Nilson,
would be the most permanent presence in their lives.

Attending Minneapolis Central High, Harriette's excellent musical prowess included a lovely lyric soprano voice, as well as her accomplished violin
and piano playing. At an early age she also demonstrated great skill with musical composition. Teaching her at
the McPhail School of Music was
Sophie Skjerdtingstad-Dahl and
Countess Moroztya. When not on
tour, her mother was also employed
there. Mastering Beethoven and
Brahms by the time she was eleven,
Harriette's composition, "Study in B,"
was performed professionally by the
Minneapolis Symphony Orchestra
when she was thirteen. Later, she
was sent to Detroit to play her own
compositions at the National Music
Supervisors Conference. These won
her three prizes, three years in a row.
These awards were "The Minneapolis Journal Prize for Piano Competition"—City Final, 1924 (1st)—1925
(2nd) and 1926 (1st). She also composed works for the violin and was

CENTRAL HIGH '26
MINNEAPOLIS, MINNESOTA

☐☐☐   ☐☐☐☐☐☐
Latin Club; French Club; Girls' Club; Press
Club; news staff; comedy concert; music con-
test winner.
*"Emotion is the summit of existence; music is
the summit of emotion; art the pathway to
God."*

praised for her contributions to chamber music. Harriette graduated from Central High in 1926.

HARRIETTE LAKE AT THE
UNIVERSITY OF WASHINGTON

With her mother's decision to move with her two younger daughters to Los Angeles, Harriette joined her father in Seattle, Washington. The Lakes were finally divorced in 1927 and Annette found work initially as a vocal coach at Warner Bros. Walter now had his own import-export company and his dealings with the stock market had a decided influence on his now-reconciled daughter. Attending the University of Washington in 1928 was a decision that greatly pleased her academically-minded father. This choice was made initially to further her musical studies, but her dislike of mathematics caused problems at home. The announcement that she would be seeking a career in the theatre caused another estrangement from her father. He blamed the entertainment industry for his marital breakup and cited his wife's career ambitions as the reason he walked out on them. This bitterness now escalated into an uncompromising resolution and he ceased all support payments for Harriette.

With no finances to continue at the university, she left Seattle and journeyed south to join her mother and sisters in Hollywood. These were lean times for Mrs. Lake and her three daughters, and Harriette realized she'd have to be the breadwinner. Mrs. Lakes' duties in Hollywood had become fewer and fewer as the silent star pupils to whom she was teaching diction and vocal technique were being replaced by artists with theatre experience and trained voices. Harriette, at her mother's prodding, began the rounds of studio casting offices. At this time she had no desire to be in films but, as they needed the money, thought of it as a temporary stop gap to her goal as a singer. An encounter with a Minneapolis friend, William Koenig, a studio

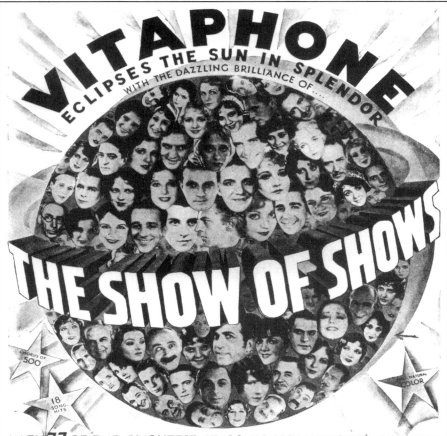

VITAPHONE

ECLIPSES THE SUN IN SPLENDOR

WITH THE DAZZLING BRILLIANCE OF....

THE SHOW OF SHOWS

CHORUS OF 500

18 SONG HITS

NATURAL COLOR

WITH 77 OF THE BRIGHTEST STARS IN HOLLYWOOD'S HEAVEN

Since their first startling introduction of *Vitaphone* Warner Bros. have gradually massed wonder upon wonder until it seemed that talking picture progress had surely reached its peak.

But now suddenly at a single stride *Vitaphone* comes forward with an achievement so immeasurably superior to any that have gone before, that the history of screen development must be completely rewritten and revised.

"THE SHOW OF SHOWS" is a connoisseur's collection of the supreme examples of almost every form of stage and screen entertainment.

Only *Vitaphone* could assemble the names of John Barrymore, Richard Barthelmess, Beatrice Lillie, Ted Lewis, Georges Carpentier, Irene Bordoni, Dolores Costello, and enough more for 20 average pictures, all

"Vitaphone" is the registered trade mark of the Vitaphone Corporation. Color scenes by the Technicolor Process

on one prodigious program.

And you'll remember as long as you live such sensational features as the Florodora Sextet composed of headline screen stars — the Sister Number with eight sets of celebrated screen-star sisters—the stupendous Lady Luck finale with a chorus of 300 and fifteen specialty "acts."

If you could see only one motion picture this season, that picture should be "The Show of Shows." Don't dare miss it—for·you may never look upon its like again!

The Show of Shows (Warner Bros., 1929)

manager at Warner Bros., led to a
screen test there. She passed and
joined the studio stock company
with a contract paying $75 a week.

A petite 5'1", the blue-grey-eyed
Harriette obtained her first film job
because Warners was looking for a
tiny gal to play sister to an even ti-
nier one, actress Marion (Peanuts)
Byron. Playing an Italian, she dark-
ened her auburn hair to brunette.
The film was the all-star-revue-type
extravaganza, *The Show of Shows*
(1929), boasting some two-color
Technicolor sequences. The Byron
"Sisters" were in the production
number "Meet My Sister," where a
number of real or reel sisters were
featured: Loretta Young and Sally

HARRIETTE LAKE AT
WARNER BROS., 1929

Blane, Helene and Dolores Costello and Sally O'Neill and Nell O'Day. The
final result was only mildly successful and Harriette became very despondent
just sitting around doing nothing. Her debut film's cast boasted a host of talent and the likable Harriette became a lifelong friend to Lila Lee, and Loretta
Young also instantly warmed to the charms of the fledgling performer. Her
next two films were further discouragements. *Hearts in Exile* (1929) starred
Dolores Costello and Grant Withers, while Harriette was merely an unbilled
extra. Following this came the Warners' comedy *Hold Everything* (1930), starring Joe E. Brown, in which she had a brief moment with Bert Roach. Marion
Byron had befriended her during the *Show of Shows* shoot and she found a
spot for her in *Song of the West* (Warners, 1930). Marion also gave her advice
on make-up and hairstyles and in this, her final Warners contract film, she
photographs much more pleasingly.

Ivan Kahn, who took an interest in new faces for films, thought she had
possibilities, became her agent and organized a screen test at MGM. Once
again she was signed, but dejection soon set in as most of her time there was
spent posing for hundreds of stills. These were often used for hosiery and

HARRIETTE LAKE, VIVIENNE SEGAL AND MARION BYRON IN
SONG OF THE WEST (WARNER BROS., 1930)

HARRIETTE LAKE IN SWING, JOE E. BROWN (CENTER) AND
BERT ROACH IN *HOLD EVERYTHING* (WARNER BROS., 1929)

beauty advertisements, and her presence was also required at premieres of MGM releases. In *Doughboys* (1930), starring Buster Keaton, she made a scant appearance falling off a motorcycle. She was also seen in *Free and Easy* (1930), again a Buster Keaton comedy, but in this one she was just one of the girls in a musical number. She described MGM producer Paul Bern, who tried unsuccessfully to help her career at MGM, as a genuine person. After providing the voice of a barking dog in one of the Pete Smith comedy short subjects, her dreams of film stardom evaporated.

All the love in the world
To my darling Mama!

SIX MONTHS AT MGM, AS POSED AND POSED FOR STILL PICTURES. IT WOULD BE THREE YEARS BEFORE SHE WOULD APPEAR IN FRONT OF A MOVIE CAMERA.

Her boyfriend at the time was the brother of Fanny Brice. Fanny was greatly impressed with Harriette's singing voice, describing it as "pure and lovely, with an incredibly sweet top C." She'd just finished *Whoopee!,* an Eddie Cantor film for United Artists (1930). Virginia Bruce, Betty Grable and Paulette Goddard were all showgirls in this Samuel Goldwyn extravaganza. Harriette appeared in a musical number with western costuming. Florenz Ziegfeld and his manager, Stanley Sharpe, first noticed Harriette at Malibu Beach, where they were sunning and she was swimming. Asking her if she could sing, she replied affirmatively and mentioned that she was in Ziegfeld's film version of *Whoopee!* At a cast party, Fanny Brice had her sing, as she felt her mentor Florenz Ziegfeld, who was also present, would be impressed. He was, and found a place for her in *Smiles,* a new Broadway musical he was producing with Marilyn Miller starring.

The friendship with Paul Bern was beneficial in obtaining a release from her MGM contract. Also, her agent, Ivan Kahn, who had such faith in his client, released her from his pact as well. Quitting Hollywood, which had brought her such disillusionment, she arrived with her mother for rehearsals in New York. In addition to Marilyn Miller, *Smiles* starred the dance team of Fred and Adele Astaire, with whom Harriette found empathy. A Minneapolis acquaintance, the blonde and beautiful Virginia Bruce, was one of the show-girls. Miss Bruce, or Briggs as she was known in Minneapolis, was also a pianist of note and their paths would cross again and again. She, like Harriette, had been seen briefly in *Whoopee!* This was Harriette's first visit to New York and she was very nervous, even though her mother was there to offer support. Virtually inexperienced as a stage performer, her confusion was noticed by cast member Tom Howard, who took her under his wing and taught her all the technical terms she needed to know. Her role as Glory was not large but she did have two songs, plus a little solo work in "Dance Wedding." *Smiles* had a two-week tryout in Boston and its Vincent Youmans score was praised. Harriette Lake was also singled out, with the *Boston Post* review stating, "H.L.

CLIFF EDWARDS, HARRIETTE LAKE AND SALLY EILERS
IN *DOUGHBOYS* (MGM, 1930)

who sings 'Blue Bowery' and 'More than Ever' is a welcome newcomer to the Ziegfeld stage gallery." *The Boston Daily Record* reported, "It's a good enough score with here and there a bit of blues sung by the quite decorative H.L." She was also among others selected for mention in the *Boston Daily Globe*.

Fred Astaire had given her much encouragement during their rehearsals, which were held on the roof at the New Amsterdam Theater. They had dated too when he learned her mother had returned to Los Angeles. Knowing she'd be lonely, he escorted her to many social events and parties with Adele also in the car that transported them. Discovering her musical talent also included piano, in which he also indulged, they often enjoyed playing duets.

HARRIETTE LAKE IN
FREE AND EASY (MGM, 1930)

Ann remembered him bringing the fifteen-year-old Larry Adler to rehearsals. Adler, who would later become a world famous harmonica player, then joined the company of *Smiles*. In his autobiography, *It Ain't Necessarily So*, Larry Adler recalled, "Harriette's 'Blue Bowery' was a hit in Boston causing friction with star Marilyn Miller who then told Ziegfeld she wanted Miss Lake out of the show." "Dance Wedding" had originally been a solo for Harriette, but it was given to other cast members as well, which reduced her participation greatly. When MGM filmed *Till the Clouds Roll By* (1946), with Judy Garland emulating Marilyn Miller, an incident similar to the one experienced by Harriette was enacted by Lucille Bremer. Despite her excellent press notices she lost a second solo, again to the star, and Fred Astaire was there to comfort her and allay her feelings of doubt and humiliation. Ann told reporter Adele Whitely Fletcher, "But for Freddie's assurance I easily might have gone to pieces. He managed to make me feel it was all in the

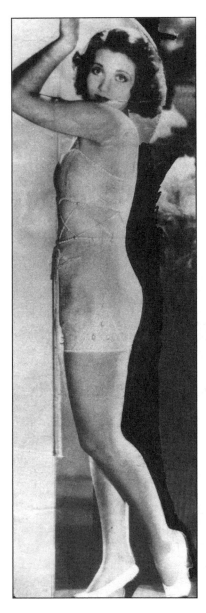

HARRIETTE LAKE
IN *FOOTLIGHT PARADE*
(WARNER BROS., 1932)

game and it would be very silly and foolish to allow myself to be humiliated by any part of it. He helped me keep my perspective and remember that there were many reasons why numbers were taken away from people and that many of them had nothing to do with the performer's ability at all." *Smiles* opened in New York on November 18, 1930, and Marilyn Miller had her way: Harriette Lake was not in it.

Composer Walter Donaldson introduced her to Larry Schwab (of Schwab & Mandel), and her unemployment was short lived. With the enthusiastic notices she'd received for *Smiles,* this meeting led to an audition for Richard Rodgers. *America's Sweetheart* was the show and, following a week's tryout in Pittsburgh, Harriette Lake made her Broadway debut (1931). According to Jan Clayton, who, with Samuel Marx, co-wrote *Bewitched, Bothered and Bedevilled*, a dual biography of Rodgers and Larry Hart, Richard Rodgers did not want her in the show. Clayton said, "He found her voice small and nasal but producer Larry Schwab went to bat for her." Asked for recollections of the team, Harriette [Ann] said, "I remember Richard Rodgers scared me to death. He was a very stern man, very very stern. I auditioned but it seems Rodgers did not want me. It was Larry Schwab who absolutely insisted that I be in the play. Laurence Schwab and Frank Mandel were the producers. Larry Schwab thought I'd be divine in the part and I got it." In his autobiography, *Musical Stages,*

Richard Rodgers commented, "For the female lead we auditioned a number of actresses and then settled on a tiny, round-faced blonde [sic] with an oddly appealing nasal voice."

Time magazine's review of *America's Sweetheart* gave a lovely synthesis of Harriette: "one part Ginger Rogers, one part Ethel Merman," saying she was "Pleasantly healthy and unmannered with a jolly smile and agreeable voice." The *New York Times* said, "Jack Whiting of the blonde hair and baritone voice and Harriette Lake are a personable pair of musical comedy bandmasters. 'I've Got Five Dollars' is far more romantic than it sounds. It is the pet melody of Jack Whiting and H.L. the inevitable love interest." *Variety* was more negative. "H.L. is a mild mannered pleasing morsel, if void of any particular animation," but *Billboard* raved, "The most important thing is to introduce one newcomer who is sure to be seen and heard many times in the future. That charming person is Harriette Lake...H.L. is simply grand." Virginia Bruce was also in the cast, as was comedienne Inez Courtney, who would also reappear in Ann's film future. In one light moment of conversation with me, Ann sang a few bars of "I've Got Five Dollars." Very wryly she said, "My worst memory of that show was being doused in a fountain and having a wet fanny every performance for over four months. Luckily, intermission gave me time to dry off before Act 2." This memory is also included in *Bewitched, Bothered and Bedevilled.*

Her next Broadway show was *Everybody's Welcome* (1931), adapted from *Up Pops the Devil.* Oscar Shaw was her leading man and the cast also included Roy Roberts, Ann Pennington and the Dorsey Bros. Orchestra. By this time she was engaged to their trumpet player, Mickey Bloom, who unfortunately had a roving eye, and this soon led to a breakup. Although the romance department was not progressing well, otherwise things were doing better. *Billboard* said, "H.L....was adequate in her lines though there is nothing to rave about her singing ability; but then there is no denying the fact that she is one of the most beautiful ingenues hereabouts." *Variety* said, "H.L. is both personable and capable. Hers is no strong voice but she plays smoothly opposite [Oscar] Shaw and impresses as sincere and vigorous."

I had the great pleasure of seeing Elizabeth Welch when she was doing her one-woman show in Sydney, Australia. Then in her eighties, she was singing up a storm and delighting audiences with her witty repartee. During her act she mentioned being in *Everybody's Welcome,* which had introduced the

HARRIETTE LAKE IN *BROADWAY THROUGH A KEYHOLE* (20TH CENTURY-UNITED ARTISTS, 1933)

classic Herman Hupfield song "As Time Goes By." Meeting her afterwards, she chortled on about "Everybody's Welcome—but nobody came." When asked about Harriette Lake, she said, "Harriette became Ann Sothern, you know. Nice gal, with one of those true voices, perfect pitch. 'As Time Goes By,' with a slightly different lyric, was not a hit back then. The show closed just short of a five-month run and Harriette then returned to Hollywood."

Ivan Kahn, still her agent, got her a stint in *Footlight Parade* (1933), shot at Warner Bros. in 1932, starring James Cagney, Ruby Keeler and Dick Powell. She is one of the Busby Berkeley girls in the "By a Waterfall" number. Also in this sequence was Jean Rogers, who always found Harriette remote whenever their paths crossed years later. "She was probably afraid I'd talk about our days in the chorus with *Footlight Parade*," Jean said. While working at Warners she met the head of their sound department, Lou Silvers. He took a liking to her and so admired her singing that he told her, "You know music and you can sing. All you've got to know is how to sing for pictures and I'm going to see that you learn." There were lots of lessons with microphone technique but, just when she was ready for tests, the stage beckoned again.

Of Thee I Sing was a huge Broadway hit and the national tour was being cast. Oscar Shaw was signed and at his suggestion Harriette Lake was offered the co-lead. The Pulitzer Prize-winning show opened in Detroit (1932) and toured for seven months. Audrey Christie, who was Harriett's understudy and also had a small role in the production, later told me, "Harriette had this gorgeous puss and a most ingratiating manner. When she became ill, I dreaded going on for her. Her pure soprano just soared to the top notes of Gershwin's score while my vocal ability was more rough and ready."

The longest run of the tour was in Chicago where Roger Pryor, a band-leader, was moonlighting as an actor in *Blessed Event*. When introduced, there was an immediate mutual attraction but, as he had a wife, Priscilla, conventions prevailed. Following the San Francisco season, the tour of *Of Thee I Sing* concluded and Harriette returned to Chicago for a rest and to visit her mother. Her notices for the tour had all been excellent. *The San Francisco Chronicle* was especially exuberant: "Harriette Lake is slim and blonde, a graceful dancer and an excellent singer." Needing a replacement for Lois Moran, the original Broadway lead, the producers had the stage man-ager, Max Siegal, contact Harriette with a firm offer to take over. Naturally, she accepted and her opening night on Broadway was June 3, 1933. Unfortu-nately, New York was in the midst of an unbearable heat wave and bad busi-ness caused the show to close six nights later. One of Harriette's closest woman friends in New York was Marilyn Hare of the vaudeville team "Eddie & Marilyn." Marilyn's influence was responsible for Harriette adopting softer make-up and the blonde hair change. She had pointed out that Harriette's features, especially her eyes, were similar to those of Virginia Bruce, dubbing her a pint-size Virginia. Reading of Virginia's recent marriage to John Gilbert and her emergence as a Hollywood actress, Harriette decided to give the West coast another try.

The faithful Ivan Kahn found her a spot in a United Artists feature, *Broadway Thru a Keyhole* (1933), starring Russ Columbo and Constance Cummings. A blonde Lucille Ball was seen with Harriette in a brief beach scene. Lucille had some lines, but H.L. did not get to speak. Harriette and Lucille formed a friendship then that lasted throughout their lifetimes.

Columbia needed a Scandinavian-type who could sing for a little musical called *Lets Fall in Love*. Her Warners mentor Lou Silvers' words of praise reached the ears of mogul Harry Cohn, who tested and eventually signed her.

With this, her first leading role in a movie, it meant the exit of Harriette Lake and the entry of Ann Sothern.

SINGING
"LOVE IS LOVE EVERYWHERE"
IN *LET'S FALL IN LOVE*
(COLUMBIA, 1934)

WITH EDMUND LOWE
IN *LET'S FALL IN LOVE*
(COLUMBIA, 1934)

ONE OF ANN'S FIRST
COLUMBIA PORTRAITS, FOR
LET'S FALL IN LOVE (1934)

Chapter Two: "Ann"

Harry Cohn had caught her performance in *Of Thee I Sing* when it played the Biltmore in Los Angeles. When he offered her the role in *Let's Fall in Love* he was insistent on a name change. There are conflicting reports as to how the name Ann Sothern was chosen. The first stated that a Paramount starlet, Mary Mason, was given that name by producer Charles R. Rogers. When illness forced her to drop out of the Paramount film which was set to launch her, she became Mary Mason again. Then Harry Cohn grabbed the name Ann Sothern for his newest leading lady. On the American Movie Classics cable channel Ann stated in 1987, "Harry Cohn said, well you can't have the name of Lake as there are too many Lakes. There's Arthur Lake, Veronica Lake, Florence Lake, Alice Lake…too many Lakes! He made out a list and called me in. On the list there were a lot of names there. Having been a good student of Shakespeare and that sort of thing, the name E. E. Sothern was there. I admired him because he was a very fine Shakespearean actor, so I took Sothern. My mother's name was Annette so I chose Ann. And that is how I became Ann Sothern." (An error on Ann's part: In 1933 Veronica Lake was 14-year-old Constance Ockleman, who worked firstly as Constance Keane, becoming Veronica Lake in 1941 for the film *I Wanted Wings*.)

Let's Fall in Love starred Edmund Lowe and he and Ann proved to be an excellent romantic team. She sang the title song and "Love is Love Everywhere," both written by Harold Arlen and Ted Koehler. Sound expert and good friend Lou Silvers had a sneak preview of the finished product and suggested some redubbing of her songs. Ann remained grateful to Lou and said, "He fought to have parts of my songs re-recorded for the soundtrack."

WITH LANNY ROSS IN *MELODY IN SPRING* (PARAMOUNT, 1934)

Silvers was quoted as saying, "They might have gotten by, but if they had they would not have helped a newcomer." When the film was publicly previewed, a highly satisfied Harry Cohn signed Ann to a multi-picture contract. Her reviews were positive, with *The New York Times* praising her "personal charm" and "pretty voice." The film would be re-released years later as *Scarlet Blonde*, with Ann getting top billing over the title.

Oddly, her second film was a loan out to Paramount, who having previously spent time and money publicizing the name Ann Sothern could now take advantage of it. The movie was *Melody in Spring* (1934), and top cast were Charles Ruggles and Mary Boland, who played Ann's parents. Lanny Ross, a popular radio singer, had the romantic lead opposite Ann. For some unknown reason the lovely score by Harlan Thompson and Lewis Gersler was solo sung by Ross. Ann never sang a note, though the storyline, with its Swiss setting, cried out for a duet. Once again the reviews were good, with both the *New York Times* and *Variety* giving her favorable mention.

CHARLES RUGGLES, MARY BOLAND, LANNY ROSS AND AS IN *MELODY IN SPRING* (PARAMOUNT, 1934)

The Hell Cat, a Columbia programmer, cast her as a spitfire heiress with dark hair. With a battling newspaper reporter, Robert Armstrong, as her opponent, the *New York Times* thought it "unoriginal." *Variety* summarized the routine storyline: "Armstrong is a tough newspaper mug. He covers a society assignment and when Ann Sothern socks him, he socks her back. She masquerades as another person, gets a job on his paper, and vamps him." The film did boast good performances from both J. Carrol Naish and Ann, who plays half her screen time as a blonde. Noted *The New York Times*, "Miss Sothern is equally attractive as blonde or brunette."

Keeping her busy, Columbia immediately put her in another second feature, *Blind Date*. A neatly turned film, it was directed by Roy William Neill. With a "Kitty Foyle"-type character to portray, *Variety* found "her shop girl very irritating." However, most other reviews were

MINNA GOMBELL, ROBERT ARMSTRONG AND AS IN *THE HELL CAT* (COLUMBIA, 1934)

high in their praise for the film, its direction and the believable family scenes. Mickey Rooney was Ann's young brother; Joan Gale (from *Melody in Spring*), her sister; mother was the reliable Jane Darwell and father, Spencer Charters. Ann had to choose between wealthy Neil Hamilton and garage owner Paul Kelly in the romance department. Way ahead of its time, she ends up with

WITH PAUL KELLY IN *BLIND DATE* (COLUMBIA, 1934)

Hamilton. Wrote *Picture Show,* "The financial troubles of the family are amusingly shown and provide just enough relief from the charming love scenes between Ann Sothern and Neil Hamilton, whose worlds are apart but whose hearts are one." Having worked particularly hard with this last role and winning the praise of her director, her aspirations for an "A" feature seemed attainable.

WITH STUART ERWIN IN *THE PARTY'S OVER* (COLUMBIA, 1934)

This was not to be, for *The Party's Over* with Stuart Erwin, another minor comedy, was her next assignment at Columbia. Walter Lang directed it well enough and it had a supporting cast of skilled comedians, Chick Chandler, Patsy Kelly, Catherine Doucet and Arline Judge, with Ann in a more serious vein as Erwin's love interest. Patsy Kelly remembered, when I asked her about this film, that "It was a quickie and we were all hired as we were workhorses and knew our way around a comedy scene. Ann [played] Erwin's secretary, and was totally professional and got on well with all the character ladies in the cast."

Her wish for a major feature came when she was borrowed by Samuel Goldwyn for *Kid Millions* (1934). Eddie Cantor was the star and Ann, second billed, played the ingenue lead opposite newcomer George Murphy. Ethel Merman was also top cast and the two women hit it off right away. Goldwyn Girls Lucille Ball and Lynne Carver would also be befriended by Ann. *The*

New York Times felt that "Ann Sothern and George Murphy form a pleasant romantic team," and together they sang "Your Head on My Shoulder," which showcased Ann's lovely soprano to advantage. With a deep South setting on a ship's deck and costumed along with all the Goldwyn Girls in crinolines, Ann never looked lovelier. A full screen close-up of her face at the number's conclusion also rated critical approval. "Mandy," an Irving Berlin standard, was sung by the whole cast with Ann very glamorously clad in top hat and lame' tails. The Nicholas Brothers were also featured prominently in this production number. Weirdly though, the Murphy and Sothern characters disappear 2/3rds through the footage, missing out on the Technicolor finale.

At this time, she stated: "I've always been very definite. I've always done the things I wanted to do. I've always believed that an indefinite woman is a failure before she ever begins." This philosophy was shared by her friend Lucille Ball, whom Ann helped decorate an apartment. Ann later recalled for *People Magazine,* "When I first knew her she had a little apartment some

Kid Millions (United Artists, 1935)

EDDIE CANTOR, GEORGE MURPHY
AND AS IN *KID MILLIONS*
(UNITED ARTISTS, 1935)

funny place somewhere and she asked me to come over and help get it together. I said, 'Lucy, we need to get some curtains,' to which she replied, 'I just can't afford it.' I knew damn well she could, so I just went out and bought her some. She always said I was the most extravagant person she ever knew."

George Murphy had some amusing recollections of Ann, especially in regard to her costume for their duet, "Your Head on My Shoulder." In his autobiography, *Say ... Didn't You Used to be George Murphy?*, he recalled: "Annie was wearing a big circular bouffant skirt and when I put my arm around her, the other side of her hoop would fly up. So a man was assigned to hold it down. Because of the skirt she couldn't see her feet so another man was assigned to guide her. A third man was steering my feet and two more were holding special lights to accommodate the cameraman."

Her friend Walter Donaldson, the composer of "Your Head on My Shoulder," had also written songs for *Whoopee!* He reminded Ann of the time she had tried out for a role in *Waltz Dream.* He thought the part of a French girl who played the violin and sang would be a "shoo-in" for her. Paramount made the Oscar Strauss operetta as *The Smiling Lieutenant,* with the role eventually played by their contract player Claudette Colbert. The star was

FOLIES BERGERE
(UNITED ARTISTS/FOX, 1935)

WITH MAURICE CHEVALIER IN *FOLIES BERGERE*
(UNITED ARTISTS/FOX, 1935) REMADE LATER AS
THAT NIGHT IN RIO AND *ON THE RIVIERA*

Maurice Chevalier and he remembered the test she had made and liked what he saw of the petite, then-redhead.

His latest film, *Folies Bergere*, needed two leading ladies and Ann was selected to be his song-and-dance partner. Portraying two characters, a Folies Bergere entertainer and a Baron, Chevalier excelled in this 20th Century-United Artists musical confection. Merle Oberon, playing the Baron's wife, was the second leading lady. The film was shot in late 1934 and Miss Oberon recalled how Ann was very close to her mother and sisters. When the company stopped shooting for Christmas, she was very excited about spending Christmas Day with her family.

Opening in 1935, *Folies Bergere* was a resounding success. Directed by Roy Del Ruth, who also helmed a French version simultaneously, it won choreographer Dave Gould an Academy Award for his staging of "Singing a Happy Song," which cost $100,000, and featured the singing and dancing of Maurice and Ann. Joined by a large chorus, the two stars perform on a tier of three gigantic straw hats standing 48 feet high. Both this and "Rhythm of the

WITH JOHN BUCKLER IN
EIGHT BELLS (COLUMBIA, 1935)

Raindrops," which Ann again duetted with Chevalier, was given Busby Berkeley-style presentation. Dave Gould's Oscar win also included recognition of his staging of "I've Got a Feeling You're Foolin'," from *Broadway Melody of 1936*. As for Ann's work in the snappy musical, *The New York Times* commented, "As the cabaret grisette, Miss Sothern displays a neat and captivating talent for the song and dance," while *Variety* thought her singing and dancing made "a definite sock impression." In the years ahead the film would be remade as *That Night in Rio*, with Don Ameche, and *On the Riviera,* with Danny Kaye. Carmen Miranda and Corinne Calvet, respectively, essayed the role Ann originated.

At this time Ann was seriously dating Roger Pryor, who was currently seeking a divorce.

Meanwhile, Columbia cast her in *Eight Bells* (1935), which, by coincidence, had her playing the role for which she had originally been screen-tested there. Based on a play by Percy C. Mandley, it was made acceptable by the capable direction of Roy William Neill, whom Ann respected. Her leading man was Ralph Bellamy and they got along "just fine," as Ann told me. Still, the film was very much a second feature and was not given a major press release. *Photoplay* gave it a brief mention: "Just medium well done, as they say in the better restaurants. But you'll find it worth an evening's entertainment."

RKO then borrowed her for *Hooray for Love* (1935), a musical with catchy songs by Dorothy Fields and Jimmy McHugh. Ann sang "I'm in Love All Over Again," which proved to be a popular hit, and then rendered a lovely wistful version of "You're an Angel." She was also in the group numbers "Palsy Walsy" and "Hooray for Love." With guest appearances from Fats Waller, ballerina Maria Gambarelli, Bill Robinson and Jeni Le Gon, it boasted good entertainment. Ann's leading man was Gene Raymond, with whom it has been said she didn't get along. In this scenario it works well as they battle throughout before love takes over. There's good support, too, from Thurston Hall, as her father, and Georgia Caine, as his wealthy pursuer. Most of the reviews were negative, but *Photoplay* thought "Ann looks like a million and acts when she gets the chance," and *Motion Picture* pointed out that "Ann's singing was better than ever and the hit song 'I'm in Love All Over Again' will long outlive the picture."

Dissatisfaction caused Ann to comment after *Hooray for Love* was reviewed, "Give me parts I can get my teeth into. I'd trade a 'pretty girl' role any day of the week for that of an old hag, if the hag was a real character. Right now I stand a good chance of being a 'looker type.' I don't want that."

After seething inside and appearing outwardly calm for so long, she could stand Columbia's apathy no longer. Going to the powers that be, she asked for better parts and major scripts. To appease her they signed Roger Pryor to be her romantic lead in *The Girl Friend* (1935). Apart from his dating of Carole Lombard, they'd been seeing each other intermittently and although Ann too would date others, including Gene Raymond, it was Roger

GEORGIA KANE, THURSTON HALL AND AS IN
HOORAY FOR LOVE (RKO, 1935)

AS, JACK HALEY AND HER FIRST
HUSBAND, ROGER PRYOR, IN
THE GIRLFRIEND (COLUMBIA, 1935)

who remained foremost in her thoughts. Jack Haley was also top cast in the "putting on a show in the barn" musical, and he had the most to do. Ann did get to sing two songs in the "Napoleon" musical-within-a-musical: "Two Together," a particularly melodic piece, and the other, a duet with Haley, was witty and fun to watch. "Mildly amusing entertainment if you are not too critical," said *Picture Show.* "Ann Sothern looks lovelier than ever but acting honors go to Jack Haley." Concurred *Variety,* "Miss Sothern has less to do than the other principals, although she again looks well and also sings nicely. As far as the story is concerned she just walks through." *The New York Times* thought the whole thing "A minor lark, designed for the assassination of empty hours in the shopper's schedule, it is happy in the presence of the comical Jack Haley and the entirely lovely Ann Sothern."

Grand Exit (Columbia, 1935), directed by Earle Kenton, gave her a strong dramatic opportunity, her best to date. Playing a very enigmatic role with strength and plausibility, she was again cast opposite the dapper Edmund Lowe. The reviews were generally excellent with *Variety* extolling: "Aside from the all-round superb performance by Edmund Lowe, Ann Sothern and Onslow Stevens chip in with two excellent jobs. Miss Sothern, providing the romantic interest, handles two or three dramatic scenes with restraint and poise." Lowe and Ann would also star in "Kick In" for *Lux Radio Theatre* in 1936.

Despite her hammering at Columbia's executive doors for better material, and the good notices she was getting, her next assignment was *You May Be Next!* (1936). Starring with the always natural and in control Lloyd Nolan, she played a niterie singer with radio ambitions. Her singing was heard only

JACK HALEY, AS, ROGER PRYOR, VICTOR KILIAN, INEZ COURTNEY
AND RAY WALKER IN *THE GIRLFRIEND* (COLUMBIA, 1935)

in snatches and her share of the dialogue was scant as well. *Picture Show* said, "This film shows up yet another gangster racket—with broadcasting. Apart from this novelty it moves on conventional lines but it is excellently acted and moves briskly." *Variety* thought her "more fetching than ever but gets little chance to handle other than routine lines." Incidentally, her and Nolan's unobtrusive romance blends nicely with the main musical theme. Some of the film's background scoring contains melodies from Grace Moore's Columbia films and it is probable that Miss Moore's arrival at Columbia, which was such a huge success, caused Harry Cohn to lose interest in Ann as a lead singing star.

She did enjoy her stint working opposite Lloyd Nolan, even if the material gave her little personal opportunity to shine. Columbia next scheduled her for *Don't Gamble With Love* (1936), opposite an actor with whom she did not have any rapport whatsoever, Bruce Cabot. Again top billed in Columbia's *Hell-Ship Morgan* (1936), Ann's name was being used to sell an inferior product, and her role was secondary to those of both Victor Jory and George Bancroft. She allowed her feelings to be aired, declaring that she was tired of all those "sea" pictures. (*Eight Bells* being the other.) Still, *Variety* liked her performance. "Ann Sothern brings a touch of wistful sincerity to the role of down-and-out Mary. Her thespian effort is far above story and direction." However, to Ann, this was the nadir of her Columbia pictures. Reportedly, she heard of Frank Capra's plans to film *Lost Horizon*, and asked to be considered for the part of the critically ill good-time girl, the role eventually played by Isabel Jewell. Neither Capra nor Harry Cohn took her seriously and would not even consider testing her. This incensed her so much that she sought a release from her Columbia tenure and Harry Cohn, probably relieved to be rid of what he considered a rebellious woman, let her go.

With this release she let her hair go natural and she found the former auburn hair she'd been born with was now a honey brown. In New York, on March 17, 1936, Ann spoke openly about being kept in a rut and not being built up at Columbia, stating that a month or so earlier she'd signed a contract at RKO. Before reporting for work there, her services were employed by

ONSLOW STEVENS, AS AND EDMUND LOWE
IN *GRAND EXIT* (COLUMBIA, 1935)

Paramount in *My American Wife* (1936). Francis Lederer and Ann were billed above the title and she was beautifully photographed by Harry Fischbeck in a superb wardrobe designed by Travis Banton. In this satirical look at snobbery, the stars teamed brightly and Ann became a lifelong friend to her mother in the film, Billie Burke. On radio's *Hollywood Hotel*, Ann and Lederer repeated a scene from the film.

Leaving Columbia, as far as publicity was concerned, seemed the right move as *The New York Sunday News* now had her as their Color Cover Girl on May 3, 1936. *Screen and Radio* had her and Francis Lederer in a color cover pose and her face began to adorn all the fan magazine covers. A letter from Harry Cohn, expressing regret for her departure, arrived belatedly.

At this time Ann's name was linked with that of Norman Krazna's, the gifted writer and producer, but, romantically, Roger Pryor was still in the picture, so much so that while he was touring, her main date was with the "safe" Cesar Romero. He was her escort to the Academy Awards that year and would continue to be forever her friend. Of her women friends, she spent a lot of time with Joan Bennett. They attended the *Born to Dance* premiere together and Ann also got on well with Joan's then-husband, Gene Markey.

With a tendency to plumpness she began playing social tennis and swimming during her spare time. When in town, Roger Pryor would take her to the fights, the races and tennis matches. Priscilla Pryor had started divorce proceedings in 1934, but left Reno before the six-week residency period was up. Now having a new man in her life, she divorced Roger in 1936 and married again the following day.

Ann's first RKO film under her new contract was *Count Pete* with Gene Raymond. A good script, it

LLOYD NOLAN HAD A RARE CHANCE TO PLAY THE HERO IN *YOU MAY BE NEXT!* (COLUMBIA, 1936), OPPOSITE AS

AS, GEORGE BANCROFT AND VICTOR JORY IN
HELL-SHIP MORGAN (COLUMBIA, 1936)

BRUCE CABOT AND AS IN *DON'T GAMBLE WITH LOVE*
(COLUMBIA, 1936)

also boasted songs by Bert Kalmar and Harry Ruby. Excellent performances from Henry Stephenson and Jessie Ralph, as Ann's father and aunt, also added to the fun. Newcomers Anita Colby, Patricia Wilder and Alan Curtis were also seen in small roles. Retitled *Walking on Air* (1936) for its release, it proved to be a most scintillating little comedy. Ann and Gene Raymond teamed well, though Ann did say that his singing was not good enough for him to be cast as a radio singing star.

FRANCIS LEDERER, BILLIE BURKE AND AS IN *MY AMERICAN WIFE* (PARAMOUNT, 1936)

She liked him for his other musical talents, mentioning his ability with composition. *The New York Times* enjoyed *Walking on Air*, calling it "a gay, frothy comedy," while *Time* praised the "breezy comedy" for its "pleasant new melodies ["Cabin on the Hilltop," "Let's Make a Wish," and "My Heart Wants to Dance"]. As for Ann, she looked lovely and duetted on "Let's Make a Wish," in a plaintive, soulful style, with Gene Raymond.

 The Smartest Girl in Town (1936) was another teaming with Gene Raymond, but this time it was strictly lower-bill material. Ann adored working with and learning from Helen Broderick, a former Ziegfeld beauty now character actress. The cast also included Erik Rhodes, Eric Blore and Frank Jenks to bolster the comedic content. One reviewer thought it "an Astaire, Rogers film without the music," while *Screen Play* felt that Ann and Gene "top their last performances together in this frothy, delightful and sparkling comedy." *Variety* was divided: "Flip comedy in which Ann Sothern, in her first starring venture, shares billing with Gene Raymond, but film hasn't enough

HENRY STEPHENSON, AS AND JESSIE RALPH IN *WALKING ON AIR* (RKO, 1936)

REHEARSING MAKING BREAKFAST
FOR *WALKING ON AIR* (RKO, 1936)

substance to be anything beyond the duals." *The Smartest Girl in Town* has the very brief running time of just less than one hour. Ann always claimed she hated the word temperament and was never temperamental. However, she would always stand up for her rights and if things in the script or in the lyrics of the songs didn't suit her, she would say so. Her quick departure from the set of this film may have been part of the reason for its hurried completion.

During the making of this film Gene Raymond became engaged to Jeanette MacDonald and Roger Pryor wired Ann that he was returning to Hollywood. Ann drove to the airport to meet him and when he alighted from the plane, he swept her into his arms and proposed. His divorce final and with a year's contract for his orchestra to play at the College Inn in Chicago, his marriage proposal was opportune if overdue. Having had their initial introduction at the College Inn four years previously and considering it a good omen, they decided to marry immediately. However, being so much in love, they completely overlooked that there was a mandatory three-day notice period which needed to be observed before the union could take place. After filing and hoping for a Wednesday ceremony, they were informed it would have to be the following Sunday. This last-minute obstacle was solved by having the wedding at one minute past midnight on the Saturday evening.

WITH GENE RAYMOND IN
SMARTEST GIRL IN TOWN
(RKO, 1936)

SIGNING THE MARRIAGE LICENSE WITH ROGER PRYOR

HONEYMOON-BOUND WITH
HUSBAND ROGER PRYOR,
EN ROUTE TO CHICAGO,
SEPTEMBER 27, 1936

ANN MARRIED ROGER AT ONE
MINUTE PAST MIDNIGHT ON
SEPTEMBER 27, 1936
AT THE HOLLYWOOD
CONGREGATIONAL CHURCH

Roger had to be back in Chicago to rehearse his band for their opening at the College Inn.

When asked to appear on NBC radio's variety show *Shell Chateau*, to be broadcast on September 26, they at first declined. But, choosing a romantic scene from *There's Always Juliet*, the excited and soon-to-be-wed couple again thought this a good omen, and agreed.

Best friend Joan Bennett came to Ann's aid in helping her with arrangements for the reception and packing. Roger's failed first marriage caused him to dislike bridal gowns of white so, although this was her first wedding, Ann compromised and wore a pale-blue bridal creation designed by Irene. Photographs of the event attest to Ann's loveliness on this long awaited day for the jubilant couple. The movie wedding with a difference took place at the Hollywood Congregational Church at one minute into Sunday, September 27, 1936. Reverend J. Hamilton Lash officiated at the ceremony and the reception was held at Ann's English-style home, lasting until the early hours of the morning. Boarding the plane, she remarked that with all the haste she hadn't time to think about a trousseau but would do that in Chicago. The ecstatic newlyweds were again delighted to find their seats on the plane had been covered in decorative pink and white satin, courtesy of their kindhearted and genuinely rejoicing friend Joan Bennett.

AS, HELEN BRODERICK AND ERIC BLORE IN
SMARTEST GIRL IN TOWN (RKO, 1936)

Chapter Three: "Mrs. Roger Pryor"

Roger Pryor was born on August 27, 1901, in New York City. His father, Arthur Pryor, was a prominent musician first associated with John Phillip Sousa. Forming his own orchestra, the elder Pryor's band proved second in popularity only to the great Sousa's. A handsome lad with dark wavy hair, Roger's first stage appearance occurred when a family friend offered him an ailing juvenile lead's spot in a play he was producing. This was against the wishes of his father, who did not want his two sons in show business. Roger overcame this family objection and later toured in repertory. *The Backslapper* (1925) was his first New York appearance. Other Broadway roles included *The Sea Woman, Saturday's Children, The Royal Family, The Front Page* and *Blessed Event* (1932). His first wife was Priscilla Mitchell, whom he wed in 1928, and a daughter was born to them in 1931.

Now sporting a finely trimmed moustache, the suave-looking actor made his film debut in a couple of short subjects in 1930 and made his feature debut in *Moonlight and Pretzels* (1933). Priscilla and his daughter remained in New Jersey; they were considered a separated couple.

A 1936 MGM PORTRAIT

WITH ROBERT YOUNG IN
DANGEROUS NUMBER
(MGM, 1936)

Occasionally, there would be a good lead, like in *Lady by Choice* (1934), opposite Carole Lombard and May Robson, and *Belle of the Nineties* (1934) with Mae West. The latter was filmed twice as the preview of the first version worried Paramount executives because of likely censorship.

Roger was at Columbia before Ann, and among his many credits were *I Like it That Way*, *Romance in the Rain*, *I'll Tell the World*, *Wake Up and Dream*, *Straight From the Heart* and *The Man They Could Not Hang*. He also had his own orchestra in the late 1930s, and one of his vocalists back then was actress Adrian Booth. With his marriage to Ann Sothern, he also found great success on radio and she was his guest-vocalist on a tour in 1938. As well as conducting, he played trombone. Never happy with acting, he always stated the music side of his career gave him the most pleasure. The producer of *Cavalcade of America*, his other radio achievements were hosting both *Screen Guild Players* and *Theater Guild on the Air* and narrating NBC Symphony broadcasts. Ann would star in many of these productions, including "I Met Him in Paris" (1940), with his best friend at that time, Melvyn Douglas, and her friend Robert Young.

Returning to movies, he was usually cast as a heavy, probably because of his rich, deep voice and brilliantine-wavy hair. Some of the programmers he played in were *The Man with Nine Lives*, *A Fugitive from Justice*, *She Couldn't Say No* (all 1940), *Power Dive*, *Bullets for O'Hara* (both 1941), *I Live on Danger* (1942), *Lady Bodyguard* (1943), *High Powered*, *Scared Stiff* (both 1945), and a couple at Republic, *Thoroughbreds* (1944) and, his last film, *The Man From Oklahoma* (1945).

Continuing with his orchestra (1941-1945) proved to be a mistake as the changes in popular music led to fewer bookings, smaller audiences and eventually bankruptcy. A tour with Kay Francis in *Windy Hill* (1945) helped him recoup and he also directed three "B" pictures, which he, mercifully, asked to have his name omitted from the credits.

His brother was vice-president of programming for Batten, Barton, Durstine & Osborne in New York City. Roger took a similar position with Foote, Cone & Boldings (1947) and remained vice-president in charge of broadcasting until he retired in 1962. With his third wife of many years he moved to Pompano Beach, Florida, where he indulged in his favorite pastime, fishing. Ann told me she continued to see him over the years and that he had

DEAN JAGGER, AS, ROBERT YOUNG, REGINALD OWEN IN *DANGEROUS NUMBER* (MGM, 1936)

moved back to Southern California. When I visited her in 1974, she was visibly upset, having just received a telephone call from Roger who was very ill. He died soon afterwards and Ann mentioned that his love of cigarettes was a major cause. Their love affair, marriage and divorce seemed to be secondary to the truly remarkable loving friendship which had evolved between them.

The Pryors' honeymoon was just over three weeks long. In addition to his engagement at the College Inn, he had a twice weekly coast-to-coast radio broadcast from Chicago. Combining a little business with this idyllic period, in October Ann was offered a singing engagement at The Palace Theater. Ann was a huge success. "She sang her way into the hearts of the audience making no reference to her motion picture life, but chalking up a hit on singing merit alone," wrote *Billboard*. Chicago audiences had taken her to their hearts when, as Harriette Lake, she had starred in *Of Thee I Sing*. The mutual love affair between Ann and Chicago would continue through many decades and many engagements. In her

AS, GORDON JONES, RICHARD LANE, FRANK JENKS AND GENE RAYMOND IN *THERE GOES MY GIRL* (RKO, 1936)

ANN AND DON AMECHE DUETTED
"NEVER IN A MILLION YEARS" IN
FIFTY ROADS TO TOWN (FOX, 1937)

Palace act, she sang songs from *Hooray for Love* and *Folies Bergere*, including "I Was Lucky" and, of course, "Let's Fall in Love." The standard "I'm Getting Sentimental Over You" was given a vigorous reception from a rapt audience.

Ann was an adept swimmer and generally an all-round keen sportswoman. She'd had some unlucky escapes with horses, but still became a capable equestrienne. Roger introduced her to the relaxing pastime of fishing and this, along with skiing, became two of her favorite forms of enjoyment away from the soundstages.

Known as the commuting bride, she would be immediately on a flight to Chicago between pictures. Sometimes the studio would require her for retakes and she'd have to fly back to Los Angeles after only a single day there. In one hectic fortnight she made four trips, and the strain was beginning to show.

Ann always liked little "pooches" and over the years there were poodles, terriers and occasionally white cats to receive her pampering and love. In this year of frustrating separations, Roger suggested a puppy, the idea of which came to fruition and provided some small relief from her terrible loneliness. Before they wed there had been a long discussion on the subject of Ann dating during their periods of separation. Both agreed that it would be okay if the man involved was a friend of Roger's and that there were no romantic intentions.

A PORTRAIT FOR *SUPER-SLEUTH*
RKO, 1937)

Cesar Romero was sympathetic to their situation and would always be available, should she need an escort. Another friend who obliged was RKO publicist Jerry Asher.

RKO lent her to MGM upon her return from Chicago for *Dangerous Number*, in which she would be cast opposite one of her favorite leading men, Robert Young. Reginald Owen, who would also figure prominently in her film future, was also cast as were Dean Jagger and two other players from her movie past, Spencer Charters and Franklin Pangborn. Cora Witherspoon, as her wacky ex-burlesque queen mother, was in good form. Coiffed, dressed and photographed with all the MGM gloss, Ann was well directed by Richard Thorpe. Said *Photoplay*, "Ann Sothern playing the actress-bride, who can start an argument over breakfast coffee and dramatize it and herself indefinitely, displays a surprising and spirited comedy sense that is as devastating as it is restrained." Another review called Ann "delectable," mentioning she'd been at MGM as Harriette Lake seven years earlier.

An even better loan out was to 20th Century-Fox for *Fifty Roads to*

JOAN WOODBURY, AS JACK OAKIE, EDGAR KENNEDY AND
PAUL GUILFOYLE IN *SUPER-SLEUTH* (RKO, 1937)

ACCOMPANYING CESAR ROMERO TO
THE 1936 ACADEMY
AWARDS DINNER

Town. This one starred her with Don Ameche and drew comparison to *It Happened One Night.* Her work in this was duly noticed by Darryl F. Zanuck, who thought her a likely prospect as an Alice Faye backup. He'd liked what he saw when she appeared in *Folies Bergere,* and would continue to try and get her under contract. Ironically, he'd directed her first test at Warner Bros. With most of the action in *Fifty Roads* taking place in a deserted hut, hit by a blizzard, the lighting was not always flattering. Vocally, though, Ann was in great voice and her duetting with Ameche on "Never in a Million Years" (previously in the Jack Haley-Alice Faye musical, *Wake Up and Live*) allowed her soprano to soar at its melodic conclusion. Spencer Charters, Jane Darwell and John Qualen were again in the cast, with Slim Summerville and Stepin Fetchit providing additional comedy relief. For once *Variety* approved, feeling she "has made progress and now qualifies for good comedy leads." Years later, Pelican records would release the LP *The Feminine Touch,* with Ann singing "Never in a Million Years." Though claiming the selection to be from a 1937 radio show, it sounds exactly the same as the film track with Ameche's contribution missing. To publicize the film the duo would perform a scene from their movie on The Chase & Sanborn radio show on July 18, 1937. In 1937 Ann also guested on *Your Hit Parade,* the NBC radio program, with Mark Warnow's orchestra.

That year also found Ann the recipient of a medal, awarded by the American Cosmeticians Association. Her make-up was deemed to be the most consistently fashionable of any actress in the movies. She'd also tied for second place with Anita Louise in a "Most Beautiful Blonde" line-up. Virginia

Bruce got the No. 1 spot. Nineteen Thirty-seven also found Ann often up at Lake Arrowhead, where she'd partake in her love of skiing during the winter months and, of course, fishing during the summer.

Reporter Virginia T. Lane, in an article on Ann, mentioned that Norman Taurog, the director of *Fifty Roads to Town*, told her this anecdote: "We rigged up Annie's dressing room on the set, like an old shack...there was even a wooden

WITH EDWARD EVERETT HORTON
IN *DANGER – LOVE AT WORK*
(FOX, 1937)

horse tethered at the door and the crew solemnly presented her with a striped blue and white nightgown, vintage 1890. You should have seen Annie's face when she walked in...then we pulled another gag on her. She had to shoot a gun in the picture and I told her to go out and practice, because she was scared to death of firearms. Well, she shut both eyes and pulled the trig-

THERE GOES THE GROOM
(RKO, 1937)

ger on a blank shot—and a stuffed rabbit fell at her feet! One of the electricians had dropped it from the catwalk. A photograph, with a poster outside reading 'Annie doesn't live here anymore,' was taken so Ann could share the fun with Roger. She took the nightgown and the rabbit to show Roger when she flew to Chicago immediately after shooting was finished."

Ann had been very blue at the commencement of making this movie for it was just after Christmas and she had spent the holidays with her family, without Roger. Movie magazine writer Anthony Curtis reported on Ann's very real misery

THERE GOES THE GROOM (RKO, 1937) WITH AS,
MARY BOLAND AND LEONA ROBERTS

at this time. "Last night was one of those nights. I thought I couldn't stand being alone another minute. I was trying my best to be brave about it. I knew in my heart Roger was going through the same thing. I was just about to give up and give in to one of those fits of the blues when a special delivery letter arrived. It was the first letter Roger's mother had ever written me and nothing could have been more perfect at that moment. She seemed to know exactly what I was going through. You see her husband is a famous bandleader—Arthur Pryor. I believe I can quote her letter almost by heart, I read it so many times. She wrote in effect:

"'...I can guess what you are going through this very minute. It is the holiday season and you are separated from the one you love. But perhaps I can tell you a few things from experience—so similar—that will give you the courage to face your loneliness.

"'When Arthur and I were married, he left almost immediately after the ceremony for a tour. He was gone three months. I saw him for two weeks and he left on a concert tour of Europe. In fact, during that first two years of our marriage, I don't think we were together more than three months. Imagine! I had two children and brought them up to the point where they could talk before they even knew their own father! So, when you get lonely, my dear, just remember that Arthur and I have celebrated our golden wedding anniversary together. And I sometimes think it is because we learned so well, just as you are learning, how dear and precious we were to one another in the bitter school of separation that our married life proved to be such a happy one. And while I hope and pray that your two careers won't keep you separated as long as we were, I know that the knowledge of the wonderful marriage we have shared will help give you courage now while you are apart.'"

"Ann was talking through a lump in her throat as she finished the contents of that letter. She didn't say anything for a minute—and then, 'Maybe Hollywood's right. Maybe ours is a marriage gamble. But something in my heart tells me that Roger and I are gambling on a sure thing.'"

RKO found a vehicle for Ann, *There Goes My Girl*, and, as their last two efforts had been audience pleasers, Gene Raymond, top billed, was signed as her co-star. Joan Woodbury, whom Ann had befriended on the set of *Folies Bergere*, was in the supporting cast and would again be cast in *Super-Sleuth*, Ann's followup film. In 1975, when I visited Ann, I had with me a large selection of recently purchased movie stills. Ann always liked to look at these pictures as I acquired them each year and she would comment on the film and her co-players. There was a scene from *Super-Sleuth* and, spotting Joan Woodbury, Ann said, "Colin, isn't that Ann Miller?" When I identified the person as Joan, she looked closely at the shot and said, "Of course, she was such a nice girl and a terrific dancer, no wonder I mixed her up with Annie Miller." We talked a bit more and

A PORTRAIT FOR
SHE'S GOT EVERYTHING
(RKO, 1937)

she said she called Jack Oakie "'Jokey' Oakie as he was always such fun to work with." Then she grew serious and said, "Do you know what happened to Joan Woodbury? She married Henry Wilcoxon, you know, and it was one of the longest marriages and to my amazement after so many years they divorced." I told Ann that Joan had remarried and became a well-known theatre personality in Palm Desert. She seemed happy to know that Joan was doing okay.

There Goes My Girl was a fast-talking, rapid-fire newspaper comedy, with editor Richard Lane out to prevent his reporter, Ann, from marrying rival reporter, Gene Raymond. The reviews were not good. *Photoplay* rated the film "second rate entertainment," and *The New York Times* "couldn't understand after watching the Sothern-Raymond method of covering a story...why he [Lane] wanted them around at all. We wouldn't trust them at a pet show." *Modern Screen* was more positive: "Ann Sothern—best dressed reporter in the World...she runs through a series of gowns that would make Kay Francis rush for the nearest journalism school. Ann does well with her assignment,

HELEN BRODERICK AND AS IN SHE'S GOT EVERYTHING (RKO, 1937)

but Gene Raymond is not at his best in this sort of thing…Joan Woodbury furnishes an attractive Spanish dance."

The Pryors now had two residences, an apartment at the Ambassador in Chicago and their specially-built rented Los Angeles home which included a bedroom for visits by Roger's daughter. Ann seemed happy as she decorated and furnished this new abode, but when all that activity ceased, she found the idleness unbearable. Work seemed the best solution and RKO's decision to keep her busy on loan out, as well as with their own productions, was the best tonic imaginable. Ann stated in *Film Fan,* "Husbands should have a lot of attention and interest from their wives." Ann had also become a tireless knitter on the sets of her films and could be seen settled in an old rocking chair pursuing this pastime.

Super-Sleuth, directed by Ben Stoloff, is generally thought of as inconsequential but, nevertheless, it's a very funny movie. Jack Oakie, as a film detective who undertakes to solve some real-life "poison pen" celebrity killings, was a hoot. Boasting a huge ego, his office sports a large self-autographed photograph, inscribed "From Yourself to Me with Sincere Admiration." Ann played his exasperated girlfriend and studio publicity head. *Modern Movies* thought "The team of Oakie and Sothern is an excellent one. Both turn in delightful performances and Miss Sothern is unusually lovely." *Modern Screen* seconded that, calling Ann "attractive and capable in the feminine lead."

Six months had now elapsed since the Pryors' wedding and Ann, dubbed "the travelingest" wife in filmdom, had flown back and forth to Chicago innumerable times. Despite an inherent fear of flying she estimated that between them, Roger and she had chalked up some 50,000 miles.

Darryl F. Zanuck then requested Ann for the lead in the Fox comedy *Danger—Love at Work,* a *You Can't Take It With You*-type farce about an even zanier family. Reunited with Jack Haley and Mary Boland, she found this one to be a most pleasurable experience. Again, Ann sang a reprise of an Alice Faye tune, as she and Jack Haley duetted the title song most charmingly in a stable setting. (Alice Faye had previously sung the title song in *You Can't Have Everything.*) The cast seemed to enjoy the romp, with such experienced farceurs as Walter Catlett, Edward Everett Horton, Etienne Giradot and even John Carradine entering into the spirit of the crazy goings on. Otto

Preminger directed at a strenuous pace, and it was generally well received. To its credit, it was made a year before *You Can't Take It With You*.

While making this film, Ann joined escort Cesar Romero as guests at a premiere of another Fox feature, *Ali Baba Goes to Town*. As it starred her good friend Eddie Cantor, she was glad to do this bit of moonlighting. Apart from Fox contract players like Phyllis Brooks, Tyrone Power, Sonja Henie, Shirley Temple and The Ritz Brothers, other celebrities joining Ann and Cesar included Dolores Del Rio, Victor McLaglen, Douglas Fairbanks, Sr., and Lady Sylvia Ashley (who would later marry Clark Gable).

It was then straight back to RKO for *There Goes the Groom*, an "entertaining farce" (*Variety*). Joseph Santley was at the helm again, and Ann had found him an excellent director when they had done *Walking on Air* together. Once again her pal Mary Boland was cast as her mother, and her leading man was the gifted stage actor Burgess Meredith, and he brilliantly brought to life sequences that would have defeated lesser talents. Considered an all-round "good egg" by the crews of all her pictures, Ann became a good buddy of Meredith. A man of immense intellect and unfathomable talent, he was not overly impressed with "Hollywood actors." Ann's down-to-earth good nature and complete professionalism helped change his mind.

The year at the College Inn was almost up and Ann's wish that Roger would get bookings closer to Los Angeles came true. He was engaged to appear at one of San Francisco's top hotel's cabaret room.

She's Got Everything would prove to be the final film of her RKO contract. Directed by Joseph Santley and with Gene Raymond as co-star, she had hopes it would be better than the script promised. Helen Broderick tried hard to give it a decided lift, and Ann had her first acquaintance with a comedian from Milwaukee, Jack Carson. There was a song, "It's Sleepy Time in Hawaii," which Ann crooned wistfully in a bar setting. *Variety* gave it a dreadful panning: "Helen Broderick and Victor Moore go through heaps of words and passes without nudging into a solid laugh and the results aren't much better for Parkyakarkas and Billy Gilbert…with Ann Sothern and Gene Raymond posed for their parts." Other reviews weren't much better, with even the direction being slated.

Feeling her career to be at a standstill, and with the offer of only a supporting role in *Joy of Living* at RKO, she obtained her release in late 1937,

WITH RALPH BELLAMY IN TRADE WINDS (UNITED ARTISTS, 1938)

though she, Victor Moore, and Gene Raymond would publicize *She's Got Everything* on the *Hollywood Hotel* radio show in 1937.

There had been more trips for her as an orchestra wife and she'd even flown to Dallas in order to see Roger. Admittedly, when she arrived there was usually his band playing a song of welcome, but the stress of all the traveling became too much. Deciding to take a total break from filmmaking, she would hold out until something worthwhile was offered. *The Woodbury Radio Playhouse* provided two anthologies with Tyrone Power, "Trinidad Dryad" and "Fifty Roads to Town."

Most of 1938 was spent in idleness, but later during that year she did make *Trade Winds*. In 1939 she undertook a vaudeville tour with her husband's orchestra. Commencing in Newark, New Jersey, the three-month concert tour covered Baltimore (Hippodrome), New York (Loew's State Theater), Cleveland (Palace), Akron (Palace), Youngstown (Palace), Montreal (Loew's), Hartford (State), and their beloved Chicago (Chicago Theater). Their pro-

grams boasted star names in support, which, owing to their film commitments, would vary from city to city. For example, Nick Lucas and The Con-
dos Brothers were in Newark, Eleanor Whitney in Cleveland and John Boles
in Hartford. Ann sang "With a Song in My Heart," "My Cigarette" and "Deep
in a Dream." The act's review in *Billboard* was typical of the praise she was
receiving. "Show builds up a custom-made entrance for Miss Sothern, who
further ingratiates herself in amiable banter with her husband. Her clear soprano and microphone poise in three ballads enhances her as even more of a
treat to the eyes on the stage than on the screen. She sings with a sweet and
pleasing voice, her three offerings being well selected."

During the season she had an offer from Universal to play opposite Bing
Crosby in *East Side of Heaven*. Not one to desert a project to which she was
committed, she declined the offer, which Joan Blondell quickly grabbed. Bing
Crosby had been most complimentary to her when she guested on the *Kraft
Music Hall* radio variety show twice in 1936. With Jimmy Dorsey's orchestra
she sang "Where's the Boy, Here's the Girl" on her second appearance on the
show.

Trade Winds (1938), a Walter Wanger production starring Fredric March,
was released just before she went on the vaudeville tour. Her success in this
film and the large audiences who saw her ensured there was good box office
for the tour. Director Tay Garnett had written a rough draft of the *Trade
Winds* script three years earlier and then embarked on a world cruise with
his wife, ship's crew, camera crew and a complete film laboratory. With *Trade
Winds* in mind he shot 70,000 feet of travelogue film for background material. Wanger had bought the story and acquired Garnett's services as director.
He then hired Dorothy Parker, Alan Campbell and Frank R. Adams to flesh
out the story with humor and geographical facts. Joan Bennett was signed for
the lead role of a runaway heiress wanted for murder. It proved to be the role
which would change the whole course of her career. Up until then she'd been
a blonde leading lady usually cast in stock heroine roles. Playing an escapee
from the law, the script required her to become a brunette and a brunette she
would remain.

Ann Sothern also underwent a metamorphosis which would establish
her as a new and different screen personality. Her friendship with Joan Bennett led to her being considered for the part of private eye March's secretary.
She was playing a game of "Quotations" when her gift of mimicry with a

AS AND JOAN BENNETT IN TRADE WINDS (UNITED ARTISTS, 1938)

comic line alerted Walter Wanger to her suitability for the part. During the RKO years Ann admired and was friendly with Irene Dunne and also kept in touch throughout her life with Ginger Rogers. Although they shared the same drama teacher, Ann was not always impressed with Katharine Hepburn. Visiting the set of *Mary of Scotland* (1936), she was enthralled with the performance of Florence Eldridge. In fact, they had a sort of mutual admiration society and would always greet each other with enthusiasm at premieres and parties. When her husband, Fredric March, received the script for *Trade Winds*, Florence read it and also suggested Ann for the comedy role. March agreed and with Joan Bennett on her side as well, Ann, after a little hesitation, accepted the part. Also part of the *Trade Winds* team was Ralph Bellamy, who excelled in playing the "dumb ox"-type he'd made his own since *The Awful Truth*. Ann scored with critcs. *Variety* said, "Greatest surprise of the picture is the acting of Ann Sothern as March's tough, acquisitive, amorous secretary. Completely reversing the romantic roles she usually plays, Miss Sothern gives by far the most plausible performance of her career. She catches the proper combination of hardness and sentimentality in the character and gets every ounce of its humor across." *Film Digest* noted, "She steals all her scenes."

After seeing the film alone and listening to the audiences' reactions, Ann said: "I had my fingers crossed throughout but the laughter and the comments in the foyer afterwards were all so positive. I've never had a New Year like this one." With her usual sense of gratitude, she descended on director Tay Garnett. Describing her visit in his autobiography, *Light Your Torches and Pull Up Your Tights*, he wrote: "The Jeanie character, a lightheaded, softhearted dizzy babe, was played to the hilt by Ann Sothern. Several months after the film's release, I was working at my desk at U.A. when a blonde blur burst through the open door, body surfed across the desk and landed in my lap, wiping out the two of us onto the floor. I had my arms full of glorious girl, but she was giggling, which unnerved me. 'What the hell goes on,' I managed to say. Kiss on the forehead, kiss on the cheek, kiss on the chin—'Oh Tay, You'll never guess! You've done it this time—you've really done it. MGM has stolen your Jeanie character out of 'Trade Winds' and they're going to build a series around her for ME. They're going to call her Maisie,' chortled Miss Sothern. And they did." Garnett also added, "The picture was a smash and Walter Wanger, newly divorced at the time of its making, would wed Joan Bennett after its release."

Still worth a return visit, *Trade Winds* owes much to Tay Garnett's skilled direction and Alfred Newman's haunting musical score, as well as benefiting from the emerging comic talents of Ann. At the time of its making she debated the difficulty of playing a drunk scene. Bringing it off with aplomb, she would further demonstrate her ability to portray inebriation later, most notably in *Brother Orchid*.

Chapter Four: "Maisie"

Before she finished making *Maisie* at MGM, Ann accepted a top billed role in Elsa Maxwell's *Hotel for Women*. Marking the debut of beautiful 15-year-old Linda Darnell, Ann's name was sought to give the film stronger box office appeal. Her pal June Gale was in the cast and she and Chick Chandler renewed their friendship. Ann remained totally estranged from Jean Rogers, with whom she'd worked alongside in *Footlight Parade* as Harriette Lake. Jean recalled, "My best friend Lynn Bari and I worked together for the first time in *Hotel for Women* and we dubbed Ann Sothern 'Miss Aloof.' She was chummy and helpful with Linda Darnell, but it seemed Lynn and I didn't exist." Asking Lynn Bari of her experiences on the film, brought this response: "That movie was designed to showcase Linda Darnell and Zanuck gave her the full star treatment. Pev Marley, the cameraman, whom she later married, was totally rapt in her, even then. This was so much so that I always felt when he photographed me, being in many ways her competition, it was to my disadvantage.

AS and Robert Young in *Maisie*
(MGM, 1939)

AS, Robert Young and Ruth Hussey in *Maisie* (MGM, 1939)

My hairdresser on that film went ruthless with the shears and I had to wear little hair pieces and hats to cover her mistakes. As to Miss Sothern, she was professional and knew her lines but was rather frosty with the other players in our scenes. To me she seemed to be very antisocial except with the director, Gregory Ratoff, and society matron, Elsa Maxwell. Despite my hating the way I looked and was photographed, I experienced some of the greatest moments I've had on a set. These were meeting my lifelong friend, Jean Rogers, and receiving an ovation from the actors and crew after a big dramatic scene where I shot John Halliday."

With *Hotel for Women* in the can, Zanuck viewed it and asked Ann to sign a seven-year deal. A month earlier *Maisie* had been previewed and MGM, elated at the audience reaction, also offered her a contract for seven years with a stipulation that there would be more *Maisie* films included. Talking it over with Roger they decided the MGM deal was the more secure as she would at least know what some of her future projects might be. This displeased Zanuck so much that he had a lot of her footage scissored from the release print of *Hotel for Women* and in the accompanying publicity her billing was lowered.

Woodbury Radio Playhouse summoned Ann to appear in "Goodbye Again" and as it was with Charles Boyer, a favorite of hers, she readily accepted. On the homefront things were also much happier. Roger was now spending more time in Los Angeles and would attempt to revive his movie career.

Jean Rogers, Linda Darnell and AS in *Hotel for Women* (Fox, 1939)

On one of her trips to visit him in Dallas for Thanksgiving, her maternal instinct was aroused. A young ten-year-old newsboy, David Hobbs, was the recipient of her warm affection. She'd first met his family when delivering baskets of food and goodies and money to the poor in Dallas, during one of her many excursions which she undertook each Thanksgiving and Christmas. She would visit Welfare to obtain names and addresses of the most needy. The Hobbs family was on her list that year in Dallas. Chatting with the kids she mentioned where she was staying and offhandedly asked them to come and see her. Early the next day David and his brother arrived on her doorstep and Roger, too, got to meet them. He, influenced by Ann, became protective of David, who came from an overlarge and poor family. He had twelve siblings. Approaching the boy's family, the Pryors were able to convince them that if they would allow David to live with them, he would receive the best of care and advantages. To be fair, initially, the boy was uncertain about the move and the family said no to adoption, but prevailed on his behalf and David left with Ann and Roger for Hollywood "for a while." Unaccustomed to luxury living, David was, at first, thrilled with all the attention, love and outings that Ann provided. When Roger was home the three were always doing things together and all seemed happy. Ann gave David piano lessons and his education was of the very best they could provide. He had his teeth straightened and Roger had him coached in boxing and sporting activities. Couples like the George Murphys, the Herbert Marshalls, the Ray Millands and their families would often accompany the Pryors and David on visits to the circus and zoo. The Pryors next sought to have David, now 12, legally adopted. His family visited but when the time came for their departure, the boy became distraught, begging them to take him with them. A heartbroken Ann said

WITH FRANCHOT TONE IN
FAST AND FURIOUS (MGM, 1939)

FAST AND FURIOUS (MGM, 1939) WITH AS, FRANCHOT TONE AND RUTH
HUSSEY, WITH ALLYN JOSLYN AND LEE BOWMAN IN THE BACKGROUND

goodbye to this boy, who she had truly loved as any real mother would. The
Hobbs family was now living in a tent on a California ranch where the father
was employed. Despite all the love and first-class care he was given by Ann
and Roger, David, understandably, missed his brothers and sisters. They were
for the most part children too, and no doubt the fun and games they shared
was to David something Ann and Roger could not provide. Marion, Ann's
sister, who was now working as a newspaper writer, would tell reporter Lup-
ton A. Wilkinson, when he asked for Ann's reaction to this tragic occurrence,
"I can't [talk about it]. Ann would never forgive me. None of us speak of it."

Guesting on radio's *Screen Actors Guild Theater* in a variety program, she
again worked with Mickey Rooney. He, in turn, introduced her to Judy Garland, who always had a liking for Ann as both a singer and as a person. Roger
Pryor was also featured and he, Cary Grant and Ann played in a sketch together.

Maisie was originally earmarked as a vehicle for Jean Harlow. Based on the novel *Dark Dame* by Wilson Collison, MGM producer J. Walter Ruben had been trying to find the right actress to fill the deceased Jean Harlow's shoes. Ruben's wife, Virginia Bruce, was considered but was thought to be too ladylike. Una Merkel came close, but was she sexy enough? When Ruben saw *Trade Winds* he was sure he'd found "Maisie" at last. MGM executives, who'd recalled Ann's work in *Dangerous Number,* were not overly enthusiastic, but, with Ruben's prodding, they gave in. George Murphy was on the set the first day to welcome her to MGM, as was Lynne Carver. Robert Young, her co-star from *Dangerous Number*, was her leading man. They always got along just fine and Ann was very pleased with the British Ian Hunter, who also had an important role. The socially-conscious side of Ann was always aimed at impressing the British Colony in Hollywood. The Ray Millands were the first couple she embraced and Mal Milland would become one of her closest friends and confidantes, remaining so for her entire life. Ann's voice and dic-

AS, Marsha Hunt and William Gargan in
Joe and Ethel Turp Call on the President (MGM, 1939)

tion were highly praised by reviewers, but many thought her speech too pseudo-British and affected. This Anglophile fanaticism also extended to her signature for autographs which, for the most part, bore the ultra-refined and very British "Cordially." By way of total contrast Ann also befriended the earthy character actor George Tobias.

Her friend RKO publicist Jerry Asher wrote a very probing piece on Ann titled "Languid Lady." This revealed something of the enigma she had become through the constant reinventing of herself. Here, in part, are his observations of the contradictions that were Ann Sothern, at the time she was making *Maisie*:

"Hollywood has never really known Ann. As she says, 'Everyone expects me to be as hel-l-lpless as a humming bird. No-o-o one ever gives me credit for being sensible.' In speaking, she has an inimitable way of forcing certain words which gives them an exaggerated importance. Everything she says sounds funny, because she is always so serious when she says it. She always affects a confidential tone. Even if she's telling you about a hangnail.

"Ann looks like a fugitive from a hothouse. She is definitely a dual personality, herself and the girl you expect her to be. There's an air of indifference about her which makes her different. It also gives people the impression that she is snooty. Ann does have a charming way of looking at you, through you and beyond you. It's unintentional and there's a good reason.

WITH JOHN CARROLL IN
CONGO MAISIE (MGM, 1940)

"It all started way back when she suffered from anemia. She was a diffident child, bursting with talent and never finding quite enough energy to express it. She was always cold and listless. A lassie who lived in lassitude. (Today, she has one of the warmest hearts in Hollywood. But she wears fur coats in July.) She was trained to conserve her strength. Not an ounce of effort was ever wasted. At four she toddled out

WITH RITA JOHNSON IN CONGO MAISIE (MGM, 1940)

on the local stage to sing a chorus of 'Pretty Baby.' In the middle of the number she stopped. For the first time she noticed the theater was half-empty. Deeming such a small audience unworthy of taxing her talent, she went toddling off again.

"At fourteen she rode to school in a taxi. At the junior prom she got every dance. Sat them all out. By the time she became an actress 'Languid Lady' was her greatest role. Having suffered herself, worked under trying conditions, Ann developed an extremely sympathetic nature. On the sets everybody calls her 'Doc' Sothern. She's always pursuing someone with a pill. She has a remedy for everything from fallen arches to floating kidneys. Her favorite drink is cucumber juice. Because it's good for her, she 'just knows' it's good for you.

"Because there is no meanness in her nature, it's impossible for her to carry a grudge. She couldn't stay mad even if she wanted to. Her nicest quality is finding an excuse for everyone. She won't listen to gossip and generally forgives all sinners without knowing the circumstances. She reasons, 'The po-o-r darling was probably sick.' Even if people cheat her, she's convinced it's all

LOOKING STYLISH FOR *BROTHER ORCHID*, (WARNER BROS., 1940)

a mistake. But when she's through she's through. It's impossible to win her back.

"She has a terrific curiosity about people. Swears she knows the life story of every Pullman porter on the Union Pacific. She's a pushover for a sob story and, because she's a good listener, she frequently gets stuck with a tale of woe which is dull and uninteresting. When these sob stories get too long, she's trained herself to look as though she's paying the closest attention. Mentally she's arranging the furniture in her living room.

"She has a flair for dramatizing life. She can make a thumbtack seem like something rare and beautiful.

The fact that she's discovered something makes it news to her. Even if she's heard about it a dozen times before. Phyllis Laughton has been a successful dramatic coach for years. Ann went to her about *Maisie*. She received so much help she couldn't wait to tell the world about Phyllis. Spent hours bending people's ears, telling them why they needed Phyllis. Is the same way about her dentist, her masseuse, Pete the gardener and the woman who 'does' her hair. A mere vegetable man becomes 'great' once she's discovered his existence.

WITH EDWARD G. ROBINSON IN *BROTHER ORCHID* (WARNER BROS., 1940)

"Her loyalty to her friends is a rarity in Hollywood. She was delighted when Matty Melneck became the musical sensation of Hollywood. When she struggled for recognition in musical comedy, Melneck played in Paul Whiteman's band. He was a friend in need.

"She loves dogs and right now owns 'only four.' Apologizes to them personally because she can't allow them to come in and spoil the new furniture. Loves fishing and is 'so-o-o mis-s-er-able' every season if she doesn't catch a big one.

"She calls everyone 'darling.' Never remembers their names. She constantly complains about her memory, though has never been late on the set and has never forgotten her lines.

"Her motto, cleanliness or else! In her own home she's a clothes-hanger-upper, an ash-tray emptier, a bed smoother, a drawer fixer, a magazine folder and a picture straightener. She loved working with Jack Oakie because, 'He looks like a baby that's just been spanked and scrubbed.' She's also a bathtub knitter and a draft-seeker-outer from way back. When her own house is finished (a rented one), she goes calling on 'Mama' and her two sisters. She always gets them to try their furniture a new way. They change it back the minute she goes home.

"She adores jokes at her own expense. Was pretty upset when a Hollywood columnist erroneously printed an announcement of her pending divorce. For the first time since their wedding, she and Roger Pryor are able to have a home together. He's out of the band business and back on the screen. Things are working out beautifully. She thinks it's very odd that good-looking men never attract her. She tells you this in the presence of Roger, who has long since resigned himself to the pet name of 'Poppy.' Even if you don't ask her, she'll tell you that 'Poppy's legs are much prettier than Dietrich's.' Once she sent him a wire addressed to 'Legs Pryor.'

"Ten years ago she started at MGM. As a lukewarm redhead she thought she was pretty hot stuff. The studio's interest was cold. When they asked her to do extra work she refused. So they settled it by allowing her to make a sound track. She put her 'art' and soul into her voice as she spoke her lines. After they let her out, she learned her voice was used in a dog comedy. Today they are so doggone glad to have her back, they are the ones who are howling with delight.

SLIM SUMMERVILLE, AS AND LEE BOWMAN IN
GOLD RUSH MAISIE (MGM, 1940)

"Down underneath that maze of contradictions in La Sothern's nature, there's an awful lot of good common sense. She's suffered a lot. She's learned a lot. She can tell you all the answers. She's terribly grateful for her break. But she hasn't forgotten the way she was shoved around when nobody wanted her. When MGM decided to launch this big publicity campaign, she was called in on the meeting. For hours she sat there listening to them rave and plan her future in a supercolossal sort of way. Finally they asked her if she had any ideas she'd like to suggest.

"'Why yes, I have an idea that will sla-a-ay you,' said Ann Sothern in her most languid manner. 'Why don't you just call me the 'Scr-r-oomph girl?'"

There was no way she could forget her humble beginnings at MGM, for also cast in *Maisie* was Cliff Edwards. Together, between scenes, they composed a song, "We Meet Again," and Roger was so confident of its success, he used it as the theme for his orchestral introductions.

Variety was fully complimentary in their review of the first *Maisie* (1939). "Ann Sothern stands out prominently in the title role...she's sexy, smart and resourceful...and decidedly likeable throughout." *Time* made the astute observation, "As Maisie she's a healthier Jean Harlow, an untarnished Mae West."

As to *Hotel for Women*, *The New York Times* said, "She is Hollywood's best least recognized comedienne. Some day a script, a director and Miss Sothern are going to meet and bring the house down." *Variety* admired the "incidental comedy and smart cracks by Ann Sothern," adding that she "carries bulk of picture's interest with her flippant quick-witted and expected wisecracks."

MGM then cast her in *Fast and Furious* (1939), whose cast included Ruth Hussey, who'd also scored in *Maisie*. Lee Bowman and Bernard Nedell would also find friendship with Ann, who played the wife of book-dealer Franchot Tone. Socially, she had met Tone's former wife, Joan Crawford, through their mutual dating friend Cesar Romero, but apart from "on the set" knitting they shared little in common. Tone was urbane, well educated and from the type of socially connected family

WITH VIRGINIA WEIDLER IN
GOLD RUSH MAISIE (MGM, 1940)

Ann aspired to associate with. He also had an irresistible charm which usually proved fatal to his leading ladies. In Ann's case he recognized her ladylike manner and, being acquainted with Roger Pryor, respected her. As a team they were terrific and, though the script at times was ridiculous, they managed to rise above the material. Ruth Hussey was again on board and gave her aggressive, rude and arrogant character amazing realism. However, Ann's friendship with women was still reserved for the character ladies in her movies. Even Lucille Ball, who would later join her at MGM, had been neglected. Joan Bennett's presence was rarely mentioned and it appeared that a certain coolness had developed in their relationship after working together on *Trade*

WITH JUDY GARLAND BACKSTAGE
AFTER A RADIO BROADCAST IN 1940

Winds. Reasons may have been competitiveness, or, with Joan herself now married to Walter Wanger, less free time available.

With the male members of her casts and crews she was always considered fun to work with. Clark Gable worked with her on radio in "Red Dust," which found her playing the Jean Harlow role. He warmed to her immediately and said he hoped they could make a picture together. Also in "Red Dust" was Rita Johnson, who had been cast in a loose remake of that film, *Congo Maisie.* Ann, of course, was top billed, but there was no Clark Gable for her leading man. John Carroll, whom MGM used as a back-up for Gable and who could emulate his style, got the job.

Before *Congo Maisie* went into production, she'd made *Joe and Ethel Turp Call on the President* (1939). With William Gargan as Joe and Ann as Ethel, they depicted Damon Runyon-type characters. Lewis Stone was the President and in pivotal roles were Walter Brennan and Marsha Hunt. I spoke with Marsha many times about Ann as they had appeared in four films together. Marsha, a beautiful, intelligent and literate lady, said that "though we worked together frequently, I never really got to be close to Ann. *The Turps* was an especially rewarding part for me as I aged from 18 to around 65. I also thought working with such 'pros' as Walter Brennan, Lewis Stone and Ann, an added bonus."

With Ann's career booming, she had become the family breadwinner. Roger Pryor would file for bankruptcy on July 7, 1939, as his return to films in mostly secondary roles was not financially successful. This led to friction in the rented home that was newly built for them as Ann was constantly purchasing antique furnishings. Another setback was a fire caused by a cigarette which had destroyed the guest room earmarked for Roger's daughter. Most of the roles he got in films required only little over a week's work and he missed his musician buddies, and the conducting and prestige of having his own orchestra. Admittedly, he had the radio programs, which paid well enough, and he and Ann would work on songs and arrangements in their leisure time at home. They collaborated on a number of dance tunes and she studied orchestration. Never giving up her composing, Ann also orchestrated her own composition "Cinema Symphony." Expressed musically, this was her conception of the tempo of working and living in Hollywood.

Loretta Young was once again a friend and Gail Patrick along with Jeanne Cagney were gals she socialized with. As she had done with Lynne Carver, Ann also befriended Adele Pearce, a young actress who started her career at RKO. With a name change to Pamela Blake, she, with Ann's help, got a contract at MGM and would later work with her. Pamela Blake shared Ann's diminutiveness in height and she knew how this had handicapped her own career. This may have influenced the warmhearted Ann to help the starlet.

At this time Ann was named, along with Clark Gable, Ann Sheridan, Bette Davis, Spencer Tracy, Tyrone Power, Hedy Lamarr, Don Ameche and Vivien Leigh, as one of "The Stars"—"Nicest"—in person. "They never forget to be nice even under pressure. Courteous and considerate to all with whom they come in contact." Ann was also judged to have the "perfect face" for the new medium of television.

The Pryors indulged in weekend fishing excursions. For them both this was their favorite recreation. Conscious of her tendency to gain weight, Ann continued with lots of tennis, swimming and horseback riding between pictures in an effort to keep herself in shape. Reading at night when she wasn't learning lines had this ever-creative and inquisitive gal discovering a love of old

As *Dulcy* (MGM, 1940)

Russian history. *Under the Double Eagle* got her started on the subject and an extensive study found her fascinated by Catherine the Great.

The release of *Congo Maisie* led to loads more fan mail and Ann's reviews were splendid, with *Modern Screen* stating that the movie featured "her best comedy work," and *The New York Times* applauding her "flounce and impudence."

Following the loss of her foster son, David, Ann suffered appendicitis and was rushed to the hospital in the early part of 1940. The operation was without complications and after three weeks' recuperation, she became restless and eager to work again. Her hospitalization had cost her the second lead in the classic *Waterloo Bridge*, which starred Vivien Leigh and Robert Taylor. Looking forward to a big-budgeted "A" film, in which she would be afforded

WITH IAN HUNTER IN *DULCY*
(MGM, 1940)

equal star billing in accordance with her contract conditions, she was very disappointed in missing out. The fine English actress Virginia Field replaced Ann and gave the role a worthy interpretation.

Having given many interviews about her previous studio contracts and how she was relegated to "B" pictures, Ann again began to worry that MGM would do the same. Warner Bros. came to her rescue with an offer to play the girlfriend of Edward G. Robinson in *Brother Orchid*. The cast also included Humphrey Bogart, Donald Crisp and Ralph Bellamy, so this one was an "A" all the way. With an excellent screenplay by Earl Baldwin, the film continues to delight film devotees today. Edward G. Robinson was overjoyed with his charming leading lady, for not only was she talented, but her 5'1½" height made him look taller. Like *Congo Maisie*, this one did excellent box office business and garnered Ann some of the finest reviews in her career.

When Warners couldn't locate a rocking chair for Ann's knitting relaxation, they had to borrow and transport the one she used at MGM. This was said to have created quite a stir as the truck drove through the streets with its aged cargo bearing a large "Ann Sothern" on the headrest. Edward G., too, had his favorite chair on set—a large comfy red leather one with "private" on the headrest.

Returning to MGM, Ann was delighted to be assigned *Dulcy*, a Broadway success which had starred Lynn Fontanne. But, once again, a major star was not cast as her leading man. Ian Hunter, whom she liked, got the role. Reliable as he was, he never aspired to be, or considered himself, a star personality. It was a happy set as Billie Burke, Roland Young and Lynne Carver were all in the cast and Ann was encouraging to newcomer Dan Dailey. Having used a Brooklyn accent for Ethel Turp and a different New York twang for her *Brother Orchid* part, plus the special dialect she'd developed as Maisie, Ann was pleased to be able to use a more elite tone for the dumb but socially upperclass Dulcy. *Picture Show* said, "Ann Sothern's saucy, wise-cracking performance is the mainstay of the film."

Before starting *Dulcy*, she had to fulfill her promise to Louis B. Mayer to make another *Maisie* movie. *Gold Rush Maisie* (1940) was in a more serious vein, which made it more appealing for Ann in view of her feelings about being typecast. With a *Grapes of Wrath* realism, there was some fine dramatic moments for Ann as Maisie. Particularly heart-wrenching were the scenes involving her with Mary Nash, who played the tragic mother of a penniless brood. Virginia Weidler, as her daughter, was also in fine mettle and Ann and she became pals. A sweater Ann was knitting for Virginia grew larger and larger as other members of the cast, including Virginia herself, took part in its making. *Variety* was more specific: "Ann Sothern ably carries the burden of the title role…her one scene in which she becomes drunk on one swig and tells off Lee Bowman, is one of the best and well timed episodes of its kind to hit the screen."

In his second appearance with Ann, Lee Bowman had a difficult and unlikable role to play. Years later he would be the compere-advertising front man for television's *Max Liebman Presents*, and Ann would star in the second of the series, "Lady in the Dark." Always praiseful of Ann's accomplishments, he stated, "All of us who know and have worked with Ann can be certain of a fine performance."

C. AUBREY SMITH, MAUREEN O'SULLIVAN, AS, LEW AYRES,
RITA JOHNSON (REPLACED BY JOAN PERRY) AND EDWARD ASHLEY
IN *MAISIE WAS A LADY* (MGM, 1941)

On radio in 1940 she played in the aforementioned "I Met Him in Paris," with *Variety* enthusing, "Ann Sothern again demonstrated the sharp touch Hollywood belatedly discovered not long ago."

With the release of *Dulcy* (1940), Ann must have thought her fears of being typecast in "B" material had indeed come true. *The New York Times* summed it up: "Ann Sothern must be awfully tired of displaying her particular talent for acting nit-wit dames, especially in second rate films." Having been filmed twice before, with Constance Talmadge (1923) and Marion Davies (1929), *Dulcy* showed its age. *Picture Show,* however, still enthused, "Those who like Ann Sothern's work in the Maisie series are almost bound to like her even better as Dulcy, for she gives a delicious portrayal." *Variety* and *Photoplay* were equally firm in their praise for Ann.

Louis B. Mayer, thrilled with the profits from her reasonably inexpensive *Maisie* films, guaranteed her an "A" film if she would do just one more *Maisie*. She'd been studying singing once more but, apart from "St. Louis Blues," which she'd warbled a cappella in *Congo Maisie*, she had done no singing at MGM. Roger Edens got to hear her and with his help and composer/musician Earl Brent's accompaniment, she recorded four operatic arias. Armed with these, she invaded Mayer's office and had him listen to them. Impressed by the great feeling she gave the lyrics, Mayer, as he often did, turned on the tears. Eleanor Powell told me, "He was emotionally moved by her voice, he said she was going to be the new Jeanette MacDonald." In actuality, Miss MacDonald was only eight years older than Ann, but MGM always shaved years off the ages of their stars. Ann's birth date was now 1911, and Jeanette's went from 1901 to 1907; probably the most subtractive was June Allyson's, which became 1924 in lieu of 1917.

Assured now that there would be an "A"-grade musical coming up, Ann commenced work on *Maisie Was a Lady* (1940). With stock situations and characters, it was very predictable and most of the critical response proved on the whole to be negative except for Ann's own work in it. Nevertheless, with the many showings of the *Maisie* films on television *Maisie Was a Lady* is usually rated as one of the best in the series. Lew Ayres was her leading man and there's more than a hint of a wedding at its conclusion. Probably this was the idea of Louis B. Mayer's to convince Ann that it would mark the finale of the series—which, of course, it wasn't.

Maureen O'Sullivan and Rita Johnson were cast in the other female roles and Ann was friends with them both. Rita became ill and her replacement was Joan Perry, who later married Harry Cohn. Seen briefly, too, is Hillary Brooke as a snooty party guest. Ann would remember and suggest her when they cast a later *Maisie* adventure. Most of the humor in the film came from Ann's impossible behavior as a servant and its effect on manservant C. Aubrey Smith. They played beautifully together and it is obvious they are enjoying themselves. *Maisie Was a Lady* would be a *Lux Radio Theater* presentation in November 1941 and Ann, Lew Ayres and Maureen O'Sullivan would reprise their roles. Henry Stephenson substituted for C. Aubrey Smith, who was working on another project.

To placate his popular star, Louis B. Mayer had her take over Greta Garbo's dressing room, when the Swedish star quit the studio. This paved the way for her acceptance of another *Maisie* script as her next vehicle.

Things at home had worsened and Roger and she would begin a trial separation that September. Ann believed the *Maisie* debacle was becoming threatening when a lot of

RINGSIDE MAISIE (MGM, 1941)

her fan mail was now being addressed to "Maisie c/o MGM." One lengthy magazine piece featured letters from the public to Maisie requesting personal advice a la "Dear Abby."

Now feeling she was losing her own identity, it was with extreme trepidation that Ann began filming *Ringside Maisie* (1941). But, with her good friend George Murphy cast as her leading man, she began to feel more comfortable with the assignment. Another MGM newcomer in the cast was Virginia O'Brien and, just like before, Ann took her under her wing. I met Virginia, firstly at a party hosted by Betty Kean. A warm, friendly gal, she could not speak highly enough about Ann saying, "She is one of the 'real' people. Down to earth, a nice person and a lady. We did four films together and she was always the same – never assuming to be the star, just a hard-working actress, who knew her stuff. Years later she had me guest on her *Private Secretary* TV series and she was just as regular as ever." To jog Virginia's memory a little more, I suggested we sing "Let's Be Buddies" together, which she'd performed in *Panama Hattie.* "Why not," said Virginia, "if you, Colin, sing the Ann Sothern chorus first." We did it and the guests, including Patsy Kelly and Elliott Reid, and, of course, our hostess Betty Kean, seemed to welcome the diversion.

Most criticisms of *Ringside Maisie* are that Maisie is not the focal point of the screenplay. Robert Sterling, playing a young boxer, was the hub of the plot. There must have been an initial attraction between Ann and him, for she allows him to dominate many scenes, and she often takes a backseat in others. *Photoplay* hit on the film's main problem: "The weakest in the series.

It's okay for MGM to build up their fledgling star, Mr. Sterling, but not at Maisie's expense, please...or it gives murder we promise." *Variety* saw the positives. "Miss Sothern is a capable comedienne, distinctly pleasant to gaze upon and talented far beyond the material handed to her in the current release."

At the conclusion of its shooting Ann took off in *Popeye*, a fishing boat she and Roger used to hire every year. Holidaying at Catalina, she landed a prize catch—a 250 lb. marlin—and was presented with a Gold Medal as it was the largest of the four caught that season. She hooked the huge game fish, twice her own weight, on regulation 24-thread tackle, and hauled it aboard in 22 minutes, a feat worthy of a champion angler. This was not the first time she'd caught a "biggie" for when she first met Flo Ziegfeld, he was astounded at her having caught a swordfish weighing more than 200 pounds.

Walter Lake invited Ann and Roger to Seattle for a salmon fishing expedition. Fully reconciled with her father, she said, "He's so like me, it's amazing."

AS WITH HER SECOND HUSBAND-TO-BE, ROBERT STERLING,
IN *RINGSIDE MAISIE* (MGM, 1940)

SINGING "THE LAST TIME I SAW PARIS" IN
LADY BE GOOD (MGM, 1941)

Chapter Five: "Ann"

Lady Be Good, which began shooting shortly after *Ringside Maisie*, may have been the reason Ann wasn't unduly concerned about her part in the latter. The Arthur Freed big-budget musical gave Robert Young and especially Ann, who originally had three songs to sing, mammoth roles. Top billed, though, was Eleanor Powell, MGM's tap dancing Queen. Generous to her public and an all-round beautiful person, she was only too happy to discuss her career and *Lady Be Good*. "That film," said Ellie, "started out really great. I had three dance routines, with Robert Young as co-star. This made me very happy. Then Miss Sothern came aboard. Oh, she was friendly enough at first and we got along just fine. Then the bosses decided she needed a fourth song. This turned out to be 'The Last Time I Saw Paris,' and Louis B. Mayer was ecstatic about her singing. Okay, I thought, but I didn't realize they would cut one of my already filmed dance routines to insert it." Asking Ann herself about this incident only brought the response, "Eleanor was a beautiful girl, Colin, a fine, fine person." When Eleanor was suffering with cancer and approaching death, a Hollywood tabloid printed an article on her illness. In the article, Eleanor asked for letters from people and their prayers and good wishes. Typical of Ann's nature was to reply at once with a loving letter and prayer. The big-hearted, gregarious Eleanor died on February 11, 1982 and during my visit with Ann later that year I asked if Eleanor had the strength to reply to her letter. Ann said, "Eleanor was the most beautiful girl and she replied to my letter herself, by hand." Ann made no mention of a feud between them and seemingly had no memory of one. If there had been any ill feeling between the two ladies it was finally banished by their last correspondence.

LADY BE GOOD (MGM, 1941). LEFT TO RIGHT: JOHN CARROLL, ELEANOR POWELL, AS, ROBERT YOUNG, VIRGINIA O'BRIEN, AND RED SKELTON.

Virginia O'Brien recalled only their early comradery. "Both Ann and Eleanor were of the old school, well brought up—ladies!! My most vivid memory of that movie was that exquisite full-screen close-up of Ann's face as she sang 'The Last Time I Saw Paris.' One of the most beautiful close-ups ever."

Connie Russell, who at 16 years of age made her film debut in *Lady Be Good*, was another star with whom I discussed this film. The petite former vaudeville performer would become a household name a dozen years later with her regular singing appearances on TV's *Garroway at Large*. Possessing a voice with the caressing quality of a Rosemary Clooney, Connie could also be a Broadway-type belter and in *Lady Be Good* she delivers "Fascinatin' Rhythm" with great power and verve. "That was a wonderful experience and my first at MGM. Everyone was so helpful, both Eleanor and Ann especially. There was talk the three of us would be in *Panama Hattie*, but it never happened. After I did a song voice-over for Claire Trevor [1942's *Crossroads*] and bits in *Joe Smith, American* and *Unholy Partners*, I went back to the stage." Later television and more movies would follow in the 1950s. Connie would marry Mike Zimring, and, on becoming the mother of three daughters, would retire from show business.

Both Eleanor Powell and Ann fought against having Busby Berkeley as director and so he was assigned the role of dance director only. Norman Z. McLeod got the director's job and the Arthur Freed production cost $863,460. It was a box office success, grossing $1,692,000 in its initial domestic release. This was great, as the film's reviews mostly complained of it being overlong with too many dull stretches. Personally, Ann generally escaped criticism, with the exception being the sequence of the composing of "Lady Be Good." Both she, as lyricist, and Robert Young, as music writer, have the song started and completed in three minutes.

Author Hugh Fordin, in his book *The World of Entertainment*, stated how Eleanor Powell's "Fascinatin' Rhythm" song-and-dance number was shot after production had closed down. Arthur Freed, worried by delays caused by Busby Berkeley with the previous dance scenes he'd directed, gave him an ultimatum: "You've got three days to rehearse and one day to shoot." He started shooting at 9:00 in the morning; at 10:00 in the evening George Fol-sey, his cameraman, had to be replaced; and at 2:20 in the morning the crew walked off the set. Berkeley's total lack of discipline killed off any professionalism Eleanor Powell ever had.

During a conversation I had with Ellie, she told me that she'd had a lot of trouble finding the right dog for her specialty number in the film. After "auditioning" many trained dogs with little success she happened to notice the prop man's pet "Buttons." Buttons proved to be a quick student and got the part. A real scene stealer, he also worked well with Ann who adored him and

CONRAD NAGEL, LEFT, DIRECTED AS FOR HER "LADY WITH IDEAS" EPISODE OF *SILVER THEATRE* IN 1941. ALSO SHOWN ARE BOB MONTGOMERY AND HUSBAND ROGER PRYOR, RIGHT.

WITH DONALD MEEK IN
MAISIE GETS HER MAN
(MGM, 1942)

got him a job in one of her later films.

Jerome Kern was on the set of *Lady Be Good* and Ann got to meet not only him, but another great musical theater composer, Sigmund Romberg. Kern would be thrilled with her rendition of "The Last Time I Saw Paris" and when it won the Academy Award for Best Song, he praised her to the hilt. Controversy arose about the song's win as it was not written expressly for the film, having been recorded and played extensively a year earlier. From then on it became mandatory that all songs to be nominated for the Academy Award must be original and heard for the first time in their featured film.

I recall Ann's reaction when I asked if she'd seen *That's Entertainment!* (1974) and its sequel, *That's Entertainment, Part 2* (1976). She asked, "Is 'Paris' in it?" To which I replied, "No, not your version—they used Dinah Shore's [from *Till the Clouds Roll By*]." She remarked, "That would be Gene Kelly's input. Mr. Kelly never liked me." I mentioned that her on-the-spot composition of the lyrics to *Lady Be Good*, along with Robert Young's musical inventiveness, was included, to which she replied, "Not one of our best moments. Oh well, I'm not into nostalgia and I won't be seeing those films."

Eleanor Powell was equally upset about *That's Entertainment, Part 2*, blaming Gene Kelly for the truncating of her dances. She said, "Gene Kelly is to blame for it, not Fred [Astaire]. Fred would never be a party to the cuts in this movie. They hold some of the greats like Nelson [Eddy] and Jeanette [MacDonald] up to ridicule." Ellie was very happy with the initial *That's Entertainment!* and, of course, with the enormous response it brought her from new fans all over the world.

Ann headed off to New York City and Broadway to see *Panama Hattie*, starring her old friend Ethel Merman. MGM had announced that Ann would play the title role in their film version and a *Life* magazine layout featured pictures of Ethel instructing Ann in the movement and dance needed for the role.

Panama Hattie, which MGM purchased along with *DuBarry Was a Lady* for $200,000, was again directed by Norman Z. McLeod. Ann and he did not get along and her fears that, like *Lady Be Good*, it would be overburdened with dialogue and dull patches proved to be only too true. The usually prompt and dedicated star was reporting in late and often missing from the set through illness. With her marriage to Roger Pryor now definitely over her personal life also was approaching turmoil.

The songs she was allotted did not please her either; "Let's Be Buddies" was the exception, but she thought others, like "Salome" and "Did I Get Stinkin' at the Savoy?," inferior material. "At the Savoy" was an original song by Walter Donaldson, which was performed by Virginia O'Brien after Ann flatly refused to sing it.

Casting also suffered, as it did not now consist of the original "A" list it had commenced with. Ann's initial leading man, pal George Murphy, was out

"Cooking with Gas" was cut from *Panama Hattie*, but used in *Maisie Gets Her Man* (MGM, 1942)

Performing "I'd Do Anything for You" in *Panama Hattie*
(MGM, 1942) are Ben Blue, Rags Ragland, AS and Red Skelton.
The song sequence was deleted from the final print.

and newcomer Dan Dailey took over. Shirley Temple, who was to sing "Let's Be Buddies" with Ann, left MGM and was replaced by newcomer Jackie Horner. Eleanor Powell's suggested role went to Virginia O'Brien. "When Shirley Temple was no longer associated with the project, the song 'Let's Be Buddies' became a solo for Ann and I did a reprise with Alan Mowbray," Virginia recalled. Ann became very fond of Rags Ragland who, along with Red Skelton and Ben Blue, was part of a comedy trio of sailors. Showing her a still of them, with Ann performing the song "I'd Do Anything for You," she said, "There's my beloved Rags, he was such a dear, dear man." This song was deleted from the finished movie and I asked Ann why. She stated, "No, it was in it. They cut other songs like that awful 'Salome' and 'Make it Another Old Fashioned, Please.'" Obviously, Ann's memory was playing tricks on her as the final release print does omit this song. What a pity. But a recording of it was later released on an LP of "CUT—OUT TAKE" Records OTF3. "Salome" also got an airing on "CUT—OUT TAKE" Records—OTF1. This song would be given to Virginia O'Brien to sing in *DuBarry Was a Lady.*

When *Panama Hattie* was previewed in November 1941, the reaction so dismayed producer Arthur Freed and Louis B. Mayer, that they shelved it. Five months later, with massive cuts, they began again in an effort to salvage the product. Vincente Minnelli was given the task of staging, cutting and re-shooting the film. The total cost was now $1,174,000.

In the four-month period between the two versions of *Panama Hattie,* Ann had begun making *Maisie Gets Her Man* with Red Skelton. Since their first film together, *Lady Be Good,* he'd had a smash hit in *Whistling in the Dark,* and was now very much a popular star. Along with cronies Ann Ruth-erford and Rags Ragland, he would get to make two sequels, *Whistling in Dixie* and *Whistling in Brooklyn.*

PANAMA HATTIE (MGM, 1942). LEFT TO RIGHT: ALAN MOWBRAY, VIRGINIA O'BRIEN, RAGS RAGLAND, AS, JACKIE HORNER, DAN DAILEY, RED SKELTON, MARSHA HUNT, AND BEN BLUE.

When the second version of *Panama Hattie* was released in September 1942, Red Skelton's box office appeal afforded him top billing over Ann. However, there was no animosity between them as Ann liked him and he thought her "yummy." He admitted to having a secret crush on Ann. They would appear on television together years later and were always the best of friends.

The director of *Maisie Gets Her Man* was Roy Del Ruth and Ann and he got along so well that he got to helm further reshooting of *Panama Hattie*. His direction was uncredited, but Ann, with his help, got to sing "I've Got My Health" by Cole Porter from the original Broadway score. Another song cut from *Panama Hattie* was "Cooking With Gas," which Ann got to reprise in *Maisie Gets Her Man,* with an energetic dance routine that later included the participation of Red Skelton.

Marsha Hunt made her second appearance with Ann in *Panama Hattie* and they had a fine confrontation scene, which fortunately was not cut from the picture. Marsha said of this one, "I played a snob and there was a fun scene with Red Skelton and a strong dramatic one with Ann. She was a thorough professional and I greatly admired her lovely singing voice. About this time she'd just begun dating Robert Sterling and they made a very handsome couple."

Maisie Gets Her Man (1942) was released before *Panama Hattie* and cleaned up nicely at the box office. Ann also had Pamela Blake in the cast, playing Red Skelton's conniving fiancée, and Rags Ragland, Donald Meek and Allen Jenkins offered fine support. Ann's "consistently good portrayals in the 'Maisie' pictures rate her better stories. However, she appears a little more plumpish than usual," noted *Variety*. Addicted to ice cream, chocolate layer cake and rich foods, Ann's tendency to plumpness was probably exacerbated as a result of unhappiness.

Separated from Roger since September 1941, she explained: "Due to widely divergent activities, problems have arisen which we feel might be more easily solved by a trial separation." On April 14, 1942, she filed for divorce citing grounds of "great and grievous cruelty." Then, on May 7, 1942, she told the judge, "We separated twice before our final separation…and all three breakups were due to the same thing—airplanes. He took up flying three years ago. I am terribly frightened by airplanes and begged him not to fly. But he kept on and would make cross-country trips in his planes despite

LEFT TO RIGHT: KAY MEDFORD, JACQUELINE WHITE, ANN RICHARDS, AS
AND MARTA LINDEN IN *THREE HEARTS FOR JULIA* (MGM, 1943)

my protests. Sometimes he would go away in his plane and I would not know
where he was for a week at a time."

Roger and she would continue to see each other occasionally and they'd
talk on the telephone. Their mutual fondness for each other would never die
nor would the same sense of loyalty that Ann gave to all her dear ones.

An odd friendship had sprung up between Ann and Hedy Lamarr. They
were, along with Lana Turner, then a redhead, the beauties of the MGM lot.
Hedy the brunette and Ann the blonde. Hedy called Ann "Pluto" because of
her sad eyes while Ann tagged the beauteous Hedy, "Double Ugly." They'd
met at the Fred MacMurrays' and Hedy, having been through a recent divorce herself, understood the trauma Ann was experiencing. Hedy divorced
Gene Markey in 1940 and he had been the husband of Joan Bennett before
she had wed Walter Wanger. Wanger, of course, starred Hedy in her first U.S.
film, *Algiers*, and heightened Bennett's resemblance to her by having her go

brunette in *Trade Winds*. So Ann's friendship with both these women must have been tested. Hedy was now dating, and would later marry, actor John Loder. Her next door neighbor was actor Robert Sterling and one day when Ann was minding Hedy's adopted son, Sterling encountered them returning from a walk. They got to talking and recalled their first meeting and Sterling remembered how helpful Ann had been when *Ringside Maisie* was being made. Eventually he visited her house and ultimately they began dating. He took up tennis and she took up his favorite sport, golf. When asked how come Robert Sterling was nominated as Mr. Maisie No. 2, she grinned and said, "What makes you think I was casting?"

Also back in the picture was her Minneapolis school days' friend William Koenig. On May 12, 1942, Rosalind Russell, along with Ann, launched the Association of Motion Picture Producers USO Drive. They signed Bill Koenig up at one minute past noon at the end of a giant studio mass meeting launching the drive. Present as well, to represent the interested parties, were a soldier and a sailor. Ann would continue to be friends with Koenig until his death and he was often her escort to numerous functions and events.

Robert Sterling became a frequent visitor to the set of *Panama Hattie* and with Roy Del Ruth directing, Ann was a much happier lady. Sterling would bring along a favorite puppy too, Muggzie, and it was obvious he was out to win her heart.

Ann went on just one more date with Roger Pryor and then they dated only others; he was an item for a while with Lana Turner. Ann double-dated with Hedy Lamarr, Ben Blue and Rags Ragland. One amusing incident occurred when she went to Ciro's one evening and met Roger with his date, Olivia de Havilland. Accompanied by her escort Robert Sterling, Ann said to Roger, "How are you, darling?" before she introduced him to Robert and he to Olivia.

There were radio appearances too. "My Life With Caroline" for Roger's *Screen Guild Theater*, co-starring William Powell, in December of 1941; "The Awful Truth," for *Silver Theater*; and, again for *Screen Guild*, "Bachelor Mother" with Fred MacMurray and Charles Coburn in November 1942. Sandwiched between the radio plays she was heard with Charlie McCarthy on the *Chase and Sanborn Hour* and a variety show with Frank Morgan, *Post Traction Time*. Later, *Globe Theatre* utilized Ann, Chester Morris and Lee Tracy in an airwave's version of the comedy "Boy Meets Girl."

Her service record during World War II was excellent with Hollywood Canteen volunteering, entertaining servicemen at her home, working for children who were disadvantaged by war and donating station wagon equipment for civilian evacuations. The latter charitable endeavor may have been brought home when she appeared in a short subject at MGM entitled *You, John Jones* (1943). Playing the wife of James Cagney and mother of Margaret O'Brien, its patriotic message had Margaret play several children in war-torn countries of the world. This was then contrasted with the safe homelife of the typical American "Jones" family. Made by the Department of War, it reunited Cagney and Ann (she had a bit in 1933's *Footlight Parade*), who looked her most beautiful as the perfect wife and mother.

Panama Hattie was finally released in September of 1942, and to the studio's surprise grossed almost $4,500,000.

A complete departure from *Maisie* came her way with *Three Hearts for Julia* at MGM (1943). With Roger's pal Melvyn Douglas as her leading man she felt this would be a prestigious motion picture. Maybe because of her divorce from Roger and her dating Robert Sterling, the much-needed chemistry between the two stars was sadly lacking. Pal Lee Bowman and Richard Ainley were the other two "hearts" in the labored domestic comedy. As a lead violinist in a woman's symphony orchestra, Ann got out her violin again. This beautiful instrument, which was brought back from France in 1919 by Ann's uncle, was a gift from her mother. She'd learned to play "Humoresque" when given the violin, but had subsequently abandoned her studies. On the set with 75 professional musicians around her she managed, on the first day of shooting, to recall the early training. She had to do the actual fingering and when the film was

IT'S DIFFICULT TO CHOOSE BETWEEN MELVYN DOUGLAS, LEE BOWMAN AND RICHARD AINLEY IN *THREE HEARTS FOR JULIA* (MGM, 1943)

released, her mother called and said, "If you hadn't been such an indifferent child and had persevered with your violin as I wanted you to, you could have done more than the fingering." Ann always said her mother was not a stage mother, but she proved to be the greatest influence on her career. Douglas and Ann would reprise their roles in a preview performance for *Mail Call,* a military radio program.

In 1943 MGM released the Ann Sothern "Paper Dolls" authorized edition and it was another money-maker. They also requested she sign "Maisie" for the many autograph hunters who asked for her signature. In most cases she did, but wrote "Ann Sothern" above it.

With wartime rationing, Ann decided to do her bit by conserving gasoline. She stopped using a car and began riding a motorcycle as the substitute. Bob Sterling was now in the Army Air Corps in Santa Ana and she devoted even more time to hostessing at the Hollywood Canteen. One night she was serving coffee and sandwiches, along with Jane Wyman, Irene Dunne and Hedy Lamarr, when a sailor began staring at her. Feeling sensitive, as she'd just had a wisdom tooth extracted which caused her jaw to be swollen, she believed he thought her to be strange looking. To her relief he asked, "When did you dye your hair?" "I haven't dyed my hair, sailor," she replied. "Oh, yes you have too," he insisted. "I saw you in the east last year and you were a brunette – black as the ace of spades. Say, you're Ann Rutherford, aren't you?" Ann was so pleased to be mistaken for the young and pretty Rutherford, she kept mum and forced two pieces of cake on him.

Ann's big heart showed itself again when she visited her sister in San Francisco, where a group of them dined out at a Chinese restaurant. A young sailor came up and asked, "Aren't you Maisie?" When she nodded, he asked her to dance. Explaining that her dinner had been served and she wanted to enjoy it while it was hot, the boy said, "This sure is a lousy town. Nobody will dance with me. I thought you being Maisie you'd be a swell dame and dance with me." Not wanting Maisie to be a heel, Ann suggested he dine with them and afterwards they could dance all over town. As Ann recalled, "He suddenly exclaimed, 'Jeez, I'm out with movie people. Millionaires. My mother will never believe it.'" Ann tried to explain that movie people were a long way from being millionaires, but to him they were one and the same. He wrote to Ann regularly, after that signing his letters "Your pal, Ralph."

Another amusing incident was hearing from a schoolmate in Minneapolis, now recuperating in an Army hospital. "The patients selected me as the star they would most like to meet," stated Ann. "My school friend told them he knew me and had sat across from me in school. They bet him $50 I wouldn't write him or send an autographed photo. In his letter to me he said he wasn't a movie fan but did go to school with me and would appreciate a letter saying so and an autographed photo so he could win the $50." He got his letter and photograph and Ann hoped that he got his $50. Yet another amusing happening occurred when a marine, greeting

"A winning smile for victory"
in *Swing Shift Maisie*
(MGM, 1942)

her at the Hollywood Canteen, said, "I've seen all your *Maisie* movies, Miss Sothern. I sure am crazy about you. You're a regular girl of the streets."

For her most humiliating experience Ann always named the time she failed to land even a three-pound trout in a public fishing place. This was after her landing that huge swordfish at Catalina. Bob Sterling around this time said, "Ann was great at fishing as long as someone else baited the hook and removed the fish." He could have added, "and eaten it as well," as she did not care for fish as a meal. When she had landed the swordfish, she had a moving van deliver it to Beverly Hills. Then it was sent out to be smoked and cut into portions for her fish-eating friends. The head was stuffed and mounted on her living room wall. Somehow it did not suit the décor of the room, which had been designed by ex-actor William Haines. Also, it still retained some of its odor. Offering it to umpteen friends proved useless as they would sniff it and say, "No, Ann, not even for you." Accepting it at last was Bob Sterling, even though he was not too happy about this acquisition. Lucky for Bob he enlisted and among his things for which he asked Ann to arrange storage for was the fish. "Riper than ever," Ann declared. Finally she had a brain wave and offered it to MGM's property department. They accepted, picked it up a few days later and Ann got a check for $1.00.

Three Hearts for Julia was released in June 1943, and in April of that year Ann was on the *Lux Radio Theater*. The show was "A Night to Remember," with Robert Young and Ann portraying the roles Brian Aherne and Loretta Young had done onscreen. Her only other radio play that year was "And the Farmer's Son," for *Silver Theater*, which paired her with Preston Foster.

Swing Shift Maisie was her next assignment and she looked cuter than ever as "The Girl in Overalls," the film's title in England. Once again Ann found herself cast with Jean Rogers. This time Jean, now under contract to MGM as well, had a strong third-billed second lead. James Craig was the leading man and the bone of contention between the two girls. Off set it was not a bed of roses as Jean Rogers recalled, "She had a woman employed by the studio to play music on a record player for her. The studio really spoiled her rotten. One day I had a headache and asked this woman if she'd convey to Miss Sothern that I was not well and could the music be turned down. Guess what? It became louder." Looking at Jean's earlier credits, I found she'd been teamed with Robert Sterling at Fox in *Yesterday's Heroes* and again in MGM's *Dr. Kildare's Victory*. Maybe the feeling of competition on a personal level could have caused more deliberate dislike, as the coolness to Marsha Hunt could also then be explained. Marsha had been Sterling's love interest in *I'll Wait for You* and *The Penalty*. On the other hand, Ann was at her most cordial with Marta Linden, a young character woman. They first worked together in *Three Hearts for Julia* and, in addition to *Swing Shift Maisie,* Marta would also be cast in *Maisie Goes to Reno.*

JAMES CRAIG AND AS IN
SWING SHIFT MAISIE (MGM, 1942)

James Craig was another Clark Gable-type, who rose to prominence when Gable left the studio for war service. A tall guy, Ann would complain how she wished she'd grown taller than her 5'1½. Her looking up at the mostly 6' leading men all day, usually left her with a crick in the neck. This *Maisie* adventure had her working as a riveter, so, accompanied by her director Norman McLeod, she went to a Douglas Aircraft camouflaged defense plant and sat between two girls who riveted the big bombers. As a result of her experiences during the full day spent there, she redoubled her own activities in war work. Using a line from the script of *Swing Shift Maisie* she said at the time, "Women have always been in defense work—in one form or another. Today they're just perfecting the technique." Ann went on more bond tours and was a regular blood donor at the Red Cross.

Released in 1943, the latest *Maisie* caper's success, stated *Time,* was "…due to cinemactress Ann Sothern, one of the smartest comediennes in the business." *Variety* was a little more cautious. "Miss Sothern is her customary zestful self, working overtime to breathe some reality into the overworked situations."

Thousands Cheer was a Technicolor musical extravaganza with lots of MGM guest stars performing in an Army show finale. The nominal stars were Kathryn Grayson, Gene Kelly, John Boles and Mary Astor. In her first Technicolor appearance, Ann looked ravishing; it's regrettable that there were so few of her films made in color when her beauty was at its peak. Taking part in a WAVE recruitment comedy sketch, which cast Frank Morgan as a barber posing as a doctor, Ann as herself, is good-natured and fun. Her friend Marta Linden played the nurse in this skit. The other two recruits are Lucille Ball, newly signed by MGM, and Marsha Hunt. Again a 1943 release, *Thousands Cheer* was a big grosser and with Mickey Rooney, Judy Garland, Eleanor Powell, Red Skelton, Margaret O'Brien and June Allyson among the guest stars, it is not hard to understand why. Ann's "really hilarious sketch" was among the highlights for *Picture Show.*

While Robert Sterling was stationed at Thunderbird Field, Phoenix, Arizona, in the Army Air Corps, Ann's only date had been Cesar Romero. Then he too joined the service, enlisting for active duty in the Coast Guard. Numerous magazines covered the friendship and romance between Ann and Robert Sterling, but neither would confirm nor deny any plans for matrimony.

With no man in her life Ann began work at MGM on *Cry Havoc.* Starting out with this title, the stage play had a Hollywood debut with Julie Bishop in the cast. Moving onto Broadway it became *Proof Through the Night,* and among the cast were Katherine Locke, Carol Channing, Florence Rice and

Katherine Emery. MGM bought the rights with Merle Oberon and Joan Crawford in mind for the two leads, and Marsha Hunt was pencilled in to play a pseudo-delicate girl who is actually a Nazi spy. Oberon proved unavailable and Crawford had left the studio by the time production started. Rewrites eliminated the Nazi spy element and instead the delicate girl became a victim of Japanese machine gun fire. Hunt was now given the role of the good-natured friend to all of the female cast and Ella Raines became the delicate fatality.

Margaret Sullavan was coaxed back to films after a year's absence to play the head nurse. Ann Sothern inherited the Joan Crawford role of an ex-waitress with a tough exterior who finds love amongst the carnage. Beautiful Frances Gifford, in her first MGM assignment, was the girl with men on her mind. Dorothy Morris was the girl buried alive after a bomb blast and Joan Blondell provided the humor as an ex-stripper.

It was during the making of this film that Ann's divorce from Roger Pryor became final, May 17, 1943.

Frances Gifford shared several scenes with Ann and she told me that Ann was so lonely with Bob away in Phoenix. "She had this little dog he had given her and she lavished all her love and affection on the cute little pup. When shooting began, all the crew said, 'Thirteen women, what a catfight that will be!' Every day I worked on it there were no problems or tantrums whatsoever. On the last day, Margaret Sullavan, who like myself was highly strung and nervous, gave the entire cast a gift of Phenobarbital."

Nevertheless, there were stories of conflict between Margaret Sullavan and Ann - due mainly to Margaret's need for retakes and Ann's preference for a good first take. Both Marsha Hunt and Ann championed Dorothy Morris, with Marsha still in touch with her today.

I met Dorothy in Fort Lauderdale some years ago and this was a fun experience. Within minutes of our meeting, she had my shoes off and was administering reflexology at which she is an expert. Of *Cry Havoc*, Dorothy said, "Ann Sothern was wonderful, in fact the whole cast bonded beautifully. In fact, everyone at MGM at that time was terrific. It was wartime and we were all concentrating on peace and harmony. I was born in Hollywood and grew up there so for me there wasn't the mystery and excitement that a movie career offered to, say, girls from other states. Frances Rafferty and I were good friends, in fact we started at MGM around the same time. We were called 'The Golddust Twins'...she was peppy, full of go, while I was shy. Marsha Hunt is still a lovely woman and my good friend. We still get together. I did a minute role with her in *I'll Wait for You,* in which Robert Sterling also appeared. As he, like myself, was reasonably new at MGM, we'd run into each other from time to time. He was a nice person. Marsha Hunt was my idol and a wonderful actress. We also did *Pilot No.5, The Human Comedy,*

WITH FRANK MORGAN IN *THOUSANDS CHEER* (MGM, 1943)

Seven Sweethearts and *None Shall Escape* together, as well as *Cry Havoc.*" Ann herself said, "I admired the acting of young Dorothy Morris and on one of my days off went to the studio to cue her lines off camera."

According to Heather Angel, who played the sister of Dorothy Morris in the film, "The only gal who kept to herself was Fay Bainter. She'd worked with Maggie Sullavan before and knew she could be difficult."

With both Joan Blondell and Ann Sothern in the same film, many were of the opinion they would be too much alike in appearance. "Not so," said Ann, "side by side, there was little resemblance at all. Joan was a good old pro and lightened things up generally."

Because of an emergency appendectomy, Robert Sterling was granted a two-week leave. Director Richard Thorpe's wedding present to Ann was agreeing to her absence from the set on May 23, 1943, the day she became Mrs. Robert Sterling.

A 1944 PIN-UP PORTRAIT

Chapter Six: "Mrs. Robert Sterling"

Prior to their wedding and all through the period of their courtship, magazines and newspaper articles dwelled continually on the age difference between Ann and Robert Sterling. At the time of their marriage he was 25 and Ann, 34. With an extremely boyish face, he looked younger and there was an attempt on his part to look more mature. At one stage he grew a moustache in an effort to achieve this.

A contributing factor in Ann's acceptance of his proposal was the union of another MGM star, Greer Garson, to actor Richard Ney. Also subjected to an age comparison, this difference was highlighted by the fact that Ney had played Greer's son in *Mrs. Miniver*. They first met on the set of this film. The MGM publicity department had given Greer a more youthful age, changing her birth date from 1903 to 1908. So, when their marriage took place, she was almost 40 and Ney, a youthful 26.

Mr. and Mrs. Robert
Sterling were married
May 23, 1943

THE COVERALL GIRLS FROM *CRY HAVOC* (MGM, 1943).
TOP ROW: GLORIA GRAFTON, FAY BAINTER, DIANA LEWIS.
3RD ROW: FRANCES GIFFORD, DOROTHY MORRIS, FELY FRANQUELLI.
2ND ROW: AS, JOAN BLONDELL, MARGARET SULLAVAN.
BOTTOM ROW: ELLA RAINES, MARSHA HUNT, HEATHER ANGEL.

Margaret Sullavan offered Ann a wedding ring when the couple couldn't find two due to the demand brought on by all the hurried wartime marriages. Margaret said, "If you aren't superstitious, I have a perfectly good ring in my jewel box at home. It's just the kind you're looking for. You're welcome to it, if you can't find what you want before the stores close. It's the one William Wyler gave me. It didn't work for me but it might work for you." Ann, being superstitious, declined with thanks.

Bob phoned saying he'd found a ring for her and then a jeweler visited Ann's dressing room with a ring that might fit Bob. The reason for the hurry was they'd got the license in Ventura a few days before and planned a secret wedding with only close friends present. Louella Parsons got wind of it and their marital plans were in the next morning's press. With all the country aware of the upcoming event, the couple decided not to wait and made arrangements for the ceremony to be at 2 p.m. the next day. The reception was at the Millands', with Ray missing the service as he was at home preparing the party punch.

The actual ceremony took place at the Ventura Community Church with the Reverend Theodore Henderson presiding. Mal (Muriel) Milland was her Matron of Honor. Ann's agent, Henry Willson, took the role of best man. For her second wedding Ann wore a navy blue crepe outfit with matching shoes, a fuschia head decoration and similarly colored gloves to match, plus a corsage of fuschia and white orchids.

They had planned to wait until Robert had finished his training, but they decided to take advantage of the two-week convalescent leave he was granted on account of the emergency appendectomy. The honeymoon was brief as Ann had to resume shooting *Cry Havoc* at MGM. Robert visited her on the set most days and when the two weeks were up he reported back to Thunderbolt Field to complete his primary course in flying.

Having divorced Roger because of his excessive fondness for flying, it must have seemed ironic to have her marriage to Robert begin with a separation for the same reason. On the brighter side for her, as far as airplanes were concerned, was having a plane named *Sothern Comfort* in her honor. Her popularity with all the enlisted men was tremendous and she toured hospitals and camps, which kept the boys liking her on an even more personal level.

Back on the set of *Cry Havoc*, Marsha Hunt thought Ann's reserve toward her might soften, now that she was happily married. Marsha and Bob Sterling had become firm friends when they played romantic leads in two MGM movies, and she would remain friends with both he and his second wife, Anne Jeffreys. "But, no," said the genial Marsha, "Ann kept to herself, professional as ever, but remote as ever to me off camera."

Robert Sterling's real name was William John Hart and he was born November 13, 1917, in New Castle, Pennsylvania. When taking their marriage vows, Ann would answer to Harriette and Robert to William. His father, Walter S. Hart, was a professional baseball player for the Chicago Cubs. Educated at New Wilmington High School and the University of Pittsburgh, he worked as a clothing salesman following graduation. With matinee idol looks, friends told the 6'1" adonis he should seek a career in motion pictures.

In 1938 he went to Hollywood, where he unsuccessfully tested for the lead in *Golden Boy*. But Columbia was sufficiently impressed to put him under contract. William Holden played "Golden Boy" and Sterling, in a very minor capacity, made his movie debut in this film (1939). Other fleeting appearances that year were in *First Offenders* with Walter Abel; *Missing Daughters* with Richard Arlen; *Outside These Walls* with Michael Whalen; *Those High Gray Walls* with Walter Connolly; *Beware, Spooks!* with Joe E. Brown; *Romance of the Redwoods* with Jean Parker; *My Son is Guilty* with Julie Bishop and Glenn Ford; and *A Woman is the Judge* with Frieda Inescort. By coincidence, Roger Pryor and he were cast in *The Man They Could Not Hang*, starring Boris Karloff, and, along with James Craig, he did a small bit in *Good Girls Go to Paris* starring Melvyn Douglas and Joan Blondell. He also appeared in the "A" features, *Mr. Smith Goes to Washington* and *Only Angels Have Wings*, plus two Blondie comedies, *Blondie Meets the Boss* and *Blondie Brings Up Baby*.

The 1940 release *Scandal Sheet*, with Ona Munson and Otto Kruger, was his last at Columbia. Actress Gene Tierney was there briefly too, to test for a role in *Coast Guard*, which she did not get. She and Sterling were an item for a while and both returned to New York when their Columbia deals fell through. Later in 1940 he was signed by Fox and as Gene Tierney was now also under contract there, a romance developed between them. Sterling only got to do three features at Fox: *Manhattan Heartbeat*, with Virginia Gilmore, which was a remake of 1931's *Bad Girl*, *Yesterday's Heroes*, teaming him opposite Jean Rogers, and *The Gay Caballero* starring Cesar Romero. His reviews for *Manhattan Heartbeat* called him "promising" and *Variety* gave him praise for *Yesterday's Heroes*: "Sterling looks very good, has a pleasing face, a nice delivery and with all the markings of a typical school boy. With a little grooming he might grow into a good bet." Leaving Fox, he also lost Gene Tierney, who would marry fashion designer Oleg Cassini.

MGM signed Sterling and his first two there, *I'll Wait for You* and *The Penalty*, cast him romantically opposite Marsha Hunt. He did similar fare in *The Getaway*, with Donna Reed, and then got a good role in *Ringside Maisie*, encountering for the first time, and being helped by its star, Ann Sothern.

He graduated to "A" features with *Johnny Eager, Two-Faced Woman* and *Somewhere I'll Find You*. In the latter he played Clark Gable's brother and rival for Lana Turner. A programmer, *This Time for Keeps* (1942), which top billed the vivacious Ann Rutherford, had *Variety* saying, "Team is a good working combination, but if they are going to get anywhere in double harness much better material will have to be provided them than in this instance." *Somewhere I'll Find You* earned him great press notices, but would be his final film before enlisting in the service. After completing his training he would work as an army pilot instructor and be given the rank of Lieutenant.

Ann continued working on *Cry Havoc* and with its release in 1943 she collected some impressive reviews. The script was criticized by some as too stereotypical in the manner in which the twelve women were depicted. In addition to the axing of the provocative Nazi spy angle from the original, another cut was the controversial lesbian leanings of the character played by Gloria Grafton, which, because of the Production Code, couldn't be included. Labeled a female *Journey's End*, the movie screenplay by Paul Osborne softened the play's final scenes considerably. It had originally

WITH MARSHA HUNT IN
CRY HAVOC (MGM, 1943)

AS, MARGARET SULLAVAN, JOAN BLONDELL, MARSHA HUNT, AND FAY BAINTER IN *CRY HAVOC* (MGM, 1943)

concluded with a Japanese voice ordering all the women out of the shelter; when the stage had been emptied there was heard a barrage of machine gun fire. Then—total silence, except for the crying of a native baby, which the nurses had left behind in the shelter. In Osborne's treatment, the girls all exit at the sound of the enemy's voice, with Ann and Margaret Sullavan being the last to leave. Their fate is left up in the air.

Louis B. Mayer thought Ann's Technicolor appearance in *Thousands Cheer* a revelation, but *DuBarry Was a Lady*, which was mentioned for her, went instead to Lucille Ball. But, as with *Panama Hattie*, the lead role of "Dubarry" was second-fiddle to the roles played by Red Skelton and Gene Kelly.

The Harvey Girls was selected for Ann's next film and she would share top billing alongside Judy Garland, with newcomer John Hodiak in the third top spot. Really looking forward to this big-budgeted musical, Ann rehearsed the two songs she had to sing. One in particular, the melodic ballad "Wait and See," suited her voice and the emotional impact was conveyed beautifully in her interpretation of the lyrics. Judy Garland told me when she was in Melbourne, "Ann is one of my favorite singers. When she does a number at the various parties, she always moves me to tears. There's a sadness in her beautiful eyes and so much feeling in her voice…she breaks me up."

The newlyweds got together when Bob's leave would permit. On one of these occasions, they threw a dinner party for close friends and Bob's father. As the dinner concluded and the guests were being entertained musically, Bob suggested playing a new recording Ann had made. She protested, saying it was a bad recording, and she did not want the guests to hear it. Just before this, Mr. Hart, Sr. left the room to take a telephone call in the hall. Bob had now started to play the record while Ann looked at the floor with embarrassment, making aspersions about the song and her rendering of it. Being the loving spouse, Bob comforted her by saying how cute the song was and that he couldn't see anything wrong with it. Mr. Hart now returned and heard Ann's final comment, "It's just a bad record and that's all there is to it." Beaming at Ann he said, " I agree with you, my dear, the poor girl can't sing at all."

Ann still held a heavy loss in her heart for David, the boy she'd completely thought to be her own. At their wedding reception held at the Ray Millands', Bob Sterling lifted the Millands' four-year-old son, Danny, high in the air. "Hi, son," he said. "I hope some day we'll have a dozen like you." It had long been Ann's belief that there was no substitute in the world for a happy marriage and a child. "Fame, money and adulation cannot take the place of a home with children. When any woman attempts to make a movie career take the place of children, she is asking for heartaches," said Ann.

Ann also traveled to places Bob was stationed such as Mather Field, California, which was usually an embarkment point for overseas active duty. Now a 2nd Lieutenant, his servicemen buddies called him Bob, even though a 2nd Lieutenant, his servicemen buddies called him Bob, even though his real name, William Hart, was the official title.

One town Ann never forgot was Pecos, Texas. Journeying there to catch some time with Bob, who was engaged in basic training at the time, she was inundated with requests for autographs. A week after she returned home a letter arrived from a grateful Pecos drug store proprietor. He offered Ann all the ice cream sodas, drug supplies, toothpaste, etc., free of charge, anytime she returned to that Texas town. His profound gratitude came about when he unloaded 350, previously hard to sell, autograph books. Having them on his hands for five years with little likelihood of a sale, the entire consignment sold out within four hours of Ann's arrival in town.

Discovering she was pregnant had an overjoyed Ann experiencing just one small disappointment. She would have to relinquish her role in *The Harvey Girls*. Angela Lansbury, an up-and-coming English actress, got the role, while Ann embarked on a mammoth tour of hospitals.

With the trip to Pecos, Texas and the smaller town of Maria, Texas, Ann endured the hottest summer of her life. After *Cry Havoc* finished shooting she took the time and opportunity to travel as close as possible to where Bob was stationed. This would often be by plane, to crowded bus depots, then to El Paso Railway Station and another bus to the nearest hotel. For one period of three weeks, when she was based in Pecos, they only got to see one another on three occasions. Making friends with the other fliers' wives, she also worked on a sewing machine, making hundreds of bed pan covers. Ann visited the air base as the guest of Colonel Wiseheart, the Commanding Officer. She spent time at the Base Hospital, the WAC's quarters and then the Colonel took her to Bob's own barracks. Noticing the big picture of herself by his bunk and the "neat as a pin" diggings, she left a note under his pillow, "Honey, I approve of your housekeeping." Then there was the proud day she stood with all the other cadets' wives, straining her eyes trying to pick out her own cadet husband, as the field of men marched toward their wings. This was at the Army Air Base at Maria, with officers General Scanlon and Colonel Phillips in attendance.

Bob won his wings and then in a hotel room a few hours later, while facing the inspection of her husband, Ann had a set of wings pinned on her. This was a novelty jewelry ensemble consisting of earrings fashioned to resemble wings and a gold lapel wing clip with a tiny ruby heart at its center.

WITH JOHN HODIAK IN *MAISIE GOES TO RENO* (MGM, 1944)

When opened, the heart revealed two tiny pictures of Ann and Bob taken on their wedding day.

The only radio work Ann undertook in 1944 was *The Screen Guild Playhouse* presentation of "Congo Maisie," in which she starred with John Hodiak. She liked Hodiak very much and was also friendly with his wife at the time, Anne Baxter.

Beginning in the late 1930s Ann's picture had adorned many advertisements for beauty preparations. Among the products she endorsed were LUX soap and Max Factor, who would continue to use her face to promote their new lines. Ann was one of the great beauties, chosen for obvious reasons, whose face adorned a large placard titled "The Heritage Collection." Among the other beauties pictured by Max Factor in "The Heritage Collection" were Rita Hayworth, Vivien Leigh, Carole Lombard and Marlene Dietrich.

As motherhood approached, Ann picked out the name Timothy for her firstborn, which she undoubtedly felt was going to be a boy. Fate thought otherwise and Patricia Ann Sterling was born on December 10, 1944. Mal

AS, Ava Gardner, Tom Drake, Marta Linden and Paul Cavanagh
in *Maisie Goes to Reno* (MGM, 1944)

Milland was her Godmother, while director Walter Lang was her Godfather. The child was frequently called Tricia and then, because of her own mispronouncement of her name, Tricia stuck, graduating to Trish and finally Tisha. Having put on considerable weight after the birth, Ann consulted a masseuse and attempted a diet and exercise program. At this point she was often quoted as saying that she "wanted to retire, have more kids and let my husband be the sole breadwinner."

Following Tisha's birth, Ann was treated to another lovely surprise. The wedding ring Robert Sterling had originally wanted for his bride was finally located. She felt rewarded seven-fold, having waited over a year for the Russian-type wedding ring. Encircling Ann's left-hand third finger now was a ring with seven plain gold bands held together by a heart-shaped ruby. Ann explained at the time, "The bands symbolize the days of the week."

Maisie Goes to Reno, which Ann had completed in late 1943, was released in 1944, with *Picture Show* calling it a "well staged, gay breezy comedy." Beautifully photographed with better sets and production values, it also had more of an "A" feature look about it. Running 90 minutes, it gave Ann a chance to sing again onscreen, and the song, "Panhandle Pete," is given a rousing rendition by the star. Marta Linden, Paul Cavanagh and Bernard Nedell, all pally with Ann off screen, are excellent as the "heavies" of the plot. Tom Drake and Ava Gardner were the juvenile leads, and when I asked Tom about Ann he responded, "We also did *Words and Music* together and she was polite, professional but not very tolerant if you muffed a line or lost your marks." At the time *Earthquake* was released (1974), I asked Ann about Ava Gardner. She said, "Ava was 21 when she did that *Maisie* film and looked stunning. Shy and modest too. That little gangster [Frank Sinatra] changed her. I cried when I saw her in *Earthquake.* Whoever dressed her should be shot."

Articles in 1944 and 1945 about Ann Sothern always included conflicting reports on her feelings of being typed as Maisie. *Maisie Goes to Reno* was her only released film in 1944. In 1945 MGM again only utilized her services on yet another film in the *Maisie* series, *Up Goes Maisie.* With her husband returning home in October of that year, it would appear that she decided that the financial rewards made it worthwhile continuing with this very popular character.

Radio played a large part in her working life during the final years of the war. She did "Miss Dolly Says No" for *This is My Best* on CBS and was overjoyed working with William Powell on *Screen Guild Theatre's* "The Heavenly Body," also on CBS (1945). *The Biggest Show in Town,* hosted by Frank Sinatra and Lionel Barrymore, had Ann guesting alongside Joan Davis, Jimmy Durante, Jack Carson, Nelson Eddy, Ginny Simms, Gene Autry, Arthur Lake, Penny Singleton and Ozzie and Harriet (Hilliard) Nelson.

Ann's sister, Marion, had her share of drama too, when she was held up at gunpoint by a man pretending to be a police officer outside Ann's home. Marion asked to see his credentials. He produced a gun and stole her engagement ring and a small amount of cash.

Pleased with her performances, CBS signed her for *Maisie,* a weekly series which ran from July 1945 through to March 1947. Always a camera buff, Ann would commence to keep huge albums of her friends and co-stars from films and radio and, of course, her family.

Robert Sterling had only one job offer that he accepted in 1946 and this was back at MGM for *The Secret Heart*. In this, he played the stepson of Claudette Colbert and June Allyson's brother. His role wasn't over large nor very demanding, but he acquitted himself well with charm and likability. His romantic interest onscreen was provided by Patricia Medina. Off screen, his roving eye settled on another beautiful brunette, Cyd Charisse. According to Cyd, in her duel-biography with husband Tony Martin titled *The Two of Us*, Sterling was in *The Unfinished Dance* (1947) with her. His name is not in the cast list, though a role played by Charles Bradstreet could have been earmarked for him. Cyd also mentioned in her book that when Ann was out of town, Sterling kept asking her for a date, but, as he was married, she declined. At the studio he'd walk her to her car and also persisted in asking her out with telephone calls to her home. What he did not know was that Ann had the phone tapped, heard the calls and was furious. Howard Strickling, MGM's publicity head, told Cyd of the allegations of an affair, which she denied vehemently and as far as she was concerned nothing came of it. So, maybe Charles Bradstreet did replace Sterling in *The Unfinished Dance*.

Ann was positive that there was another woman (or *women*) in the life of her husband. Years later I asked her about this and who the other woman might have been. When she replied, "Cyd Charisse, I think," I mentioned that the way Cyd wrote of the interlude made it obvious that it was all pretty innocent. Ann did say, "I caught him, though. I caught him. Gloria Grahame was a definite fling he had. She looked a little like me, but with that funny little mouth. Jimmy Stewart wanted me to play the good-time girl in Capra's *It's a Wonderful Life* and they offered to build the part up…but I said no and suggested Gloria Grahame, who did well in it." Grahame would be Sterling's leading lady in *Roughshod*, an RKO Western made earlier but not released till 1949.

Robert and Ann first separated in 1946 and then, after a brief reconciliation, parted again in November 1947. Filing for divorce, she got an interlocutory decree on January 2, 1948 and was finally divorced on March 8, 1949.

There were many reasons for the divorce, the official one being "grievous mental cruelty." Other contributing factors to the final breakup may have been that Ann was eight years his senior and that, after the war ended, he hardly worked at all.

ANN AND BABY DAUGHTER, PATRICIA ANN STERLING.
BORN DECEMBER 10, 1944, SHE BECAME BETTER KNOWN AS "TISHA."

Bitterness and hurt on Ann's part led to a deterioration of her health. It seemed that all the love she had lavished on her husband was not appreciated and, worse, hurtful rumors reached her ears that with Sterling being unemployed, she was his meal ticket. After the divorce, he would pay $200 a month for the support of their daughter. During their first separation he wooed her back with the gift of a heart-shaped key. It was inscribed, "Darling, won't you come and spend a lifetime?"

Robert Sterling did a few more films, the best of which was *Show Boat* (MGM 1951). While appearing on Broadway in *Gramercy Ghost*, he met Anne Jeffreys, who at the time was appearing in another Broadway show. She divorced her husband, Joseph R. Serence, on November 14, 1951, and on November 21, 1951 she married Sterling. They have three sons, Jeffreys (1954), Dana (1958) and Tyler (1959). Together, they found success on television with *Topper* and *Love That Jill* and he made more movies, *Return to Peyton Place*, *Voyage to the Bottom of the Sea* and *A Global Affair*.

Actress Kathleen Hughes, who was "Miss 3D" at Universal in the 1950s and is married to producer Stanley Rubin of *The Narrow Margin* and *River of No Return* fame, recalled working with Robert Sterling: "I was first under contract to 20th Century-Fox and in the Technicolor comedy *Mother Was a Freshman* was given a song to sing with Loretta Young. The film was too long and the song cut. This was my first musical disappointment. The second was when I was guesting on the TV series *Love That Jill*. It starred Anne Jeffreys, who was lovely, and her husband Robert Sterling. My first faux pas was to compliment him on a very handsome suit he was wearing. I then asked where had he purchased it, saying my husband Stanley would be interested in a similar one. His dismissive reply was, 'I had it specially made.' Realizing he was a bit of a snob or elitist, I tried to be friendly and non-intrusive. The producers had asked me to sing a line in a song, to be recorded separately in a booth. This was my first experience in one of those and I miffed my entry. The director said, 'Let's do it again,' but Sterling said, 'There's no need for her to do it. I'll sing the line with a few alterations to the lyric.' So, thanks to Mr. Sterling, I experienced my second musical disappointment." For the last twenty years Kathleen has made quite a career out of her singing, appearing in clubs, cabaret and currently in churches.

Anne Jeffreys, in an interview with Susan Katz, said, "Robert is retired from show business now, he no longer acts. It was a series he did after *Topper* that really put him out of it, *Ichabod and Me*. He just hated every moment of it so he went off into the business world." He became a computer expert, but he did do a couple of TV shows, including a segment of *Love, American Style* with his wife in 1972, and *Letters from Three Lovers*, a 1973 TV movie with June Allyson. Anne Jeffreys remains an active and still glamorous show business figure, but Sterling kept to himself and for some years was confined to his bed. He died in 2006.

Chapter Seven: "Maisie"

Taking her character Maisie to CBS for a weekly radio show enabled Ann to win a whole new legion of fans. Although she had already done lots of variety and radio plays Ann said, "Radio scares me to death. It's an entirely different medium and a hard way to make a living. Radio is the hardest thing I've tackled so far—more difficult than the movies—a million times more so. Maisie is just a little girl from Brooklyn christened Mary Anastasia O'Connor. The Ravier is her stage name, after mama's favorite sister. Her parents were poor, so that she is, as she says of herself, not dumb just uneducated."

MGM liked the publicity the radio show generated and employed Ann for two more Maisie adventures on film. She also guested on radio's *The Danny Kaye Variety Show* for CBS (1946).

Up Goes Maisie starred her opposite her good friend, and often mentor, George Murphy, in this, his third appearance with Ann. Hillary Brooke returned in her second Maisie appearance as the dastardly "other woman." Ann also welcomed

AT THE MICROPHONE FOR HER
RADIO SERIES, *MAISIE* (CBS, 1945)

AS, HILLARY BROOKE AND GEORGE MURPHY IN
UP GOES MAISIE (MGM, 1946)

two cast members of *Cry Havoc* to this latest Maisie segment, Connie Gil-christ and Gloria Grafton.

The following year, 1947, saw Ann's release from her seven-year deal at MGM. It also marked the release of the final Maisie film, *Undercover Maisie*. With two leading men, Barry Nelson and Mark Daniels, and three villains, Gloria Holden, Leon Ames and Clinton Sundberg, to outwit, this episode was full of suspense and very well mounted. Playing an undercover policewoman, Ann donned a black wig for a scene or two. She also had to learn Jujitsu and prepared for the film by training at the Los Angeles Police Academy. One publicity item at the time had Ann named as the fastest learning woman Judo thrower the Academy had seen. Another item stated that she was almost knocked out doing a Judo stunt with Clinton Sundberg.

Freelancing now, she got a call from RKO about a film titled *Indian Summer*. Finding the script intelligent and full of contemporary issues, she signed on. Co-written and starring Alexander Knox, as a judge who deserts job, home and family, it was ahead of its time. Ann played a hamburger truck-stop café owner, who hires the judge as her cook. In time they fall in love and he becomes instrumental in having a law changed, to enable her, a single woman, to adopt a young orphan girl. Their "Indian Summer" ends unhappily, but logically, with the judge returning to wife and family and a higher position. The final scenes were reminiscent of the brilliant British drama *Brief Encounter* (1945). Released in England and Australia and other countries in 1947, it was shelved until 1949 for its U.S. release under the re-worked title of *The Judge Steps Out*. *Picture Show* thought the film was "played with sincerity and a deft lightness that makes it thoroughly human, humorous and enjoyable." *Film Digest* stated that Ann "steps out of that Maisie personality with competent warmth."

Tisha was photographed visiting her mother on the set. Shortly afterwards, Ann commissioned a noted portrait artist to capture mother and daughter in a large life-like painting in oils. With her separation and eventual divorce, Ann's loyal friends were quick to offer assistance. Mal and Ray Milland, Gary and Rocky Cooper, the Zachary Scotts, the Paul Clemens, the Fred MacMurrays and Loretta Young were the most frequent seekers of her company. Knowing that heartache and ill health were taking their toll, they provided solace and also insisted on her joining them at functions, parties and premieres. A couple of years earlier she'd double-dated with Jane Wyman, Ronald Reagan and Bob Sterling. She liked Jane and Ronnie very much and was genuinely upset when their marriage broke up, coincidentally, around the same time as her own. With her health restored and the decision to move on and forget the hurtful past, she was finally ready to start dating again. One of the frequent callers who escorted her on many

UNDERCOVER MAISIE (MGM, 1947), THE 10TH AND FINAL FILM OF THE SERIES

WRESTLING WITH VILLAINS LEON AMES, GLORIA HOLDEN AND
CLINTON SUNDBERG IN *UNDERCOVER MAISIE* (MGM, 1947)

occasions was the also free Ronald Reagan. Clark Gable always liked Ann
and compared her to his beloved late wife Carole Lombard. He'd been seeing
a lot of Virginia Grey, who wanted to be his wife, but he was also calling on
Ann. However, their meetings and outings were strictly of the "buddy"-type,
for he admired Ann's skills as a sportswoman and angler. Van Johnson would
say, "Annie Sothern would have a group of MGM stars, Gable and me included, over to her house for card games. She would regularly be the only
woman present and most often was the winner at the poker table. She played
like one of the guys." Ann was also friendly with Evie, Van's wife. The ever-
gallant Cesar Romero again escorted Ann when she was in need of a companion for a party or a dance date. One of her new best friends and confidantes was Gloria, wife of actor James Stewart.

In 1948 she played on *Lux Radio Theatre's* "I Love You Again," which reunited her with William Powell. As before, they had a rollicking time and the
audience lapped up their great repartee. Ann was a good friend of Diana
Lewis, whom she had met at MGM, and Diana was now Mrs. William Powell.

WITH SHARYN MOFFETT IN
INDIAN SUMMER (RKO, 1947).
NOT RELEASED IN THE U.S.
UNTIL 1949, IT WAS RETITLED
THE JUDGE STEPS OUT.

This was a CBS program, but NBC used Ann along with Jack Carson and Eve Arden in their variety show *The Village Store*. CBS obtained her services again for *Suspense* ("Beware the Quiet Man") and *Command Performance USA*, which featured her in a Christmas variety special with a host of big names, including Bing Crosby, Lauritz Melchior, Gene Autry, Harry James and The Andrews Sisters. For NN Broadcasting she also did *Background for Stardom*, which included a revealing interview with Erskine Johnson, and for MGM's *Theatre of the Air* she did "Three Loves Has Nancy."

The emotional and mental upheaval brought on by her marriage breakup caused a lot of changes in Ann's personality. There was a marked wariness and her magazine interviews began to reflect a frank and more informal image. Having concluded *Maisie* on radio, her coworkers on the CBS series vouched for her lack of temperament, of never trying to show off or grab the limelight. Not being a telephone addict, Ann preferred to visit in person. Robert Alda recalled her as "straightforward, honest and blunt, sometimes to the point of rudeness. Her own voice had a trace of affectation, but it was a trait she could not abide in others and that's when her bluntness rose to the surface."

AS AND ALEXANDER KNOX IN
THE JUDGE STEPS OUT
(RKO, 1947)

WITH JACK CARSON IN APRIL SHOWERS (WARNER BROS., 1948)

In one of her most open interviews she stated, "I'm never satisfied with my own performances. In fact I didn't go and see the daily rushes or previews of my pictures. There's so many of them I've never seen."

Beautifully photographed in color by Gene Richee, she was the "Girl of the Month" in a double-page spread in January of 1948. This would be part of the publicity campaign for *April Showers*, for which "leg art" photographs were widely circulated.

Following her return to RKO Ann must have felt very nostalgic when she went back to Warner Bros. for the light musical *April Showers*. With *Maisie* at CBS now reaching its conclusion, she

APRIL SHOWERS
(WARNER BROS., 1948)

forsook her blonde image, darkening her hair to a becoming honey-colored hue. Jack Carson and Robert Alda were her leading men and a young and talented lad, Bobby Ellis, played her son. Ann liked Carson very much, but referred to him as a "sad man." James V. Kern, who helmed the production, was one of her favorite directors. He would be remembered by Ann when *The Ann Sothern Show* on TV hit the airwaves in the years ahead. "Ann Sothern's warmth, her vibrant acting style and her very special way with a song and dance make one realize how versatile she's always been," reported *Film Digest*.

Years later, when Ann caught a rerun of *April Showers*, she raised quite a few eyebrows by criticizing both the film and her own acting. I brought this up to her in the 1980s, but by this time she had softened considerably saying, "No, it wasn't too bad! That was the first time I'd seen it, but it cropped up on TV a couple of years later and, as some friends wanted to see it, I took another look, too. You know, Colin, I was never a great dancer. I learned early on how to fake it. There were so many lovely color pictures from that film published, including portraits of myself, that everyone assumed that the picture was in color."

Ann Sothern as she appeared in *Words and Music* (MGM, 1948)

Chapter Eight: "Ann"

With the completion of *April Showers*, the ex-Mrs Sterling suddenly became the "gay divorcee." Among her many dates at this time was Cy Howard, writer John McLain, Vosco Bonini and, on a trip to New York, Roger Pryor.

Having scored her first Broadway success in a Richard Rodgers musical comedy, it must have felt rather like turning back the clock to be cast in a film based (loosely) on his life. *Words and Music* was the project, which also highly fictionalized the life of his lyricist, Lorenz Hart. Ann played a thirtyish Broadway star with whom a twenty-ish Rodgers, played by Tom Drake, becomes infatuated. In a warmly played scene, she offers him tea, some sympathy, plus a lesson in age mathematics. Her musical number is "Where's That Rainbow," a big production number, which also features the talented Blackburn Twins.

TOM DRAKE AND AS IN *WORDS AND MUSIC* (MGM, 1948)

She remained enigmatic as ever when discussing her career. A preference for character parts, rather than glamorous ones, was denied vehemently here. Nothing but praise and pleasure was expressed as we talked about her singing, dancing and especially her costume. "That

ANN WAS A MUSICAL COMEDY STAR IN *WORDS AND MUSIC*
(MGM, 1948), WITH MARSHALL THOMPSON, TOM DRAKE,
PERRY COMO AND MICKEY ROONEY

was a yellow confection with a large hat and there was a rainbow trim and layers of rainbow petticoats," she said. "I tried to have the petticoats seen as much as possible. There were lots of color stills shot of me in that outfit and many of these ended up in magazines. In the close-ups I'd lift one end of those layers so they'd be seen in each pose."

Signs of contentment and forgotten heartache were evident in the blossoming weight Ann gained at this time. Her yellow "Rainbow" gown had a little frill at the end of the bodice which cleverly disguised this. Facially, though, at the age of 39, she was still incredibly photogenic and a full-screen close-up captured her perennial beauty. Ann also mentioned that a second song, "Spring is Here," had been slotted for her but was never filmed.

Words and Music was far from being a critical success, but audiences did not care and it made a mint for the studio. Perry Como was the principal vocalist and what was his first feature at MGM also proved to be his last. Being under contract to a different record company precluded any of his hit songs in the film being included on the MGM soundtrack album. Ordered by his boss, Louis B. Mayer, to sing a personal "Happy Birthday to you— Louis B. " at a party to celebrate the occasion, Como reluctantly obliged, but added an expletive which infuriated Mayer. The enraged mogul retaliated by having him blackballed throughout the film industry. Mr. Como thankfully survived that injustice and became the host of one of TV's brightest and longest running variety shows.

A Letter to Three Wives (1949) was Ann's next picture; one of the finest of her career. Originally, it was A Letter to Five Wives, and Darryl F. Zanuck wanted Alice Faye to play Ann's role. Alice has stated that a disagreement with Zanuck caused

KIRK DOUGLAS AND ANN PLAYED
HUSBAND AND WIFE IN
A LETTER TO THREE WIVES
(FOX, 1949)

her to depart from 20th Century-Fox after making *Fallen Angel* (1945). As she still owed the studio a picture, she said that Zanuck made it impossible for other studios to hire her. With Alice declining his offer, Zanuck immediately thought of Ann, remembering her work in three previous Fox films. The project now became *A Letter to Four Wives*, with Anne Baxter cast, before it became, finally, *A Letter to Three Wives*, with Linda Darnell and Jeanne Crain joining Ann to make up the trio.

Written and directed by Joseph L. Mankiewicz, the company went on location to Lake Mahopac, just up the Hudson River from New York City. Following completion of shooting there they relocated to Connecticut. Here, Ann, in her off camera moments and weekends, was able to browse to her heart's content among the many fascinating antique shops in the area. Since her homemaking days with Roger Pryor she'd been a keen acquirer of rare china and other collectibles, including furniture. Her astute business sense was apparent for, even when dealing sight unseen with merchants, she would have the items delivered to "Harriette Lake" c/o a downtown Los Angeles address. There was good reason for this as she said, "Often when the purchaser is a known celebrity, the dealer boosts the price." There were also fantastic restaurants and eating places in Connecticut and, being a gourmet, Ann indulged at many of them.

With three female stars, the billing problem was solved by having them listed alphabetically. The male leads were Paul Douglas, Kirk Douglas and Jeffrey Lynn. Mankiewicz liked Ann and her work in the film and he once described her as having the sexiest mouth in films. When Kirk Douglas wrote his autobiography in the late 1980s, Ann's friend and neighbor Sarah Mitchell queried a passage in the book. Ann had driven Sarah, myself and a friend in her Rolls-Royce to a new "in" waterside restaurant, "The Warehouse." It was over lunch that Sarah wanted to know if Kirk's allegation was true that, during the making of *A Letter to Three Wives*, that he and Ann had "rehearsed at home." When Ann confirmed it, Sarah, a big fan of Kirk's, was over the moon. As he was, like Cy Howard, also seeing Evelyn Keyes, this romantic fling did

LINDA DARNELL, AS AND JEANNE CRAIN IN
A LETTER TO THREE WIVES (FOX, 1949)

ZACHARY SCOTT, AS, TOM HELMORE AND KRISTINE MILLER IN
SHADOW ON THE WALL (MGM, 1950). IN A COMPLETE CHANGE OF TYPE,
ANN PLAYED THE KILLER OF HER SISTER, KRISTINE MILLER.

not last past the film's wind up. Ann herself said, "It was a very brief affair in more ways than one."

Due to start *Death in the Doll's House* at MGM, Ann spent the weeks between assignments taking Tisha camping. Like her mother, she found fishing a favorite pastime and they would often journey to a lake in the San Fernando Valley to enjoy this activity together. Filled with trout, it also catered for the youngest of fishermen and women.

Lawyer Greg Bautzer, then one of Hollywood's most eligible bachelors, sought out Ann for dates. Ronald Reagan was also constantly seen with her and she was regularly in the company of the Ray Millands and the Gary Coopers. Clark Gable had Ann and Tisha visit his ranch and he was so entranced by the four-year-old that he took great delight in showing her the horses, the barns and the orchards. They became great friends. Gable did not try to see his own daughter, Judy Lewis, apart from one brief visit to the home of her mother, Loretta Young, with whom she lived. The unwillingness of Loretta to admit to the supposedly adopted Judy the facts of her parentage, made Gable realize his presence would lead to gossip. In a sense, Tisha was like a substitute child and so the affection between them replaced the natural father and daughter relationship denied both Clark and Judy.

Ann would also date Don Russ and actor Jim Davis during this time and would appear on radio in *Duffy's Tavern* with Jimmy Durante and in "Burlesque" with another great comic, Bert Lahr, for *Theatre Guild on the Air.*

While shooting *Death in the Doll's House,* Ann joined more than fifty other MGM actors for a group photo "The Jubilee Stars of Metro-Goldwyn-Mayer." Seated next to Alexis Smith, she found that she liked her immediately. When the film *Once is Not Enough* (1975) opened, Ann attended and mentioned that she did not like it at all. However, she did say, "Alexis is class all the way and I hated seeing her in that situation." Once again Sarah called in and we both asked if Ann knew who the real people were that Jacqueline Susann had based the characters of Melina Mercouri and Alexis Smith on. I mentioned Barbara Hutton and Doris Duke, but Ann said no, "Doris Duke is still alive." She did offer the tidbit that situations involving Melina Mercouri's character could have contained incidents from the life of Claudette Colbert.

Death in the Doll's House underwent a title change, becoming *Shadow on the Wall.* Zachary Scott was the male lead and this made for a jovial set as Zach and his wife Elaine were close friends of Ann. She would later regret, for Zach's sake, having introduced Elaine to novelist John Steinbeck, whom Elaine would marry following their divorce. Also in the cast was child actress Gigi Perreau and Kristine Miller, who plays Ann's sister and Scott's unfaithful wife. Both Ann and Zach got the chance to play the complete opposite to their normal screen characterizations. Ann is a murderess, who later attempts to kill Perreau. Zachary Scott, usually the suave villain, is Gigi's dad and, though innocent, is accused of the murder of his wife. New to MGM was Nancy Davis, who had a strong supporting role in the thriller. Years later Ann told me, "Nancy has never liked me! I was dating Ronald Reagan when that film was in production and he would often telephone. Maybe she remembered."

The "Foster Parents Plan" honored Ann that year for her World War II work assisting waifs. Also, she joined Claudette Colbert, Norma Shearer and others on the Sun Valley Ski School's Board of Directors.

SNAPPING A PICTURE OF KRISTINE MILLER, TOM HELMORE AND NANCY
DAVIS (REAGAN) ON THE SET OF MGM's *SHADOW ON THE WALL*, 1949

A Letter to Three Wives opened to rave reviews and would go on to win
two Academy Awards (screenplay and direction) for Joseph L. Mankiewicz.
For one, Louella Parsons thought that "this picture should open up a whole
new career for Ann Sothern. She is so good."

According to Ann, MGM renegotiated her contract while she was making *Words and Music*. It was a non-exclusive deal with a special clause in-
serted that she must have top billing over any other female player and equal
billing, if not top, with any male. The billing stipulation probably came about
because of what had transpired when *Panama Hattie* was released; Red Skelton's huge popularity at the time had MGM move Ann's name to second place
after his. She would later decline roles in *Without Love* and *Adventure* knowing her billing would be either smaller than the stars or beneath the title.

MGM also made available to Ann details of the grosses made by her
Maisie films. Adamant that she would not reprise the role, she was, however,
persuaded to accept another *Maisie* radio series. Titled *The Adventures of*

RECEIVING A HUMANITARIAN
AWARD FROM WALTER BLUE OF
THE FOSTER PARENTS PLAN FOR
WAR CHILDREN IN 1949

Maisie, she began the MGM-produced show in November 1949. Naturally, with photos required for advance publicity on the series, Ann, with her signature on the dotted line, became a blonde again. This blonde image had commenced with *A Letter to Three Wives*, which she had completed shooting just after signing the new radio deal.

Nancy Goes to Rio (1950) is a favorite Ann Sothern appearance for many. Ann herself liked the role and the glamorous clothes and hairstyles created for her. She told me it was also a favorite of her granddaughter Heidi's. "She liked the gloss, the fairy princess image," Ann said. Earl Brent, always a champion of Ann's singing voice, wrote a beautiful duet, "Time and Time Again," for her to sing with Broadway's Danny Scholl. Another melodic song, "Magic is the Moonlight," originally in *Bathing Beauty*, was revived here as a duet for Ann and her daughter in the movie, Jane Powell. Barry Sullivan was Ann's leading man, while Louis Calhern played her father. Carmen Miranda enlivened the proceedings with a couple of songs. It was MGM's remake of Universal's *It's a Date* (1940), which had starred Kay Francis and Deanna Durbin. Universal first remade it in 1945 with Donald Cook and Donald O'Connor in a father and son story variation, *Patrick the Great*. Producer Joe Pasternak obtained the rights for his MGM version, which was a big-budget Technicolor extravaganza. Ann does get onscreen top billing in *Nancy Goes to Rio*, but the cagey studio gave this spot to Jane Powell on most of the publicity material. The first issue of the LP soundtrack recording also gave Jane the top spot, but a few years later a reissue had Ann back in her rightful position. With Jane no longer at MGM and Ann now having a highly successful television career, the studio headlined the star who would be likely to generate the most sales.

Jane Powell and Ann got on fine and Ann once said to me, "I just watched *Royal Wedding* and, you know, Janie was really a wonderful dancer." The two singers at one time even considered doing a niterie act together, which sadly did not eventuate. I met Jane Powell on several occasions, the first being when I was playing in *Brigadoon* and she came backstage afterwards. Accompanied by her daughter, she was vivacious and easy to talk with. We spoke about Ann and Jane was very complimentary, saying that Ann was "busy as ever in movies," mentioning the film *Sylvia* (1965).

When the filming was over in October 1949, Ann went to New York. While there, she was stricken with a throat problem and given penicillin. A negative reaction resulted in penicillin poisoning and a doctor and a nurse were in constant attendance. Back home, Ann, who remained quite ill, was visited by her ex-husband Robert Sterling and radio and movie producer Cy Howard.

NANCY GOES TO RIO (MGM, 1950)
WITH JANE POWELL AND GLENN ANDERS

PLAYING THE ACTRESS-MOTHER OF JANE POWELL AND RIVAL FOR BARRY
SULLIVAN IN MGM'S 1950 RELEASE, *NANCY GOES TO RIO*

In December 1949, asked to represent MGM, with her frequent co-star and friend George Murphy to accompany her, she flew to London. This was for the Royal Command Performance of MGM's *That Forsythe Woman*. Along with Jean Simmons, Richard Todd, Rosalind Russell, George Murphy, and Gregory Peck, she was presented to the Royal Family. Princess Margaret turned out to be an admirer of her work and they chatted briefly. At celebrations later she danced with Michael Wilding and was on a date with a young fan, Captain Hardwick. The visiting Hollywood celebrities also publicized Warner Bros.' *Montana*, and did an interview for the BBC.

Harry Cohn expressed interest in having Ann play Billie Dawn in *Born Yesterday*. His original star choice, Rita Hayworth, had married and was unavailable. Evelyn Keyes bleached her hair and padded her bust line in an all-out effort to snare the coveted role. Marie McDonald was also briefly in contention. Cohn favored Ann, having seen her splendid showing in *A Letter to*

Three Wives. Her lengthy illness kept her out of the running, however, and Judy Holliday, who'd created the role on Broadway with great success, was rightly given the part.

ROSALIND RUSSELL, GEORGE MURPHY AND AS RETURNING FROM A COMMAND PERFORMANCE FOR THE KING AND QUEEN OF ENGLAND, DECEMBER 7, 1949

Taken ill again in February 1950, she was diagnosed as having a thyroid gland tumor, a calcium deposit pressing on her vocal chords. Swathed in bandages, her unfailing good nature won over all the hospital staff and visitors. For a time, barely able to speak, she whispered to a columnist, "I wired Winchell. He said I was carrying a torch for Cy Howard. I wanted him to know the only torch I'm carrying is for myself." Cy Howard, at that time, was also dating Evelyn Keyes, but neither she nor Ann got him to the altar.

Recuperating from her throat surgery, Ann returned home and now faced an extremely slow convalescence. Seeking further medical advice, it was discovered she needed additional surgery. This major operation disclosed that she had contracted a liver virus that usually manifests itself in its final and fatal stages. Ann hovered between life and death. Infectious hepatitis was the culprit. She had been contaminated with a faulty serum-vaccine, which had been injected with the shots used for her trip to England. The weeks in the hospital were agonizing for her, as every minute sound magnified to thunderous proportions in her ears. The nurses' uniforms rustled, but to her super-sensitive hearing it was a roar. Likewise, any form of light caused her pain and, as she lay there, her whole life unfolded with a jerky mental inventory. The thyroid condition had thrown her entire nervous system off balance and the hepatitis affecting her liver turned her bright yellow. When she was out of immediate danger, the hospital sent her, accompanied by a nurse, to the Ocean House Hotel in Santa Monica for further recuperation. For nearly three years she was far from well.

In November of 1950, Ann was released from her MGM contract. With the bedridden illness she had been unable to work and her finances were

1952 PORTRAIT FOR HER
BROADWAY COMEDY, *FAITHFULLY
YOURS*, WHICH CO-STARRED
ROBERT CUMMINGS

dwindling rapidly. MGM had been able to cancel her film contract as a whole year had elapsed since she'd made *Nancy Goes to Rio.*

They did offer her financial support, though, by maintaining and signing her for more radio episodes of *Maisie.* These would continue well into 1952 and the shows were recorded at her home, from her bed. This second series had a fine supporting cast of actors including Sheldon Leonard, Hans Conried, Joan Banks (Mrs. Frank Lovejoy), who became a close friend, Lurene Tuttle, Bea Benederet, Elvia Allman and Marvin Miller; Audrey Totter and Gene Kelly would substitute for Ann as friends of Maisie in some episodes when she was too ill to record.

Nancy Goes to Rio opened and did record business for MGM. A series of *Nancy* films was planned but with Ann becoming ill, these scenarios were altered.

After one year of this devastating sickness, her agent sent out feelers for job offers. Hal Wallis expressed interest in her playing in a Burt Lancaster film and RKO had her in mind for a comedy in which she'd play a songwriter. Not yet out of the woods healthwise she could not commit to either project. By the second year of convalescence, movie offers had completely dwindled and she thought about a return to the stage. In March of 1951, Arthur Kennedy was signed to star in the Los Angeles premiere of *The Country Girl.* Sheila Graham mentioned that Ann was first choice for the feminine lead, but, again, she suffered a relapse and was unable to accept the role for the Actors Studio Production.

Tisha, now six years old, was a very beautiful child and Beverly Hills High requested her services as a model for art classes there. By coincidence,

Ann had done similar duty as a model at Minneapolis High and was chief model at the Minneapolis School of Art.

Actor and director Richard Whorf interested Ann in an adaptation of a successful French comedy, *The Philemon Complex*. Retitled *Faithfully Yours*, and co-starring Robert Cummings, it opened in New Haven on September 9, 1951, and did a further week's tryout at the Forrest Theater in Philadelphia before opening on Broadway. A last-minute cast change had British actor Phillip Friend replaced by Philip Bowineuf for the New York opening. The Broadway run was only 68 performances and the overall notices for the play and director were not good. That year Broadway had seen many Hollywood refugees attempt a legitimate stage comeback. Ginger Rogers, Gloria Swanson, Dane Clark and Melvyn Douglas were among other movie actors whose Broadway appearances in 1951 were not well received. Of *Faithfully Yours*, Tom Donnelly, in *Washington Daily News*, said: "Miss Sothern models a different gown by Adrian in every scene, and acts thruout with that air of shopgirl languor." Donnelly added, "the girl I escorted to the play loved it. It's the sort of play to go to when you're exhausted. Other women will love it too. After a hard day at home or the

office there's nothing like of a bit of froth that doesn't make you think." Said *Variety*, "Miss Sothern matches an attractive appearance with generally dexterous thesping. A fault however is a tendency to laugh along with the audience when she, as a character, is meant to be serious."

During the tryout tour Ann had Tisha stay with her sister in Chicago. After the New York opening, Tisha joined her mother to live in a Central Park rented apartment. At age five, Ann had her taught swimming by Olympic champion Dorothy Poynton. With her illness forcing her to abandon Tisha's care, Ann entered her in a private school for girls, returning to live with her mother when she was well enough.

While in New York Ann made her TV debut on *The Fred Waring Show*. Having been judged years before as having the perfect face for TV, she lived up to her publicity. Returning to Los Angeles, she played in a *Schlitz Playhouse of Stars* segment called "Lady With a Will" for CBS. Reviewers were kind, both to her appearance and acting ability. Some months went by before she was well enough to accept another assignment on the small screen. This was for NBC and the segment was "Let George Do It" on *Hollywood Opening Night* (1952). Cast opposite her was Richard Egan, an ex-serviceman who was slowly making his name in motion pictures. They had first met in late 1949 when, at the time, Egan was "quite full of himself." Introduced to Ann, he kept talking about himself declaring, "They say I'll be another Gable." Her remark, "Well, why not try acting like him," brought him down to earth with a thud. This then prompted Ann to give him encouragement and every time he got a job he'd phone her for advice. Now, Ann was in the early stages of her illness and she refused to take his calls. Learning she was in the hospital, he became a regular visitor and of great help to her during the long recovery period. He said he loved her and asked her to be his wife. After some deliberation, she said no.

First, he was ten years her junior and second he was Roman Catholic and she a divorcee. Richard introduced her to his family, who all liked and approved of Ann. She in turn was influenced by the Egans' strength as a family unit and their unitedness in their Catholic faith. Particularly inspiring for her was Richard's older brother, who was a Jesuit priest. All the horror and tribulation she had suffered during the previous three years now had her searching and seeking answers. Up to this point not a practicing churchgoer, Ann remembered and observed the serenity of Irene Dunne, the strength and self-confidence of Loretta Young and the power that dominated Rosalind Russell. All these stars were staunch Roman Catholics. Ann Rutherford once told me that Ann Sothern and she had talks about what Sunday School to send their daughters, so Ann was then very much a Protestant. Inspired by the Egans and other Catholic film star friends, she began instruction in the Catholic faith. Richard Egan's brother was an instructor and, though Richard and she parted, she was forever grateful to both him and his brother.

The Blue Gardenia, which brought Ann back to the big screen, was a Warner Bros. release directed by Fritz Lang. Written by Vera Caspary, who also had a hand in *A Letter to Three Wives,* it was a starring vehicle for Anne

JEFF DONNELL, AS AND ANNE BAXTER IN
THE BLUE GARDENIA (WARNER BROS., 1953).
THIS WAS ANN'S COMEBACK FILM AFTER HER ILLNESS.

Baxter. Ann got third star billing after male lead Richard Conte. Also cast as a roommate to Anne and Ann was the sprightly Jeff Donnell. Ruth Storey had a strong role as a murderess. Showing Ann some stills from the movie, she noted, "That's Jeff Donnell, a really nice gal, Colin," and, "Annie Baxter, she married Mr. Galt and lived in Australia. He was a real charmer. Annie had too tight a face lift, she doesn't look the same anymore." Jeff Donnell, who became a close friend, said, "Ann Sothern and I were close right from the start of the picture. Fritz Lang was one of my favorite directors, but he could be tough. Both Anne and Ann were subjected to his wrath. Baxter, because of her interpretation of the role, and Sothern, because of her gaining weight after the film was well into production."

Marjorie Reynolds, who worked earlier with Lang on *Ministry of Fear,* had nothing but praise for the director and the admiration was mutual. Completely opposite was the opinion of English-born Anna Lee, who played in *Hangmen Also Die* directed by Lang. When asked to smash a window by hand, she hesitated only to be bullied by Lang into doing it. "My hand and wrist were severely cut," said Anna. "That Fritz Lang, he never properly apologized or admitted he was wrong in saying the stunt was quite safe."

"Susie" in *Private Secretary* (1953)

Chapter Nine: "Susie"

With the completion of two TV anthology plays and the film *The Blue Gardenia*, Ann felt ready to tackle a TV series. In a statement, she said she planned to resurrect *Maisie* as a TV regular. When the rights proved unavailable, a project based on a theatrical agent's private secretary was judged and finally accepted. Now playing Susie Camille MacNamara, the series *Private Secretary* debuted on CBS on February 1, 1953. Sponsored initially by Lucky Strike, it would later include Slenderella commercials. Susie differed from Maisie in that she wore smarter clothes and, being better educated, the character was more articulate with an excellent command of the English language spoken with a more "polished" delivery. One attribute they did share was the same genial warmth, plus the Pollyanna "Miss Fix-it" qualities. Don Porter played Peter Sands, her theatrical agent boss, with other regulars being Ann Tyrrell, as the switchboard operator, and Joan Banks as Sylvia, another secretary, who is Susie's best friend. Frank Orth, who'd done films with Ann, played Sylvia's boss, and semi-regulars included Jesse White,

AS AND DON PORTER IN THE TV SERIES *PRIVATE SECRETARY* (1953)

A *PRIVATE SECRETARY* (1953) POSE

George E. Stone, Franklin Pangborn and Frank Wilcox. The character of a drugstore clerk, played by Joseph Martorano, was promoted to office boy and the young actor underwent a name change, becoming Joseph Corey. One surprise guest on the show was the wife of Van Johnson, Evie Abbott Johnson, in a rare acting appearance. Though Ann would testify for Evie when the Johnsons later divorced, Van bore no grudge. He guested on *The Ann Sothern Show* some years later.

Private Secretary would play five seasons, airing more than one hundred segments. Among the guests stars Ann employed were friends Virginia O'Brien, Hillary Brooke, Cesar Romero, Hans Conried and an RKO pal, Frances Mercer. Jacques Bergerac, ZaSu Pitts, Jean Parker, Ann Doran, Natalie Schafer and Sherry Jackson also appeared on the series. Ann was particularly impressed with guest comedienne Pat Carroll, and suggested her for other projects, including a TV series for Ann's own production company.

One guest star not impressed with Ann as a co-worker was Marguerite Chapman. A straight-shooter, she said, "Both Eve Arden and Ann Sothern were businesslike and far from sunny of disposition in person. They were bitchy." However, Marguerite was renowned for "jokey" behavior and it is more than likely that Eve and Ann were only too aware of what they considered to be "time wasting" antics, which they would find unacceptable. Marguerite did not hesitate in guesting again, this time on Ann's followup TV show, *The Ann Sothern Show*, so obviously the "bitchiness" could not have been too unbearable as it did not prevent this return bout.

Ann's delineation of the character Susie would earn her four Emmy nominations by the time it folded in March of 1957. She lost out to her friends Loretta Young and Lucille Ball, with Nanette Fabray winning over Ann's final two nominations. Luckier, was her win as the "Most Popular TV

Actress of 1954," presented by her friend June Allyson. A silver cup award, it was voted by the readers of *Modern Screen* magazine. That year she also accepted a bronze shorthand book when named "Favorite Private Secretary of the Year." The National Secretaries Association (Los Angeles Chapter) were the presenters. Ironically, Ann could not type and she got mail telling her she was not doing it right when using the carriage return too often. Later, she'd have the keys removed as her "speed" would cause them to jam much too frequently. Her ever-loving Chicago "Sales Executives Club" presented her with a trophy for being "The Most Distinguished Secretary of 1957." Ann good-naturedly agreed to be the prize in a couple of newspaper contests and as a result she got to work as a real-life secretary for a day in a "Why I Like My Boss" competition. Replacing the winning secretary, Ann did lots of filing and some dictation. The other one had her performing similar duties at a leading hotel.

Forming Vincent Productions in 1953, Ann again mentioned retirement for herself and her interest in promoting young talent. Named after her favorite Saint, Vincent Productions also took charge of her finances for *Private*

AS and daughter Tisha at home in 1954

Secretary, sought pilots for possible TV series and looked after the careers of her discoveries. Among these were Pat Carroll, Stephanie Powers and two under contract, singer Ginny Saturday and actor Tony Remo. Ann said, "Ginny was in the chorus line of my nightclub act and I noticed her during rehearsals. She had very real talent. I later signed her. My company also stages acts for people and Tony came to see us to do this job for him. I thought he had talent and signed him. I'm looking for other promising kids but right now I've had to fight off the applications. I can only handle so much."

Other business interests she developed were A-BAR-S Cattle Ranch with her now reconciled father in charge and the Ann Sothern Sun Valley Sewing Center in Idaho, which opened in 1956.

More popular than ever, movie producers were knocking on her door. MGM wanted to sign her yet again and an independent film, *The Easterner*, almost got her attention. Raymond Burr, an admirer since *The Blue Gardenia*, wanted her to play his wife in *Desire in the Dust*, a film to be shot while his *Perry Mason* series and Ann's *Private Secretary* were in recess. As Ann had vacation plans for herself and Tisha, she declined his offer and the role was subsequently accepted by Joan Bennett.

The Blue Gardenia did not get much in the way of positive critical assessment, but Ann's own performance was generally praised. *Variety* felt the film had "an occasional bright spot, mostly because Ann Sothern breathes some life into a stock character and quips." Now 44 years old and having been ill for three years, Ann herself was concerned about her appearance on the big screen, but she need not have been worried for most reviewers welcomed her back and thought her the saving grace of the film.

Private Secretary became *Susie* when it went into reruns on NBC. Not content with being typed, as she had been with *Maisie*, Ann guested on other TV shows in 1953. There was *What's My Line*, in which she was the mystery guest, and *The Red Skelton Show*, playing Daisy June to Skelton's Clem Kadiddlehopper.

In 1954 her musical talents were revived when she undertook a niterie act. Now a platinum blonde, she commenced in Reno then rocked them in Las Vegas at the El Rancho and wound up in Chicago at the Chez Paree. *Variety* said of her Vegas stint: "She can pour flavor into a song like a soda jerk, whether it be gusto and bounce or romance and beauty." Earl Wilson said, "I've never seen a woman entertainer with more warmth or charm. She held that audience completely in the palm of her hand…She is the new charm girl of the cafes, the new sweetheart of the saloons."

Later in 1954 she starred in a live color telecast of "Lady in the Dark" for NBC. A Max Liebman production, it was hosted by Lee Bowman. Her dance sequence was adroitly handled and she played the role of Liza Elliott to the hilt. Being live, there were times when some of her vocals were inaudible. This was a pity as an LP album she recorded later revealed how effective her interpretation of the score was. This recording has often been touted as the best version of *Lady in the Dark*

IN THE FINAL SEASON OF TV's *PRIVATE SECRETARY*, 1956

and its quick sale and limited release made it a pricey and valuable collectors' item. More recently it has made its way onto compact disc.

Since her relationship with Richard Egan had folded, Ann had not been steadily dating any one man. When her friend Lillian MacMurray died, she did spend time consoling widower Fred MacMurray. Then there was the director of her niterie act, John Beck, who was a little older than Ann, and dancer Bill Andrew, but neither got the twice-bitten star to the altar.

She hosted a party for Ethel Merman when she returned to Hollywood and was supportive of Judy Garland. "Her poor little body was wracked by pills," Ann said. "Such talent, such waste! One had to lock up their medicine cabinet when Judy was a guest in your home."

To keep her acting skills stretched, she was elated to play an elderly schoolteacher in ""With No Regrets" for *The Ford Television Theater* (1957). Her role was of a young teacher, but most of the scenario had her aged 65-plus, as she defends a young lad accused of trying to burn down the school. Again, her reviews were complimentary and she expressed a desire to do more roles in contrast to *Susie*. In 1955 she had guested on *The Milton Berle Show* in "State of Confusion." Milton and she were a couple of con-artists in this original comedy written by Gore Vidal. When her friend Loretta Young became ill, Ann was one of several stars who took on the hosting of her show, *A Letter to Loretta*, until Loretta was well enough to resume. Ann's segment as hostess was titled "Man in the Ring" (1955).

There had been rumblings with producer Jack Chertok over the distribution of finances on *Private Secretary*. When he sold the rights to the series to Television Programs of America, she sought a new contract, with her fifth and final season of her existing contract as the negotiating point. Wanting to

As an elderly teacher, Ann forsook her usual glamour in the 1956 TV play, "With No Regrets."

produce the series herself, she refused to film any more episodes until the financial deal she wanted was secured. The whole thing was settled out of court, but no further episodes were made. Virginia Grey, Penny Singleton and June Allyson were mentioned as replacements, but the sponsors wanted only Ann. Grey's participation may have been a sly dig of Jack Chertok's at Ann's increasing weight. Virginia was one of the skinniest women in the industry at that time and, as one of the show's sponsors was Slenderella, Ann also copped a few barbs about being "broad across the beam" from some newspaper reviewers. Australian actor Ted Lansdowne met one of the directors of *Private Secretary* who said he liked Ann very much. However, he did say that on the last day of shooting the final episode, Ann had a fit of pique and threw the gauze chin-strap she wore as Susie at the feet of the producer. Ann professed never to have had a facelift and, like her contemporary Lucille Ball, relied on strings, tapes and make-up to present a youthful appearance.

Celebrated make-up artist Gene Hibbs, who was an expert in rejuvenating older actresses like Lucille Ball, Rosalind Russell, and Loretta Young, was Ann's make-up artist. He dropped a bombshell in 1960 when he declared

Ann was one of the most beautiful actresses. He said, "She was a natural beauty and needed little in the way of artifice." The two other lovelies named were Arlene Dahl ("putting make-up on her would be ridiculous") and Elizabeth Taylor. Dahl interviewed Ann for her beauty column and remarked on her clear, fresh complexion. Asked by Arlene what she accredited it to, Ann replied, "Baby oil." In a later spot in Arlene's column, she also said, "Good old soap and water. There's no substitute for that. Someone told me the trick of spraying perfume on my petticoats so that in motion the breeze surrounds you with the fragrance. I have always used the one fragrance so that often people identify with it."

Private Secretary placed Ann Sothern in the top echelon of television artists. She, Eve Arden and Lucille Ball were undoubtedly the top three comediennes as far as popularity with audiences was concerned. Her name, too, became more marketable than ever and her visage endorsed many products, continuing with Lux, Max Factor, Camel Cigarettes and later Lucky Strike, whom she'd first endorsed in the 1930s. Tang Orange Drink had her featured in color advertisements and Avon cosmetics also used her picture for promotion of their products. There were advertisements too nominating her personal choice of cameras and she personally kept her own photographic equipment up to date.

Ann wrote me on November 22, 1955, "Last summer I made a nightclub tour—yes, singing, dancing and comedy. I enjoyed the tour so much, but it was too exhausting to try again." The word "exhausting" would be frequently quoted in future letters. She did say in yet another communication, "I am also happy to report that I have fully recovered from my illness," but it did seem that the legacy of the hepatitis was continuing fatigue.

With *Susie's* demise, Ann reinvented herself once again, taking a full-page advertisement in the trades. Sporting a large black picture hat, pearls and a longish hairstyle, she headlined the page with, "The Kaleidoscopic Ann Sothern."

Chapter Ten: "Ann"

The Kaleidoscopic Ann of 1957 was incredibly busy with television guest spots. Invited to work on a Desi-Lucy special led to their interest in co-producing a new TV series for her. It was to be titled *Career Girl*. Ann remarked, "It has great possibilities and my production company will pursue the idea and develop the format." She also said, "I am developing another series as well, one which I'll produce but not act in. It's about the emergencies of a fire service." The new Ann gave up the white platinum hair color in favor of a softer honey-blonde hue.

Washington Square, a variety series hosted by Ray Bolger, was one of her 1957 TV guestings. Sister Bonnie Lake, with the help of Buddy Ebsen, composed a song, "Walking the Beat," for Ann to sing. She also duetted "Steppin' Out with My Baby" with Bolger and performed "Shake Rattle and Roll" with Stubby Kaye and the whole company.

Another appearance in 1957 was on *The Steve Allen Show*. Steve found Ann a charming woman, admiring her intelligence and her versatility. On this one she sang "That's Right, Woman is Smarter," a calypso number that was a popular hit of the day. Steve and she were together in a comedy skit and, for "Be a Clown," she joined other guests Bert Lahr and Brenda Lee, for the finale. There was also an appearance on the much-watched *The Perry Como Show* in 1957 and she then joined Lucille Ball and Desi Arnaz in the special mentioned earlier. Titled "Lucy Takes a Cruise to Havana," Ann was paired with longtime pal Cesar Romero. Vivian Vance, William Frawley, Rudy Vallee and Barrie Chase were also featured and the ratings "hit the roof," with it becoming one of the most watched shows of the year. This was to be an hour-long special, but the final running time was 75 minutes. Desi was able to negotiate with U.S. Steel, whose anthology followed the special, to cut their show by the necessary 15 minutes, thereby allowing the "Havana Cruise" show to escape the scissors and be shown in full. Ann played her Susie character, who was a friend of Ball's on the show. The special dealt with how Lucy first met Desi and had Hedda Hopper asking for the details. Some critics were very unkind as to the appearances of both Ann and Lucy, with Ann receiving criticism about her blossoming weight. A jail cell sequence involving the two ladies ending up drunk got good laughs, but even this did not escape a barb from *Variety*, who said it was "too long." Ann and Lucy had not worked together since *Thousands Cheer*, but they were always friendly and this teaming was enjoyed by both. The special's high ratings prompted Lucy and Desi to undertake several more of them. Betty Grable and Harry James, June Haver and Fred MacMurray were guests on other highly-rated "encore" specials.

Ann's final appearance for 1957 was *Holiday in Las Vegas* for NBC, where she was given the task of Mistress of Ceremonies. Presenting guest stars Jayne Mansfield, Vic Damone, Sammy Davis, Jr., Tony Randall and Mickey Hargitay, Ann exuded both sex appeal and charm. She liked Jayne Mansfield and thought she was "quite bright." The show had Neil Simon among its writers and was quick, fast-moving variety. Ann sang "You Can't Do a Show Without a Showgirl" and the whole company was featured in the finale, "Holiday in Las Vegas."

Shortly after her "Las Vegas" stint was over and she was back home, Ann disclosed that she got a sizable settlement from *Private Secretary*. "Susie is no more," she said. "I just could not work with the co-owners of the show. I filed suit over financial accounting." With its syndication, *Private Secretary* initially netted four million dollars. Ann's settlement gave her 25% of the first 78 shows and 42% of the final 26, which yielded quite a salary for a "secretary." A cool million dollars, before taxes, was hers for the first 78 shows. Ann had nothing but praise for the show's producer, Jack Chertok. "He's such a nice man for though he had an option on my services for another 26 segments, he released me. A wonderful producer, who I'd like to work for again. His easy manner of saying, 'do it your way, dear,' made the whole company work harder and we attained a hit show."

Tisha, through childhood to her teen years, was often photographed with her mother. The brown-haired, chubby-cheeked youngster of 1953 had developed into a very beautiful teenager by 1957. Her face resembled her mother's, with similar large expressive eyes and the same pert, delicate nose. However, she did grow to be much taller than her mother, a fact that Ann laughingly told the press, "I envy her for those long legs." There were pictures of them together wearing identical outfits, including a full-page color shot in *Family Circle*. An accompanying article, written by Ann herself, in 1955 was called "My Fountain of Youth." It dealt with positive thinking and the importance of keeping as busy as possible. She said, "The more things I take on the more wells of vitality I'm able to tap. One reason for this is I never allow myself time to dissipate useful energy brooding over the calendar." Her concluding statement summed up her philosophy perfectly. "But youth also demands that you pay attention to the spirit, because nothing ages like fear and nothing kills fear like faith."

In another interview, with Jack Holland, she spoke at length of her moving to an apartment and of Tisha's education and friends:

"'Everything has changed for me,' Ann bubbled. 'This apartment is part of my new ideas of living. I sold the big house I used to have because I suddenly didn't want any more burdens or responsibilities. I was tired of having to have four and five servants in a house loaded with a lot of furniture I didn't need. But even that house was a change for me in a way. I started out once with six bedrooms, then I got down to three or four. Now I have a penthouse and I'm uncluttered. Patricia, my daughter, and I didn't need all that room anyway. When we moved, I even changed my color scheme from a grey-green to these shades. They're so much more cheerful.' The four-bedroom, three-bathroom duplex is in a unit in an apartment building owned by Red Skelton. 'I'm renting because I don't think I'll live in California after I retire.'

"Patricia, Ann's daughter, came in at that moment and sat down quietly. She speaks so softly it's hard to hear her. But the way Ann and she look at each other, you know this is a wonderful, enduring relationship. Tish, as she is affectionately known, was playing her part in the rebirth of Ann Sothern. The cute eleven-year-old girl was going through the stages of not knowing what she wanted to be. She was studying ballet with David Lichine, she was interested in medicine even to the point of preferring to see *Medic* on TV to a roaring Western. And she was also toying with the idea of being an actress.

"'One day she said to me, "Mother, why don't you write a part for me in one of your shows?" But after thinking it over, she commented, "But do I have to act in front of all those people?" She had just enough of that attractive little girl shyness to be very appealing.'

"She was obviously growing up. It seems she had just gone to a dance at a party thrown by David Niven's son. She was escorted by Michael and Ronnie McLean, Gloria and Jimmy Stewart's sons. The evening of the party, Gloria called Ann and said, 'How is Patricia? Is she terribly excited about the dance, Ann?' Ann replied, 'She's falling apart. She's so excited. She hasn't eaten a thing all day.' 'Well, the boys are on their way,' Gloria went on. 'They were carrying so many rock and roll records they were practically staggering out the door. They're completely undone.'

"Tish, it seems, is an expert on rock and roll. She even taught Ann and Bill [Andrew] how to do the dance. 'She is now at the stage where she's borrowing scarves from mama and wearing my high heel shoes—in front of the mirror only...' Ann smiled in the way all proud mothers smile.

"'She and I have a marvelous rapport. We trust each other completely— and never go back on our word to each other. Tish also is a good student. It's been quite a job for me to keep up with her studies. When I help her with her lessons, I'm amazed at how much flotsam and jetsam I've forgotten since school days. But Tish learns quickly—and forgets quickly too at times. When she was seven or eight she had a French governess and spoke the language like a veteran. Now—nothing!!

"'Tish is probably just growing up. She is my best critic. She makes very pertinent comments about the show. She has a wonderful taste in clothes and lets me know what she likes and doesn't like about what I wear on TV. She has also a good dramatic sense about stories. Yet, on the other hand, she's quite a fan. She never looks upon me as a star. I'm just her mother, but she went to great lengths to try to get me to introduce her to Kirk Douglas, Marilyn Monroe and Fess Parker. She has one very amusing pet expression about her favorites and anything else she likes—it's 'vava voom' which means, I take it, 'The Very End.'"

Tisha would be in contact with and visit her father Robert Sterling and his wife Anne Jeffreys and their three sons. She was present at their youngest son's christening at an Episcopalean Church. Ann would say, "He was no father to Tisha," but later she remarked to me, "Tisha got to understand and like him better when she saw him with his three sons." "Mother," she said, "he treats them just the same as he treats me."

With *Career Girl* now in definite preparation, Ann formed a second TV company, ANSO Productions. Vincent Productions continued, mainly handling the reruns of *Susie,* and her A-Bar-S Cattle Company, situated in Wendell, Idaho, which proved extremely profitable. She was restocking in 1959, having sold 1,000 heads of beef the previous year. Ann also had success with the Ann Sothern Sewing Center in Sun Valley, Idaho. She designed clothes with her own label and the shop was well stocked with sewing equipment and complete lines of patterns.

Approached by Tops records to make an LP of songs, she agreed, and *Sothern Exposure* was released in 1958. What a delightful surprise when a copy arrived in the mail from Ann. The original pressing was on the Zenith label and the artwork and color was perfection. It would later be re-released by Tops with the same artwork, but with a slightly faded color process. Ann sang just one new ballad, "Another Year," written by Ian Bernard, who also conducted the orchestra for the recording sessions. Needing a publisher for the song, Ann began the Ann-Bar-S Music Company, which would later publish several numbers written by Ann and her sister Bonnie Lake. The theme song from her next TV series, *Katy,* was one and "Take Off Your Shoes," recorded by Sal Mineo and co-written by Ian Bernard, was another.

Sothern Exposure sold well despite some negative reviews. Ann's voice sounded a little gruff on some of the low notes and the keys chosen for some of the arrangements were way too low. Best of the ballads were "Another Year," "The Last Time I Saw Paris" and "Let's Fall in Love." In swinging-style, "Life is Just a Bowl of Cherries," "Ballin' the Jack," Everybody's Doing It" and "After You're Gone" received considerable airplay on the radio. The same album was reissued on the Craftsman label with a new title, *It's Ann Sothern Time.* Yet again, four songs from the album were reissued on Tiara, with *Spotlight on Ann Sothern* and the *Broadway Blues* being its headline. *Song Stylings featuring Ann Sothern* was a Sutton reissue of the previous disc.

The Steve Allen Show recalled Ann to guest again in 1958. Ann and Steve played quiz experts with a setting having them surrounded by hundreds of books. In a star-spangled finale, Steve's "This Could Be the Start of Something Big" was sung firstly by Ann and Steve, then Eydie Gorme and Steve Lawrence joined them. For the next chorus Dinah Shore tagged along and finally Frank Sinatra sang a stanza, before the other soloists combined for a socko conclusion.

Ann mentioned she'd been trying again, without success, to get the television rights to *Maisie*. Her nightclub act had a portion of its concept devoted to *Maisie* and the general audience reaction was "staggering" in its response to this favorite character. MGM flatly refused to release the rights and would make two television pilots of their own in an attempt to cash in on what they believed to be a bankable project. One, titled *Missile Maisie,* starred the clever and talented Janis Paige, who had enjoyed a successful series a couple of years prior, *It's Always Jan.* But, like the other *Maisie* TV venture, it failed to generate sufficient interest among likely sponsors.

Ann' s conversion to the Catholic faith in 1953 made her wary of marriage or even a longterm commitment. With no particular man in her life she said in 1958, "You need a certain amount of masculine drive to fight your way to the top and it's difficult to camouflage this drive when you come home to your husband. Another difficulty for the successful actress is that she's thrown in contact with actors. Many are extremely personable but have a feminine kind of vanity. It makes them selfish and ego ridden and terrible husband material. A good man is hard to find."

Career Girl underwent a name change and became *The Ann Sothern Show*. The television series debuted on October 6, 1958 and the Kalaidescopic Ann Sothern was no more. Reinventing herself, as she had done so many times before, she was now Katy O'Connor, assistant manager of a New York hotel.

Chapter Eleven: "Katy"

Of her latest character on television, Ann said, "I suppose you might say that Maisie is the mother of Susie and the grandmother of Katy. They're alike in many ways. For instance they're underdogs. The world is for the underdog. And they're always fighting fellows off. Of course Susie was a bit lighter in the romance department. But that's all over now, and they're always warm, intelligent and I should say, independent. They don't get married. You see I don't want to be different. I just want to be familiar."

Co-producing the show with Desi Amaz, she said, "It just happens that Desi Arnaz is the most successful in the business. And you don't argue with success. Lucy and I were both under contract to RKO and she used to complain about getting all the parts I turned down. There are three that I recall: *The Joy of Living*, *Beauty for the Asking* and *Five Came Back*. Now I produce the show and Lucy owns the studio. I guess that settles that. I own this show on a 50-50 basis with Desi and Lucy, who are the owners of Desilu Productions. It's costing $51,000 an episode and I think at the moment we're only get-

"KATY" OF *THE ANN SOTHERN SHOW*

ting $46,000 from the sponsor." Maxwell House Coffee and Post Cereals were the show's early sponsors and Ann said, "You can say General Foods owns me, body and soul."

Cast in *The Ann Sothern Show* were Ernest Truex, as Ann's hotel manager boss, and Reta Shaw, as his domineering wife. For old times sake, Ann Tyrrell, formerly cast as the telephonist-receptionist on *Private Secretary*, was back as Ann's secretary and roommate. Ann herself played assistant hotel manager (of the Bartley House) Katy O'Connor and newcomers Jack Mullaney (bell-hop) and Jacques Scott (room clerk) were other regulars of that first season. Ann's constant probing of public reaction had her make some hard decisions. The general consensus was that the public wanted to see Katy under the thumb of a more tyrannical boss. So, although fine actors, the Ernest Truex and Reta Shaw characters departed the series. In a surprise move, Ann hired her friend and former series co-star Don Porter to play her new and more dominant boss. There is no doubt that the show gained momentum with Porter joining the cast. As Ann said, "Until we got Don, the show was just going down the drain. There isn't any mystery about why Don is back. I wish I could show you the letters we got. In this connection I do want to be quoted exactly about Mr. Truex. He is a magnificent performer, a wonderful person but the new show was built around my dominating the boss for a change, the reverse of *Private Secretary*, but the public just didn't go for it. So when Ernest had to go the others had to go too. This series was based on that mousey little character he does so beautifully. I, for one, thought it would be amusing, but people just didn't like it. They want to see Don and me trying to outsmart each other. It's chemistry." Don Porter also revealed that he had read for two months with every possible actress when a different producer had tried to resume *Private Secretary* with him on board but not Miss Sothern. "I read with them all but we couldn't find a Susie everybody liked." Of Don, Ann said, "We worked together on the first series for over three years and never, ever had a cross word." Eventually, Jack Mullaney and Jacques Scott would also leave and Ken Berry, playing a bellhop, would join up for a two-year run. Ann showed little resentment when Louis Nye's char-acter as a dentist became a hit. She was smart enough to realize the public wanted more of him. Subsequently, Ann Tyrrell's role as Nye's girlfriend be-came larger and Gladys Hurlbut was signed on to play Nye's overprotective

JAYNE MEADOWS, DON PORTER AND AS IN *THE ANN SOTHERN SHOW* (1960). ANN GUESTED ON *THE STEVE ALLEN SHOW* TWICE AND THOUGHT HIS WIFE JAYNE WAS AS BRIGHT AS SHE WAS BEAUTIFUL.

mother. For the final season Jesse White, also from *Private Secretary*, was cast as a cigar stand proprietor.

Unlike *Private Secretary*, there were many top-line guest stars. Billie Burke, whom Ann had become close to so many years before in New York, was to be one of them. Of Burke Ann told me, "A truly lovely human being who was a good friend. I hired her for my show and it was so sad to find she couldn't remember her lines. After a day I realized it was hopeless and heart-breaking for her to try any longer, so I paid her and had her driven home. Estelle Winwood replaced her and sailed through the part." One guest star Ann did not take to was Constance Bennett. She was cast with John Emery as very theatrical parents of a young, talented actress. When I produced a pho-tograph of Constance and Ann together, she said, "That woman! If there was one person I'd never want to work with again, it's that woman." Other friends, like Eva Gabor, Van Johnson, Lucille Ball, Guy Madison, Jackie Coogan, Joe E. Brown, Gladys Cooper and Cesar Romero, would guest happily on her show. Ann was so impressed with singer Guy Mitchell, she had him back for a sec-ond appearance. This served as a pilot for a proposed TV series to star Mitchell and her protege' Pat Carroll. It never sold, nor did another series pilot which Ann used as a segment on her show. She also gave work to char-acter people and stars she'd worked with before like Fay Baker, Frances Mer-cer, Carleton Carpenter, Alan Marshall, Jeff Donnell, Charles Lane and Verna Felton.

Daughter Tisha had decided by now that she wanted to be an actress. At-tending Marymont School, she'd return home to find Aunt Marion there and would have her homework completed by the time her mother got back from work. With the new series now doing well, despite opposition from reruns of *Susie* to compete with, Ann bought a new home in Bel Air. Tisha had ballet, vocal and tennis lessons and was mad about horses. In 1960, just before her 16th birthday Tisha, billed as Patricia Ann Sterling, made her professional acting debut. It was on a segment of her mother's show; "Loving Arms" was the title of the episode and she played a teenage guest at the hotel. This seg-ment featured Van Johnson, and Tisha was involved in an elevator sequence with him and Ann.

Another discovery of Ann's was Stephanie Powers, whom she saw in a high school production of the musical comedy *Annie Get Your Gun*. So im-pressed was she that Stephanie, under the name of Taffy Paul, had a guest spot on *The Ann Sothern Show* in 1961. Also, Ann introduced her to Otto Lang, who cast the young actress in the film *Among the Thorns*. Ann gave up on her other two discoveries, Tony Remo and Ginny Saturday. "They had the talent, but they wouldn't work. Youngsters today think the magic is going to hit them overnight and they just have to be there." Reviews for *The Ann*

Sothern Show were mostly favorable. "It's safe to predict she'll have a long run with this one too," wrote Hank Grant. "Inescapably, the infectious Sothern charm is an asset and writers Bob Schiller and Bob Weiskopf gave it full opportunity to bloom." Another critic thought it was "a cut above *The Donna Reed Show* and *The Ed Wynn Show* which also debuted this season."

After a sluggish first half season, it picked up considerably and by season two it had duplicated the success of *Private Secretary*, and made the Top 10 in the Neilson ratings. On the musical front, Ann wrote two other songs for Sal Mineo to perform on her show, "Chicken Cacciatore" and "Your Crushing My Duster." Ian Bernard again supplied the lyrics. When Joel Grey guested on the show, he and Ann duetted on "Everybody Loves a Lover." Young Barry Gordon had a running part in the first season and Ann and he sang "Thanks for Everything" in a Thanksgiving episode. Ann excelled here as both singer and songwriter, with lyrics by Mal Diamond and John Kohn.

Edward R. Morrow interviewed Ann in her home on his *Person to Person* program. Televised in December 1958, his other guest was Prince Aly Khan, who, at that time, was Pakistan's Ambassador to the United Nations. Ann's various business activities were discussed, including her ranching with Blank Angus steers. Tisha also appeared on the show.

Friend June Allyson persuaded her to guest on *The DuPont Show with June Allyson* (1959). "Night Out" was the title of the segment, and Pat Carroll co-starred. It was here that Ann got to fully appreciate Pat's talent, and used her on her own show in 1961. One review of "Night Out" gave Ann's acting a plus. "As with Loretta Young I prefer small doses of Miss Allyson. However, on Monday night she came on as compere only...introducing a little piece which starred Ann Sothern as a neglected wife. And Ann Sothern, looking these days like a plump

As at the keyboard in *The Ann Sothern Show* (1959) with Don Porter and Ann Tyrrell

WITH TISHA STERLING,
WHO GUESTED IN 1961 ON
THE ANN SOTHERN SHOW

middle-aged matron, is one actress who can always be relied upon to turn in a thoroughly workman like job."

The Westinghouse Desilu Play-house showcased members of their workshop theatre on TV in "The Desilu Revue" (1959). Ann and good friend George Murphy, plus Hugh O'Brian and Rory Calhoun, were among the celebrities on hand to applaud the new talent.

Tisha's driving got her into trouble in 1961 when her car struck another vehicle on the Coast High-way. Accompanied by Ann, they were heading north toward San Francisco for a vacation. An elderly driver of 72 was struck broadside by the car Tisha was driving. He suffered minor injuries, but his 80-year-old wife was seriously injured. Ann and Tisha were treated at the hospital for multiple cuts and bruises. In a letter to me, dated April 14, 1961, Ann said, "I am on the road to recovery now and the stitches have been removed from my leg. Tisha and I were certainly divinely protected, for our injuries could have been so much worse." Many years later Ann told me that the worst thing that happened to her as a result of that accident was that "I was never able to go skiing again." A great deal of Ann's energy was channeled into caring for her daughter. The Bel Air mansion she bought was redone "English"-style and had a pool, barbecue and a soda fountain especially for Tisha.

Producer Jack Chertok, who had a love-hate relationship with Ann dur-ing the final season of *Private Secretary,* said, "If you want to classify Ann at all, you have to say that she is the most expert comedienne in the business. Ann has no weakness as an actress, she instantly knows what's good for her." Because of Ann's weakened physical condition, Chertok was forced to shoot only one TV show a week, an alarmingly slow pace. His comment on their final disagreement was, "She wanted to do another TV show which meant our show would be delayed further. My refusal had her terminate our agreement." On the lighter side, Ann said, when asked about her new show, "Well, of course, I've had hotel experience. I once danced a tango with Conrad Hilton."

Another producer spoke of Ann's dynamic drive. "She sacrificed two marriages. It's tough to say but neither of her husbands could stand her passion for perfection." Sometimes her drive for perfection was taken out on co-workers. One instance was when she insisted on casting a young man, who was training for the priesthood, in an important role. Inexperienced, in one week Ann gave him a six-month crash course in dramatics. Absorbing it all, he gave a creditable performance, but shortly afterwards he collapsed and returned to the seminary to recuperate.

At the time of making *The Ann Sothern Show* she proclaimed, "my best friends are Jesuit Priests." She also had her name Romanized when christened a Catholic; it became Anna Maria. When asked what hobby she indulged in at that time, her earnest response was very odd. "Mine is exactly what a comedienne should have. I love to read the inscriptions on the headstones of early American graves." She did dabble in painting, both oil and water colors. Her study in art had begun in 1930 at the Choinard School in Los Angeles and it was a hobby which she would continue to fall back on from time to time. When not skiing in Sun Valley, she would paint there and be tutored by artist Robert Peter May. During another vacation in Sun Valley, she became a trap shooting enthusiast and enjoyed the feel of a fine gun. "But I won't go hunting, I can't bear to kill any living thing," said Ann.

Although she was frequently listed as a shrewd businesswoman with her various commercial ventures, in 1959 she was deemed to owe $722,322.44 in income tax for the period 1953-1956. Filing a protest against the government claim, the case was settled in 1960 when Ann's tax liability was reduced to the more modest sum of $99,000. The much-touted profits from her cattle ranch dwindled to losses and she also revealed she'd lost for a couple of years on her Sun Valley Sewing Circle Center. Now in her early fifties, the plumpness, which previously had been controllable, had now become permanent. Her illness and the car accident, in addition to her penchant for rich food, all contributed to her weight gain. Unable to exercise strenuously, as she had done before the bout with hepatitis, the energy expended with her heavy workload was insufficient to cause her to shed weight. Wearing a lot of black outfits

WITH CONSTANCE BENNETT ON
THE ANN SOTHERN SHOW.
THOUGH APPEARING TO BE
FRIENDLY HERE, IT WAS A
DIFFERENT CASE ON THE SET.

with full skirts, and often having her stand behind furniture, were a few camouflage tricks employed to disguise this. On one occasion she laughingly remembered how, after having her wardrobe fitted for the next season's shows, some of the cast and crew sabotaged her first outfit by taking in the seams. "Imagine my dismay when I attempted to get into that dress. I couldn't get anywhere near it. It scared me so much I thought I'd gained even more. Ann Tyrrell's sly smile gave the game away and we all laughed."

Visiting New York in 1960, Ann spoke of going into the dress manufacturing business. "There isn't anybody designing young looking clothes for women who have bosoms and hips," she said. Yet another project mentioned was the building of a motel in a secret location in California. Her father was no longer mentioned as looking after her cattle ranch. She announced that she did not own a ranch, but tenanted her cattle on a spread at Fairfield, Idaho. She credited a man who was the head of the Idaho Cattlemens' Association as "the man who directs my cattle interests and who has been in the business 45 years. I believe it's poor economy not to go to the best." Ann's show experienced rating problems in late 1960 and she became very angry, publicly, when newspapers reported her show "DUMPED." Reporter Joe Hyams said, "She was mad enough to eat nails or at the very least chew me apart." "That word dumped really infuriates me," she said. "My contract was renewed for another year. The only change is the time slot."

This change had her pitted against *The Untouchables* and, come April 1961, the last episode was not aired as scheduled. It did get a showing via reruns and it was indicative of Ann's inability to accept its demise, by having the final frame read "to be continued…?" The episode left the fate of Ann and boss Don Porter in slight limbo, although she does get to wear a wedding dress in this final segment.

Nineteen Sixty-one was a year of mishaps for Ann. In addition to her show being cancelled and the car accident, which would eventually impair her walking, she had her bag snatched. Trying on gloves in a store, a thief grabbed her handbag. Not worried about the cash lost, she hated losing her cards and most of all her rosary beads. Then in May 1961, her mother Annette filed suit against Ann seeking support of $1,200 a month.

Ann had cared for her mother all of her working life until April 1961. Suffering from advanced arteriosclerosis, Annette, by doctors' orders, was placed in a sanitarium, with Ann continuing to pay the bills. Having spent $20,000 on her mother's medical expenses, Ann stopped the payments when her mother ignored the doctors' orders and left the sanitarium. Her sister Bonnie, now Mrs. John Dickman, had taken Annette to their home, but they were unable to pay medical bills and salary for a nurse to attend her. Ann had stopped payment because arrangements had already been made to transfer her mother to a rest home. Ann said, "While I intend to provide proper medical care for my mother, I do not wish to provide for other persons who are attempting to interfere with my mother's well being."

THE FINAL SEGMENT OF *THE ANN SOTHERN SHOW* (1961). AS IN HER WEDDING GOWN WAS ABOUT TO MARRY DON PORTER. THE SEGMENT CONCLUDED WITH "TO BE CONTINUED?"

Five physicians provided by Ann agreed that her mother should go to a rest home and even Bonnie's own doctor had recommended the same move. Judge Roger Pfaff, when considering a continuance of the case, said, "Persons who are paying bills should have some right to say where their mother is going to stay." On June 30, 1961, Judge Eugene Fay announced Marion Tetley to be appointed as guardian of their mother. He expressed the hope that his ruling be accepted graciously by all three sisters and that they could all act together for the welfare of their mother, "who may have a relatively short period to live." Judge Fay also stated that the care and support of Mrs. Lake by Ann Sothern "had been extremely generous." He also said "she should be grateful that she had a daughter with the financial ability to provide so well for her." Bonnie Dickman has been described as a strong-minded person, "who takes the bull by the horns." When the decision was announced, Bonnie burst into sobs and ran out of the courtroom. Her two sisters rushed after her, but a few seconds later a determined Bonnie quickly left the County Courthouse. Bonnie would remain estranged from her sisters for quite a stretch, but blood is thicker than water and the three reconciled permanently in years to come. With Marion being given her guardianship, Annette dropped her support suit and was again financially supported by Ann until her death on December 17, 1962 at age 78. The services were held at Hollywood Memorial Park. During the court case, Annette called her famous daughter a millionaire with an income of $240,000 a year. The U.S. Government claimed in 1961 that, in fact, Ann owed a million dollars in back taxes.

Chapter Twelve: "Ann"

In late 1961 Ann moved to New York City and retreated into what she be-lieved to be semi-retirement. In response to a birthday card I'd sent that year she said, "As of this year I have stopped having any more birthdays." Ann was living in a three-room suite at the Plaza Hotel. Tisha was enrolled in a New York finishing school and Ann enrolled in acting classes with Stella Adler to fill in some days. Although retirement was again mentioned, she said, "The classes are to extend my dramatic range and broaden my knowledge of same." Her only dramatic training had been back in the late 1930s when she engaged Phyllis Laughton, who was also coaching Katharine Hepburn.

NBC recalled Ann to Los Ange-les to shoot a pilot for a proposed TV series, *Atta Boy, Mama.* Shot at MGM, it was directed by Ida Lupino and written by Mac Benoff. Ann had the role of a deceased Lord Mayor's widow. The pilot did not sell, and, in August of 1962, it was announced that she'd open on Broadway on No-vember 26 that year. The play was *God Bless Our Bank*, penned by Mac

GUESTING ON
THE ANDY WILLIAMS SHOW, 1963

PORTRAIT FOR THE STAGE TOUR OF
GOD BLESS OUR BANK (1963)

Benoff, the author of her failed TV pilot. The planned production by the Theatre Guild and Joel Schenker was called off on October 4, with Ann explaining, "They stalled around so long with the script that they lost the theatre." Idle for most of 1962, Ann concentrated on Tisha's debut into society. Ann would say, "I never encouraged her to be an actress. I raised her for society—she came out three times." Publicity-wise, it was "The International Debutante Ball," held at the Hotel Astor in December, that got both Tisha and Ann's photograph in all the newspapers. Ann, with darker-hued but blonde-streaked hair, looked very elegant and slimmer than in her last TV series. Tisha, with an upswept hairstyle, looked every inch the society belle that Ann envisioned for her daughter. Looking at the photos taken, she has the same regal style and elegance of Grace Kelly. One of her other coming out balls was held in North Carolina.

After almost 18 months absence from the small screen, Ann returned to television as guest on NBC's *The Andy Williams Show,* in January 1963. Performing a nifty bossa nova with Andy and the rest of the company, she proved her beauty and charm were timeless. What was truly remarkable, though, was her singing voice. Selecting the soprano solo from *Kismet,* "Baubles, Bangles and Beads," it seemed a bizarre choice after the deep, husky vocals of her record album. Most critics were astounded at the clarity and purity of her rendition and there was no doubt, her voice was better than ever. The following month saw her join panelists Bess Myerson, Henry Morgan, Betsy Palmer and Tony Perkins as the celebrity guest with a secret on *I've Got a Secret.*

Definite plans to stage *God Bless Our Bank* occurred in May 1963. This time the producers were Zev Bufman and Stanley Seiden and, under the direction of Ezra Stone, it opened in Charlotte, North Carolina the following month. With the hope of a Broadway opening after a seven-week summer stock tour, it closed in August at the Westport County Playhouse in Connecticut. There was then talk of Abe Burrows directing a revised, shortened version for a Broadway season. With generally disappointing reviews of the script as a marketable project, Ann had the choice of continuing with the role, if the revisions met with her satisfaction and if she so desired. She declined; her collapse during the Johnson City, New York performance was probably the major reason, with a fear of the New York critics being another. Heat exhaustion and dehydration had her hospitalized. Once again the dreaded fatigue, an unwanted legacy from her bout with her hepatitis illness, struck.

Also, reducing her fluid intake in an effort to diet, caused the dehydration. In a letter to me, dated August 20, 1963, she mentioned having been in

MARGARET LEIGHTON, HENRY FONDA AND AS IN *THE BEST MAN* (UNITED ARTISTS, 1964)

RELAXING ON THE SET OF *LADY IN A CAGE* (PARAMOUNT, 1964)
WITH OLIVIA DE HAVILAND

Wilson Memorial Hospital and that she "was feeling a lot better." For the tour, Ann's chauffeur-driven Rolls-Royce ensured that she traveled in comfort. She had also employed a personal maid for the run of the show. The reviews, mostly unkind to the play, did give Ann some praise. Also in the cast were Roland Winters, George Ives and Jeff Corey. Corey, in addition to being an actor, was also a teacher and would become a good friend of Ann's. She would employ him to coach her for future acting assignments and was instrumental in having him cast in *God Bless Our Bank*.

Her studies with Stella Adler and Jeff Corey led to a surprise movie casting. Maureen Stapleton had been set to play the juicy role of Sade in a realistic shocker, *Lady in a Cage*, but couldn't make it to Los Angeles in time for the starting date. It seems Maureen would not fly and wanted a limousine made available to drive her from New York to Los Angeles. Jeff Corey was also cast and the title role was to be played by two-time Academy Award winner Olivia de Havilland. Ann got to play Sade, an avaricious, vicious prostitute, and made the part her very own.

Putting her Bel Air house on the market, she moved into a hotel. Eventually, her mansion was sold to Larry Doheny and she stored all her possessions. For a time Mal and Ray Milland enjoyed her company as a guest, but then she found a small but comfortable home in Westwood, which she rented for some years.

Accompanied by Jeff Corey, who played a derelict wino in the film, Ann visited Skid Row in downtown L.A. The two would have presented an incongruous sight being driven through this area in her chauffeured Rolls-Royce. Here, they researched their roles and observed the unfortunate inhabitants and their attire. Ann chose a dark auburn wig to wear, calling it "Early American egg beater," a sleazy green suit, beads and bangles. A cheap straw handbag and an over-large hat completed her chosen ensemble.

Produced by Luther Davis from his own screenplay, *Lady in a Cage* was way ahead of its time. *What Ever Happened to Baby Jane?* (1962) had proved that horror could be equally effective when played by two major dramatic stars. Bette Davis and Joan Crawford had both scored in *Jane* and Joan was then offered *Lady in a Cage*. Discovering the script was not really a horror tale, but instead a stark realistic look at contemporary living, she hesitated too long and while Joan was procrastinating, Olivia de Havilland accepted

the role. Joan cattily remarked, "I'm glad for Olivia, she needs the money."

AS AND JEFF COREY IN *LADY IN A CAGE* (PARAMOUNT, 1964)

Seeking a co-worker who knew Ann well enough to write a foreword for this book, I approached Olivia de Havilland. Ann always spoke very highly of her and, after watching a TV screening in 1975, said, "Olivia is one of the great ladies, a woman this industry should be grateful to and proud of." When I wrote a career article on de Havilland for a Hollywood-based magazine, Ann gave me the closing lines to sum it up: "Olivia is a beautiful actress, a lovely woman and a won-

JOHN CASSAVETES AND AS
IN "THE WATER'S EDGE,"
A SEGMENT FROM *THE ALFRED
HITCHCOCK HOUR* (1964)

derful human being."

In reply to my request, Olivia, honest as always, regrettably declined as she felt she did not know Ann well enough to do her justice. She said, "As to the years after *Cage,* because I live in France and my visits to Hollywood were limited to work, I do not believe Ann and I met again. It is a pity as I thought her very likable as a person while we worked together, as well as very professional and very effective in her role - as she was in every film in which she appeared."

Lady in a Cage was banned in Australia because of its excessive violence and would not surface there until the early 1990s, when it appeared on cable TV. England also banned it for a time, but its theatrical release gained Olivia de Havilland a Best Actress of the Year award from the London publication *Films and Filming.* Both Olivia and Ann were considered "sure bets" for Oscar nominations, deservedly so. Surprisingly, they both missed out. Ann said a debate over the film's sadism left a lot of voters not wanting to see the film. She was nominated for a Golden Globe for Best Supporting Actress but, due to the banning of the film in some countries, many members of the Foreign Press Association did not get to see it, so she had no chance of winning.

It was a bitter disappointment for me not to be able see *Lady in a Cage* when it was initially released. However, on a visit to California in 1975, to my surprise and delight, I got a call from Ann to say it was on TV that week. Watching it for the first time on a small TV screen in the Hollywood Roosevelt Hotel, I was unable to absorb its full dramatic impact. Now, having seen it many times on cable, I realize just how great an impact it would have caused back in 1964. The violence, then thought to be excessive, is still numbing. For audiences and critics back then the message of public apathy of getting involved in aiding a victim or the unwillingness to acknowledge that communication between human beings was being eroded, was thought to be "alarmist." Of course time has given Luther Davis's screenplay a forceful insight and, over the years, it has proven to be both sadly and alarmingly *true*.

Before its release Luther Davis was forced to make cuts. Ann's role had her locked in a closet and then, toward the film's climax, she is released only to be brutally strangled by James Caan. Making his film debut, Caan was visibly unnerved when his realistic choking of Ann caused her to blackout. This sequence was one of the cuts made when the distributors feared there was too much excessive violence. Also gone were climactic scenes with de Havilland and William Swan, the actor playing her son, being reconciled. Probably the selected ending of having her alone, crawling on the sidewalk with unheeding passers by and noisy holiday traffic, pointed up the film's message with grimmer reality. Perhaps too graphic were the close-ups of a blinded Caan attempting to choke Olivia and falling into oncoming traffic, which at last brought the roaring traffic stream to a screaming halt.

When I next saw Ann, a couple of days after my first small screen look at

the film, she asked for my opinion of the film and any thoughts I might have on her appearance as Sade. I said I thought she looked fine, to which she replied, "Gene Hibbs did my make-up and he was the make-up man on the show [TV series]." I mentioned how impressed I was with a scene in which she is threatened and appears to be visibly shaking all over. Smiling, she said, "You're observant. That was probably the hardest bit of acting I've ever had to do. Jeff Corey helped me with that."

Released by Paramount, it gained generally excellent reviews for its cast of actors directed by Walter Grauman. *Hollywood Citizen-*

A PORTRAIT FROM *SYLVIA*
(PARAMOUNT, 1965)

WITH CARROLL BAKER IN *SYLVIA* (PARAMOUNT, 1965)

News: "Miss de Havilland…to merit Oscar consideration…ditto Ann Sothern who elicits audience sympathy even though she plays the part of a conscienceless slut of easy virtue and no morals…and that's not easy to do." Said the *L.A. Herald Examiner*, "Ann Sothern will surprise all with her acting as the blowsy gal of the streets."

Tisha Sterling was very much in the news that year, when the *Sunday Mirror* called her "Miss 1964." Comparing her with her mother, they condoned her lack of make-up: "Just a touch of lipstick, a windswept wisp of hair. A natural look. Today's look." Two other young actresses were also pictured in comparison with their more famous mothers. Anne Shirley and her daughter Julie Payne and Joan Bennett with her daughter Melinda Markey. Around this time Tisha did a lengthy color test for the eldest Von Trapp daughter in *The Sound of Music*; she lost out to Charmian Carr.

AS, AS THE COUNTESS (ROSIE), AND LUCILLE BALL ON *THE LUCY SHOW* (1965)

The Best Man, a film made straight after *Lady in a Cage*, was released first. In this one, Ann got star billing along with Henry Fonda, Cliff Robertson, Lee Tracy, Shelley Berman, Edie Adams and Margaret Leighton. In *Cage* Olivia de Havilland got star over-the-title billing, and special solo "below the title" billing read, "Ann Sothern as Sade."

Cast in co-starring roles in *The Best Man* were Kevin McCarthy and Gene Raymond. Raymond played Cliff Robertson's brother and Gene's real-life sister-in-law, Blossom Rock, played a cleaning woman. Ann's role was that of Mrs. Gamadge, a bustling busybody who is head of a formidable lady delegation. Richard Arlen and Penny Singleton also make brief appearances. In reviewing the film, one critic mistook Singleton for Ann by reporting Ann as playing "a somewhat cracked southern belle." Her real notices for the film were good. "Ann Sothern is a pleasure to watch in her playing of a self-appointed expert on the 'Women's Vote,'" reported *Films in Review.* In a cast shot of the nine principal players, Ann was placed between Gene Raymond and Lee Tracy. Holding hands with them both, Ann and the group appear to be a very happy ensemble. Publicity made much of the previous teamings of Raymond and Ann, so it would seem that in view of this latest casting, any

AS AND LUCILLE BALL ON TV'S
THE LUCY SHOW (1965).
ANN GUESTED SEVEN TIMES ON HER
FRIEND'S SERIES.

former perceived grievances between them were at last resolved. Ann fell victim to one of the unkindest cuts when, due to the film's overlong running time, her big scene ended up on the cutting room floor.

Appearance-wise, Ann was heavy in this one as she had been in her previous film. However, in *The Best Man* she was beautifully costumed and groomed, which was very complimentary, but it did make the added poundage more noticeable. Massage was part of her regime and as a one-time guest at the Chateau Marmont Hotel she regularly attended sessions with the in-house masseur, Joe Leigh. Now fifty-five years of age, Ann felt entitled to eat the foods she had rigidly tried to deny herself and had scrimped on in the past. Joe Leigh said she was undisciplined and would be eating a candy bar or a banana before or after each massage session, with walking up a flight of stairs being her only exercise. Obviously the leg injury she'd sustained in the car accident in 1961 was acting up. Quite obvious, too, is the elastic stocking she is wearing in stills for *Lady in a Cage*, which was to support and protect her knee. When asked if her renaissance in films was similar to that of Olivia de Havilland, Bette Davis and Joan Crawford and their respective return to box office popularity, she replied, "In the first place each has her own audience. They got those audiences through the years. And you can't bury real talent. Talent gets better as it ages. All artists do."

Returning to television, Ann made several appearances as a panelist in 1964. *The Price is Right* was the first and this was followed by three segments on *The Celebrity Game*. *Celebrity Game* was hosted by Carl Reiner with Hedda Hopper appearing on each of Ann's three segments. Other guests included Vic Damone, Roy Rogers and Dale Evans, Gypsy Rose Lee, Mickey

Rooney and Ronald Reagan. Ann was the first star to be interviewed on *The Regis Philbin Show* in October of 1964. *Hollywood Reporter:* "Take for example his idle but warm chit chat with his 'Guest of the Week' - Ann Sothern. Philbin did nothing more than bring out the affectionate warmth and compassion that must be Ann as she is known to her intimates. The result: She looked good. Philbin looked good and viewers were pleasantly impressed."

Dramatically, she scored on *The Alfred Hitchcock Hour* in a segment titled "Water's Edge," in which John Cassavetes co-starred. The script, from a Robert Bloch horror short story, with rats being the predators, was a good one. Coincidentally, in the story Ann's character is described as a dead ringer "for that actress who plays the secretary on TV." Not attempting to look like her Susie character, Ann was excellent as a disguised frumpy woman whose greed leads to a grisly end.

Ann's faith in Catholicism had her pen columns for *Lenten Guideposts*, and other religious publications. The *Insight* TV Anthology series was a religious program for which she starred in an episode titled "Boss Toad." Ann played the mother of a teenage son in conflict with her husband, Brian Keith. Ann then ran a full-page advertisement in the Hollywood trade papers. Headed "How to Change an Image," it featured a picture of Ann as herself and included portraits from *The Alfred Hitchcock Hour, The Best Man, Lady in a Cage*, and her newest film, *Sylvia*.

THE PHOTO USED TO PUBLICIZE HER TV SERIES, *MY MOTHER, THE CAR* (1965)

Adapted from a well-liked and highly readable novel by E. V. Cunningham, *Sylvia* starred Carroll Baker in the title role. Dealing with a girl who has a mysterious background, it offered great vignettes to several big-name actors. Peter Lawford was the millionaire who hires detective George Maharis to dig and unearth all that can be found about Sylvia's past life.

Viveca Lindfors was excellent as a librarian teacher who first helps the heroine, and Joanne Dru did some of her best work as a society woman, also with a past. Ann's role as a cashier in an arcade amusement center was the most expansive of the lot. Maharis takes her to dinner and there she becomes increasingly drunk and tragically pathetic as she reveals her former association with Sylvia. For her role as (Mrs.) Grace Argona, Ann got a set of notices for which most actresses would give their eye teeth. *Film Review* thought her "so good in the film, as a very world weary cashier, that she stole every sequence of it in which she appeared." *S.F.* praised her "oddly touching performance."

To prove that she could still be glamorous, Ann accepted an offer to play Countess Framboise on *The Lucy Show*. A portrait from this series was also included in her "How to Change an Image" promotion. Ann would guest with Lucy seven times and the color photography showed her perennial attractiveness. Her character was an impoverished Countess, the former Rosie Harrigan and school friend of the star, Lucille Ball, herself. The two worked well together and Lucy wanted Ann to do more, but eventually Vivian Vance would rejoin the show and, with the set salary figure she was receiving, Ann

AS THE "WIDOW FAY" IN THAT EPISODE OF *THE LEGEND OF JESSE JAMES*, DECEMBER 20, 1965

realized that moneywise she'd be better off elsewhere. As Iris Adrian explained, "Lucy hired me and Jody Gilbert for one of the best scripts from that series. I got a lot of fan mail about that show. Most actors on her show got Scale pay. Ann may have got a little more, but I doubt it. Lucy was very much a dollars-and-cents gal. She was extremely frugal." Ann was really pleased to work with Gale Gordon on the show and she caught up with two regulars from her own series, Reta Shaw and Lester Matthews.

Queries about her thickening waistline, and even a possible pregnancy, had a worried Ann reveal that her condition was glandular. But,

BEN PIAZZA AND AS IN *THE GLASS MENAGERIE* (LOS ANGELES, 1966).
ANN WON THE MIANI HERALD BEST ACTRESS AWARD
FOR HER PORTRAYAL OF AMANDA WINGFIELD.

one reporter, visiting the set of *The Lucy Show,* inadvertently revealed she had a "very sweet tooth and was too fond of chocolates." Another said, "She adores the 5-pound boxes of chocolates an admirer sends her."

Her dates around this time included friends Cesar Romero, George Freelinghuysen and policeman Rudy Diaz. Rudy was tipped to get Ann to attempt a third marriage, but the anticipated nuptials did not eventuate.

Accepting a role in which she was heard but not seen, appealed to Ann. With no worries about her appearance or diet to be considered, and liking the financial terms of her contract, she signed up for a new NBC TV series, *My Mother the Car.* Debuting on September 14, 1965, the series starred Jerry Van Dyke as a small-town lawyer whose dear departed mother (Ann) "returns" to help and guide him with her advice, which is heard from the radio of an old dilapidated 1928 Porter touring car. Produced by Rod Amateau,

WITH STEPHANIE POWERS ON THE
SET OF "THE CARPATHIAN CAPER
AFFAIR" EPISODE OF *THE GIRL
FROM U.N.C.L.E.* (1967)

who had directed episodes of *The Ann Sothern Show*, the car was actually an antique fliver. The name "Porter" was given it, as a good luck gesture for the series, after Don Porter who had been such a successful teammate in Ann's earlier TV series.

The workload for Ann was easy to handle as she recorded all her dialogue in a booth, doing several segments at a time. She told the *Columbia Citizen Journal* why she accepted the role. "One, I like to make and spend money. I couldn't think of an easier way to make some. Two, I enjoy character roles and have no make-up problems, no hairdressers and no camera angles to worry about. It's like acting on radio for a TV stars' pay." Ann beat out both Eve Arden and Jean Arthur, who both read for the role. Describing her "emotional" role, the publicity machine had this to say: "She will be seen blowing her radiator cap when she's indignant, honking her horn to get attention, giggling uncontrollably when simonized. She has acrophobia—getting dizzy going up on a lube rack and arthritis—feeling rain in her shock absorbers. But beneath it all as in every Ann Sothern comedy, she possesses a warmly, feminine 6 cylinder heart."

The show started out well in the Neilson ratings, but the public tired of "such stupidity" and it slipped to #83 in a field of 119 shows toward

AS AS MRS. KOSSEK, MOTHER OF A
BOGUS SOCIALITE, PLAYED BY SEAN
GARRISON, IN UNIVERSAL'S TV
MOVIE, *THE OUTSIDER* (1968)

AS as Angela in *Chubasco*
(Warner Bros., 1968)

the end of its run. Ann bought a new Rolls-Royce during her run in *Car* and escaped generally unscathed in the poor reviews the show received, with Hank Grant feeling that she "shoulders most of the spoken wit and projects it with just the right combination of dryness and irony."

Although many regard the series today as a cult favorite, it does have the reputation for being one of the worst shows on television. Ann would say of its failure, "If a horse can talk [Mr. Ed] why not a car? I took it because it was something I had never done before—and I've been in every phase of show business except playing fairs or stadiums." After 30 segments, *My Mother the Car* braked to a halt with the final episode airing in 1966.

With no movie offers in sight Ann did a stock tour in Ohio with *The Solid Gold Cadillac*. Selected as her co-star was Jesse White, the character player she had employed in both *Private Secretary* and *The Ann Sothern Show*. Produced by John Kenley, the show played throughout the month of August 1965 in both Warren and Columbus. Originally, *Cadillac* had starred elderly character actress Josephine Hull, of *Arsenic and Old Lace* and *Harvey* fame, and when filmed by Columbia it had starred thirtyish Judy Holliday. Having received a souvenir program of the play from Ann, I thanked her and asked which of these two performers had influenced her interpretation of the role. She replied, "Neither, I went for somewhere in between. The play had a lot of slow passages and I remembered Helen Broderick from RKO, who could really time a good line. I guess I tried for a bit of Helen."

On another occasion, with *God Bless Our Bank* in mind, I asked if it had any connection with *I Remember Mama* as "Mama's bank account" is repeatedly mentioned in that play. "No," she responded, "that was a complete original. The character was a spinster, well-meaning but dumb, who is a longtime bookkeeper for a bank. She gives away millions of dollars to the needy customers before being found out. It sounded good at the time but never really worked. The role was very Spring Byington, so I modeled Gussie, that was her name, on Miss Byington."

Alumni Fun was one TV game show providing some nostalgia for Ann. Hosted by Peter Lind Hayes, its format had three former students of a university compete against three from a rival university. Test pilot Scott Crossfield, *Time Magazine* editor Thomas Griffith and Ann represented the University of Washington. Their opponents were actor/TV host William Lundigan, executive Robert McCaffrey and football hero John Mackey from Syracuse University.

Also in 1965, Ann was lauded critically for her in-depth acting on *The Legend of Jesse James* ("Widow Fay") for ABC. Showing Ann a still from the show she said, "They aged me for that role. Look at my hands, that's Latex." Taking a look at a rerun of that series, I saw Ann's poignant portrayal. It is a

AS AND CHRISTOPHER JONES IN CHUBASCO (WARNER BROS., 1968)

very moving and disciplined piece of work.

Ann was first choice and under serious consideration for the role of *Mame* in 1965. She loved the score and, upon reading the script, became very enthusiastic. Her eventual declinature of the role was mostly influenced by her thoughts of an inability to sustain a long run on Broadway. Tiring quickly, even with the short stock tours, brought these fears to mind. In addition, she was also concerned about the dance routines and her not always reliable knee being able to endure a lengthy season. She reasoned that to accept the role would not be fair on herself or the rest of the company. Angela Lansbury played the role with great success and other big names succeeded her - Janis Paige and Jane Morgan on Broadway, Ginger Rogers in London, Ann Miller in Florida and later on Broadway Susan Hayward and Celeste Holm in Las Vegas and, in 1968, Ann Sothern in Honolulu.

A PORTRAIT FOR *THE BEST MAN*
(UNITED ARTISTS, 1964)

Publicity photo used for the program of *Mame*, 1969

Chapter Thirteen: "Mame"

In 1966 Ann made one of her most regretted career decisions. She turned down the pilot for a proposed series to be produced by Desi Arnaz. It turned out to be the very successful sitcom, *The Mothers-in-Law*, with Eve Arden getting to play the role which had been earmarked for Ann. Kaye Ballard was the other mother-in-law. Ann said, "I made a bad choice there."

Tisha's acting career was slow in taking off but she did appear in some TV guest spots. There was talk of an estrangement between mother and daughter when she began dating a realtor and part-time actor, Lal Baum, in 1963. Unwilling to let Ann select her career path, and rightly so, she became very independent and very much her own person. There was a course in philosophy, which ultimately led to her statement, "Finally I got so screwed up that I quit." Her mother did not approve of her interest in the religions of the Far East, which, along with yoga, Tisha embraced. Like a lot of young adults in the mid-1960s she was into health foods and astrology. Despite Ann's social ambitions for her, she was very much a product of the then "now" generation. Her exclusive Duchesne College education did not inhibit her from the use of mild but expressive profanities in the course of her conversations. Ann, with her constant seeking of perfection, would contradict this behavior by saying, "Tisha's gifted but she's shy... she's a lady and she doesn't like me to get mixed up in her career."

Ann went on tour again in May 1966, this time to Miami, Florida. Here, she played Amanda Wingfield in *The Glass Menagerie* at the Coconut Grove Playhouse. Produced by Zev Bufman and James Riley and under the direction of George Keathley, Ann's performance won her the *Miami Herald's* Best

AS SCORED A TRIUMPH AS *MAME* ON STAGE IN HONOLULU, 1968

Actress award. Joan Hackett played her daughter Laura, with two excellent actors, Ben Piazza and James Olson, completing the cast of this Tennessee Williams classic. "Ann Sothern, blowsy and cozy as a stuffed koala, is the new angle on the drama," reported *The Miami Herald*. "She is enthralling as she wavers between reality and days of her youth."

With its huge success in Miami, the play was scheduled for a Los Angeles season, commencing in June. The Miami season closed on May 31. With little time for rehearsals, Piper Laurie replaced Joan Hackett for the Huntington Hartford Theatre production in Los Angeles. James Powers did not rave about Ann's handling of Amanda. "Miss Sothern is perhaps too young and pretty. She does not look the ruin Amanda should be. She has a facility for the wistful and achieves some poignant moments, but as a whole Miss Sothern is too brisk, too competent. It is difficult to believe she would be this desperate woman." Ann could take consolation with Cecil Smith of *The L.A. Times:* "Ann Sothern's Amanda is immensely valid catching both the unknowing cruelty and the rich natural humor of the faded belle. She is like a marshmallow sundae with a cherry on top…I commend it to you." Likewise, *L.A. Herald Examiner* was impressed: "Ann Sothern puts both laughter and lumps in your throat. I was unacquainted with Miss Sothern's artistry until last night…when I found how much I had been missing."

The play closed on June 25. On July 24, 1966, Tisha Sterling married Lal Baum in Las Vegas. Sheila Graham reported that Robert Sterling was present to give his daughter away but Ann was absent from the ceremony. Tisha has since said that her mother could not get there but that she did approve of the match. However, a couple of magazine items mentioned Ann being spotted swimming and sunning on the beach on the day of the wedding. The Baums would reside at Topanga Canyon in a house heated only by a fireplace. Their daughter, Heidi, would make the family a happy threesome but Ann, now reconciled with them, did not particularly like being called Grandma.

With motherhood, Tisha' s beauty blossomed even more and she was busy on TV with appearances on *Dr. Kildare, Mr. Novak, Run for Your Life* and *The Virginian*. She made her film debut in *Village of the Giants* (1965), but her first film to attract notice was *Coogan's Bluff* (1968), a Clint Eastwood starring vehicle. She was well received by most reviewers, though Susan Clark, another newcomer, and Betty Field were more forceful. Later, there would be more films: *Norwood,* with Glen Campbell and Kim Darby, and *The Name of the Game is Kill!,* a generally well acted horror opus. She also appeared in *Journey to Shiloh* and *The Wild Pack*. Tisha said later, "Being the daughter of Ann Sothern and Robert Sterling helped me to some extent, but I didn't use my mother and father's name ever. I was exposed to the business since I was a baby so I was familiar with aspects of show business. But I think it was harder for me in some ways because one doesn't want to think that they get jobs on the merit of their parents rather on themselves. I really don't think anyone that employed me gave me an acting job because of my mother. I believe I earned whatever role I got."

Stephanie Powers now had her own TV series, *The Girl From U.N.C.L.E.,* for NBC and shot at MGM. Ann was invited to guest star on the series in late 1966 and the two women made much of their reunion. With Jack Cassidy and Stan Freberg also guesting, this lighthearted affair proceeded at a merry pace. Sporting a glamorous wardrobe, Ann was the villainess out to take over the world. Playing it very tongue in cheek, for the character is also a soup manufacturer, she obviously enjoyed the experience. Not aired until February 1967, Ann did no more television until Universal summoned her for a TV movie *The Outsider*, which was televised that November. Also serving as the pilot for a TV series of the same name, it starred Darren McGavin and would be picked up by a sponsor. Written and produced by Roy Huggins, the genial Irishman who rose from writer to eventual head of Universal Television, it contained all the marks of his surety for success. Ann played Mrs. Kossek, mother of one of the suspects. Other guests were Edmond O'Brien, Shirley Knight, Audrey Totter and Joseph Wiseman, and the author's way with words and gift for vivid characterization gave the movie individuality. Director Michael Richie's treatment elevated this pilot as better than routine entertainment. Partaking in a sequence where a character on an LSD trip sees everyone in a slow motion dance, Ann wears sturdy lace-up shoes.

When I visited her in 1975, she was wearing a similar style of footwear and complained because she could not wear dressy shoes anymore. In an attempt to cheer her, I mentioned she had worn them in 1967 for *The Outsider*. This was one of a few occasions when I caught a glimpse of a short-fused Ann Sothern. She snapped, "So you remember, do you? Well, don't! I'm suing the Thunderbird Dinner Theatre as my accident there caused me to have to wear these shoes."

For the New Year of 1967 Ann was in her beloved Chicago rehearsing and eventually opening at the Ivanhoe Theatre in *Glad Tidings*. Portraying an aging actress who confronts the father of her grown illegitimate daughter, and gets him to finally marry her, Ann was at her most cajoling. A young actor, Jack Stillman, was in the cast and he recalled Ann's generosity. Achieving film fame later as the notorious Jack Wrangler, and eventually becoming a respected stage writer, director and producer, he remembered how Ann took the cast and audience of 25 to dinner when one performance was cancelled due to a blizzard.

In 1967 Ann also undertook a longer stage tour, starring in the musical *Gypsy*, in which Ethel Merman had scored a Broadway triumph. Opening late June in Cedar Grove, New Jersey, this innovative show had Ann playing Rose, mother of Gypsy Rose Lee and June Havoc. Her leading man was Alfred Sandor,

ON STAGE AS *MAME*,
HONOLULU, 1969

who had played the same role on Broadway opposite the legendary Merman. Alfred would be cast in a play in Australia, marry a local girl and settle in Sydney. A true gentleman, he attended a performance of *The Women*, the Clare Boothe Luce comedy, which I directed in 1971. Speaking with him afterwards I inquired about *Gypsy*, and in particular the season he had played opposite Ann. "She was fantastic," Sandor told me. "I did that show with Ethel and also Vivian Blaine and let me tell you, Ann was something else. She was asked to replace Ethel at the end of the Broadway season, but didn't. She should have. She gave the part a whole new dimension and the audiences just went wild for her." Of *Gypsy*, Ann herself said, "That was exhausting. Eight weeks and I used a totally different singing voice for Rose. I have a tape of it, but I'm not playing it as you may not care for my sound as Rose. At the end of the play I had to do a mock striptease and sing full out 'Rose's Turn.' My energy level since my illness remained low and after a week I was worried I'd not last the distance. However, an English friend of mine recommended something for me to take and just before 'Rose's Turn,' I'd use it. Believe me it got me through and the crowds gave me standing ovations." Ann, reported

Newsday, "makes Rose the classic stage mother, a prickly, tough and thoroughly human person. And as a bonus she adds her own sardonic sense of humor and a surprisingly effective singing voice. It is a most entertaining combination." The show closed on August 27, 1967 and though there would be requests for Ann to repeat the role, even in London, she turned them down.

Late in 1967 Ann got a call from Warner Bros. to be part of a star team in a widescreen color adventure flick, *Chubasco*. It was announced in the press she'd be playing the owner of a hamburger stand. There was a little gossip about her casting as the film would also star her old beau, Richard Egan. Long married to former starlet Patricia Hardy, and a devoted husband and father, the thought of rekindling any romance was far from his mind. Ann and he would share no scenes together and her character of Angela was not a hamburger stand proprietor. She played a friendly bar owner with girls living in her adjoining "motel." The lead players were Susan Strasberg as Egan's daughter and Christopher Jones in the title role. Although fishing occupied a lot of the 98-minute running time, the dramatic scenario was very much like *Romeo and Juliet.* Shot on location in and around San Diego, it was produced by William Conrad and directed by Allen H. Miner. Wearing the usual caftans for most of her screen time, Ann appears slimmer when she dons tight-fitting pants for later scenes. Her first feature film in color since *Nancy Goes to Rio,* showed that, facially, she was still an amazingly youthful looking woman in this 1968 release. Her character is also hinted as being Christopher Jones' mother and her sympathetic handling of scenes with him and his bride, Susan Strasberg, strengthen this notion. She said no when I asked about this. "That was just a coincidence and earlier references to the boy's mother weren't fully developed in the script."

One amusing candid photo I have from this film shows Ann in close-up poking her tongue out. I asked her "was it perhaps to the executive producer, William Conrad?" Again, replying in the negative, she responded, "No, I never met him. I wish I had as I've always admired his work. That tongue poking was done to our director, who was 'nice' and very easy to work with— Allen Miner was his name, and he also wrote the screenplay."

A more refined-looking Ann Sothern was revealed in her 1968 guesting on *Family Affair.* The long-running CBS comedy series starred Brian Keith, with whom Ann had played on *Insight* four years earlier. Her role as a comfortable widow had her setting her sights on Sebastian Cabot with plans for him to operate a restaurant.

Glad Tidings would be revived by Ann when she took on a second short run opening in Denver, Colorado on July 1, 1968 and proceeding to Connecticut with a final performance in Latham, New York on July 21. For this tour, Anne Archer, Marjorie Lord and John Archer's daughter, would be in the cast.

The highlight of 1968 for Ann Sothern was undoubtedly her appearance in Honolulu as *Mame*. Produced by the Civic Light Opera, at the enormous Honolulu Concert Hall, it proved to be a sensation, winning Ann accolades and standing ovations. The show played for the month of August. Writing to Ann in Honolulu about my disappointment in missing her triumph, brought a handwritten response. "...I am so sorry, Colin, you couldn't get to see *Mame*—I'm sure you would have enjoyed it—but I hardly think it would have been worth your spending all that money just to come here to see it. We closed on the 25th and I'm off to the mainland tomorrow (29th). Have had a marvelous, though exhausting month here, and the people are such fantastic audiences."

In the cast of *Mame*, playing Agnes Gooch, was Myra de Groot, who would later migrate to Australia. Catching up with her after a performance of *Oh Coward!*, I inquired about her working with Ann. Myra said, "That was quite a production and when she sang 'If He Walked Into My Life,' she brought the house down; the applause was deafening, it went on and on . . . They'd had three other Hollywood names headlining three musicals which preceded *Mame* and they were a disappointment for both audiences and critics, but Ann Sothern was totally embraced and got standing ovations every performance."

During our first meeting in 1973 Ann arranged for me to hear a tape of her songs from *Mame*. "If He Walked Into My Life" was, of course, her best opportunity vocally and she sang it powerfully and with incredible feeling. Myra de Groot was right, the applause and shouts of approval from the audience were showstopping and unending. When "Bosom Buddies" was played, Ann commented, "That's with that awful English girl. I fixed her on opening night." The English actress Delphi Lawrence played Vera Charles and just what Ann did I never got to find out. Mark Savage, who had played in *Mame*

BRENDA BENET, BRANDON DE WILDE AND AS IN "LOVE AND
THE BACHELOR" (1969) FROM THE POPULAR TV SERIES,
LOVE, AMERICAN STYLE

on Broadway with Angela Lansbury, was also in the cast and no doubt an important asset to the new version.

Ann flatly stated, "I don't sing music I don't like," when I asked why "That's How Young I Feel" wasn't on the tape. She would not elaborate further, but there may well have been a couple of underlying reasons which influenced her decision to drop the number, namely the lyrics and their reference to age and the rigorous dance routine that Mame performs during the number.

Joseph Maltby, of the *Honolulu Advertiser,* called it the "Production of the Year," elaborating, "For this reason I attribute the success of *Mame* to Miss Ann Sothern. Miss Sothern's a much better actress than the three previous big names of this summer's season. On top of that she radiates personality. One might argue that with all of those gorgeous costumes, it would be hard not to dazzle. But costumes don't make a star. Ann Sothern's 'Mame' is kooky and wise, wry and affectionate, graceful, sexy, full of charms. She even displays a convincing serious dimension, as in the well sung 'If He Walked Into My Life.' By the end of the run Miss Sothern will be sensational…Naturally

Miss Sothern deserved the standing ovation…For me everyone else is second to Miss Sothern." Phil Mayer, in the *Honolulu Star Bulletin,* stated, "*Mame* won a standing ovation last night…and Miss Sothern is an expert actress who is charmingly unafraid to look her age, knows what to do with a funny line and can sing…late in the second act she was astonishingly good in the matriarchal lament 'If He Walked Into My Life'…and there's similarly moving, quiet, but arresting emotion in her duet with Master Mark Savage 'My Best Girl'…Miss Sothern and Miss Lawrence are gorgeously campy in a meticulously planned disaster, a production number called 'The Man in The Moon is a Miss' in which Miss Sothern queasily rides a crescent moon which soars uncertainly across the stage."

Returning home, Ann decided to rest on her laurels for the rest of the year, and apart from social engagements and family get-togethers, remained idle. Interrupting her lethargy was the arrival of an Australian television crew at her home. She was one of several Hollywood stars who agreed to be interviewed for a popular daytime Australian series, *Girl Talk.* It was hosted by the very effervescent, English-born Hazel Phillips. A top award-winning TV personality, Hazel was blonde, lovely looking and conveyed a ladylike quality not unlike Ann's own. At one time she was a patron of the theatre company I directed for and after her attendance at our production of *Picnic,* we talked about Ann. Hazel's general consensus was that Ann was easy to interview and came across very well for her public. Ann looked okay, but complained a lot about feeling "very tired." Hazel said, "I liked her and so did the crew."

AS as the mischievous Aunt Margaret in the NBC TV movie,
The Great Man's Whiskers. Although it was made in 1969,
it was not shown until 1973.

Chapter Fourteen: "Ann"

After a considerable absence from television, Ann was cast in another segment of the religious series *Insight*, which aired in May 1969. Titled, "Is the 11:59 Late This Year?," the allegorical episode resembled Thornton Wilder's *The Bridge of San Luis Rey*. Ann played an actress, past her prime, who along with four other people are on the verge of taking the train of the title to their respective deaths. Howard Duff was also in the cast, and both he and Ann were favorably reviewed.

Much brighter in outlook was her December 1969 appearance on *Love, American Style*. Portraying Brandon de Wilde's possessive mother, she does not want him to leave the family nest, and every girl he brings home is scared off by her schemes. Brenda Benet is his latest fiancée and she bests Ann by supporting her every ruse, and eventually out maneuvers her. The cheap dinner (hamburger) prepared by Ann is praised by Brenda as healthy and Ann's hypochondria is accepted and treated by Brenda, who happens to be a doctor. Outwitted, Ann gives in and a marriage for her son is at last acceptable. Produced by William Dozier, the hour-long segment contains two other stories, one of which stars Dozier's wife, Ann Rutherford. Quite a few of the reviews mentioned the comebacks of the two former movie stars, Ann R. and Ann S. In Ann Sothern's case her increased weight was mentioned, but so was her all-encompassing charm and remarkable prettiness.

Universal made a TV movie, *The Great Man's Whiskers*, that year. Produced by Adrian Scott, from his one-act play, it starred Dean Jones, with Dennis Weaver creating a credible Abraham Lincoln. Ann played Jones' aunt, who is constantly interfering with the raising of his young daughter. An odd film, it also boasted the fine singing voice of Harve Presnell and solid character studies from Isabel Sanford, John Hillerman, Richard Erdman and Charles Lane. Executives at NBC must have doubted its salability, delaying its release for four years. Wearing a bonnet and a waisted period costume, Ann looks her heaviest, but by the time of its release in February 1973, it reflected that year's image.

With no theatre offers that year, Ann joined the many ex-movie actresses on the books of agent Ruth Webb. She had found work for many stars on the dinner theatre circuit and also for summer stock and bus truck tours. Lynn Bari, Dorothy Lamour and later Kathryn Grayson would all have their careers revitalized by Miss Webb's expertise as an agent and booker. The play *My Daughter, Your Son* was a comedy Ann undertook to tour in the summer of 1970. A popular attraction for stock productions, there would also be a company touring with June Allyson, her husband David Ashrow and son Richard Powell headlining. Ann's tour opened in St. Charles, Illinois on July 2. The show also played in Wichita and Ohio.

On returning to Los Angeles, Ann attended a number of functions with the young actor George Paulsin as her escort. He had played her son in *My Daughter, Your Son*, and the press had them linked romantically. One captioned photograph called Paulsin her real-life son, while another praised her attitude of dating younger men. Ann's interest in Paulsin was strictly a friendship thing and she remarked, "If the publicity hounds want to make something else of it, that's their mistake."

Continuing with theatre work, she returned to Chicago to play the role of the mother in *Barefoot in the Park*, with Tab Hunter as her co-star. The subsequent tour included the Meadowbrook Dinner Theatre in Cedar Grove, New Jersey.

Universal then guest-starred Ann in a segment of *The Men from Shiloh* (a.k.a. *The Virginian*), a Western series starring Doug McClure. Bradford Dillman and Carolyn Jones, portraying Ann's sister, were also cast in this episode titled "Legacy of Spencer Flats." Ann played a woman who was quick on the trigger, and also a little eccentric. The show aired in January 1971.

At the end of 1970, producer Zev Bufman brought Ann to the attention of Eddie Bracken, who was co-producing with Bufman *Butterflies are Free* for the Coconut Grove Playhouse in Miami, Florida. With memories of her great success in the Bufman-produced *The Glass Menagerie*, Ann readily signed on. Beau Bridges played her blind son in the comedy-drama, with Ann recreating the role played on Broadway by Eileen Heckart. Ann, said the *Miami Beach Sun*, "starts out as the ultimate nasty, clinging mother...a hateful, sarcastic character, but she plays Mama Baker superbly." In her opening night review of December 21, 1970, Frances Swaebly of *The Miami Herald* was most unkind: "...adequate is about all she is...not only doesn't she know all her lines, she appears to be little more than walking through the part." This review may have been a fair one as Ann was a last-minute replacement for another actress, who, because of other commitments, had to quit. Ann simply said of *Butterflies are Free*, which she later did with Brandon de Wilde, "I just got back from six frantic but fun weeks in *Butterflies are Free* and I'm starting my own Private Secretarial Service in Hollywood. There's a real need for a nationwide referral agency for business executives to find girls with swift minds and fast fingers." *Butterflies* would run into 1971 and there was also another season of *Barefoot in the Park*, with Margaret O'Brien.

Television was now marketing successful full-length movies and Ann made two in 1971. Firstly, there was *Congratulations, It's a Boy!* for ABC, produced by Aaron Spelling. Ann and Jack Albertson played the parents of swinging bachelor Bill Bixby. His discovery of a grown son due to an indiscretion years before and his need for this discovery to be kept secret from his parents and current girlfriend, Diane Baker, formed the basis of the plot. Jeff Donnell and Tom Bosley played Baker's parents. Jeff Donnell said of this production, "We had a strong cast of pros. Jack Albertson and Tom Bosley were terrific to work with and Diane Baker, such a serious, intense actress. Ann, of course, was nice as ever and I was amazed

AS USED THIS PORTRAIT TO
PUBLICIZE HER ROLE AS
CAROLE ARDEN IN
PERSONAL APPEARANCE, 1971

that the ten years or so since we had last worked together had left little or no signs of age on that fabulous face."

Her other TV film that year was *A Death of Innocence* for CBS, shot partly in New York. Originally, Ann wasn't cast in it, but she had accompanied Tisha, who had a lead role, to New York. Kim Stanley was to play a small role as mother to Tony Young, but reportedly she broke a bone in her foot and dropped out. Being on the set anyway, Ann was the quick and logical choice to replace her. Ann said of the experience, "It was a great role for Tisha so when they suggested I take over Miss Stanley's role, I agreed." She also slyly added, "Kim Stanley broke something…she said, but with Shelley Winters in a much fatter role, to me this reason could have caused her to…opt out!" Arthur Kennedy and John Randolph had the major male roles and the whole cast, under the subtle direction of Paul Wendkos, performed with aplomb.

Ann volunteered her commentary on this film when I showed her a still in which she is pictured with Shelley Winters. Putting on her glasses, Ann said, "Shelley and I look like contemporaries, don't you think, Colin?" I agreed with her and asked what she thought of the finished product. "Tisha was splendid in it and worked with Shelley again, on *Batman* I think. My part was small, but effective, and that Arthur Kennedy, in my opinion, has always been one of the best actors around."

Warner Bros. Television then came up with an offer for Ann to be a regular on a new comedy series, *The Chicago Teddy Bears*. Starring Dean Jones, as a 1920s owner of a "speakeasy," it had him matching wits with a group of inept gangsters known as "The Chicago Teddy Bears." Ann's role, of an "Apple Annie"-type character, was named Florrie the flower lady. A real con-artist, Florrie talked out of the side of her mouth and sold information to both Jones' character and the gangsters. The hilarious finale had her laid out in a basement pretending to be a victim of a fatal malaria attack. One stipulation in Ann's contract was that she must remain "pleasingly plump." Also in the cast of the pilot episode were Mickey Shaughnessy, Huntz Hall, Jamie Farr and Mike Mazurki. George Raft appeared in a cameo spot playing himself. The series did get picked up and debuted on September 17, 1971, but the pilot episode was held over until December 10, 1971. Unable to keep her weight down as specified, Ann only got to appear in the pilot. The series itself proved to be a disappointing failure in the ratings and only had a limited run.

Around this time, producer Robert Aldrich contacted Ann with an offer to star in a movie he was planning on the life of Errol Flynn. Titled *The Greatest Mother of Them All*, it dealt with Flynn's affair with teenager Beverly Aadland, and her manipulative mother. Peter Finch agreed to play Flynn and starlet Alexandra Hay was Aldrich's choice for Miss Aadland. In order to obtain backing for the project, Aldrich put up the money to pay for his cast and crew to film a mini-movie. Covering key scenes with his cast of three it was, according to Ann, "a very viable presentation, beautifully photographed with expensive production values." Legal problems with Flynn's family had it shelved for a while, but Aldrich kept right in there pitching. Only when Peter Finch died did he give up on it, not being able to think of a suitable Australian star to replace him.

No longer married, Tisha's career was now at its most productive. Guesting on most of the television drama series, she also did many movies made for that medium. Especially effective was her work in *In the Glitter Palace*, with Chad Everett, and in *Betrayal* with Sam Groom, she gave probably the best performance of her career. Playing a cold-blooded con-artist, she becomes a companion to ailing Amanda Blake. Her beautiful exterior and shy, introverted demeanor masks a devious schemer whose true character is chilling. Crooner Dick Haymes was also in this riveting little thriller. *Snatched* had Tisha as one of three women who are kidnapped. Again, she was in top form, though Sheree North, as one of the victims, had a more harrowing role, that of a diabetic being deprived of medication. Tisha made her mother most proud when she appeared in a prestigious theatre production of *The Front Page* in Los Angeles.

In the 1970s Ann, following the trend of the young actresses around, grew her hair long, just below shoulder level. She was photographed at this time with her daughter and her sister Marion.

Her summer theatre choice for August of 1971 was *Personal Appearance*, which played in the Chicago area. Roger Pryor had always told Ann that she could imitate Mae West with a lot of skill. When he was her leading man at Paramount, Ann would often "ape" the famous sex symbol when she'd see Roger after the day's filming. Of *Personal Appearance* Ann said, "That was an old play. Mae West did the movie with Randolph Scott, I think it was called *Go West, Young Man* [1936]. Years later I saw the play in Los Angeles. Louise Allbritton did it and she was excellent, but nothing like Mae West. A lot of

FOL-DE-ROL, AN ABC VARIETY SPECIAL (1972), STARRING JUDY KAYE,
TOTIE FIELDS, CYD CHARISSE, AND AS

people told me Louise was a tall version of myself. Facially, she did bear a slight resemblance but, chatting with her afterwards, I learned her favorite actress was Carole Lombard and, you know something, she'd developed her style." Ann's version must have contained a little bit of Mae West for the review in the *Arlington Heights Herald* read, "Ann Sothern brings laughs through her many double meaning retorts, almost always said with raised eyebrows." In one of his first leading roles was a young ex-sports hero, Robert Urich.

At the close of 1971, TV's *Alias Smith and Jones* was aired in which Ann had fun as a blackjack dealer, with Jessica Walter and Patrick O'Neal as the other guest stars. Their segment was called "Everything Else You Can Steal." The series starred Peter Duel and Ben Murphy in the title roles.

By the end of 1971 she had also completed a special with the Kraft Puppets. Released in February 1972, the special, called *Fol-De-Rol,* also served as an unsuccessful pilot for a TV series. Rick Nelson, whose wife Kris Harmon was a family friend, was another guest as was Cyd Charisse. Ann, wearing an ornate hairstyle of assorted plaits complete with tiara, caftan and cloak, was the "Queen of the Renaissance Fair." Totie Fields, Mickey Rooney, Judy Kaye, Lynne Thigpen and Yma Sumac, in medieval attire, were some of her "Halloween"-looking subjects. *Variety* called it "a pointless mishmash," but Ann enjoyed the romp leading a large afghan puppet around on a jewel-encrusted leash.

At the end of 1972 *The Weekend Nun*, a television film, which Ann found particularly rewarding, was released. Originally titled *Matter of the Heart*, Ann said, "I play a Mother Superior. It's a different kind of role, to say the least, and I think it's special." The nun of the title was Joanna Pettet, who worked by day as a probation officer for juveniles, returning to the convent at night and weekends. Based on the lifestyle of a real-life nun, Joyce Duco, the film also cast Vic Morrow and Kay Lenz in key roles. Ann's role was a benevolent one as the Mother Superior. She warns Joanna Pettet that it is not possible to mix her religious vows with the realistic attitudes of the outside world.

In her spare time the ever-enterprising Ann was now in partnership with Stanley, the son of composer Jule Styne. She said, "We are finishing the music and lyrics for a special theme to 'Mother Goose'—which is a long way from Mother Superior."

Her stage work in 1972 took her to Dallas, Texas where, at the Windmill Dinner Theater, she starred in *Everybody Loves Opal*. An audience pleaser, this comedy had originally starred Eileen Heckart. Interviewed in Dallas by Evan A. Crawley, Ann stated, "I never thought there was beauty in maturity. But there is. You just have to learn to accept how you are. I've learned to accept a lot in life I didn't know I was capable of. I never thought about age or changing. I thought everything just went along the same…Just recently, I went back to school, at the University of Southern California, to take classes in cinema…There are so many things going on, so many technological advances being made, that a person simply has to keep learning to keep up."

Ann also discussed her new interests in cooking, gardening and needlepoint. During another interview, she was working on a needlepoint canvas which Tisha had designed. Ann Worley, another Dallas writer, reported, "Religion is important to her. A Catholic, she has spent many days teaching the church's catechism to children in Idaho." Ann said, "Organized religion has lost many young people. But many of these same youngsters are now in the 'Jesus Movement' and that's great. I must say there is no substitute for good manners and good breeding. I will stand up when an older person enters the room. This is the era of the ugly people. Wait, maybe I should say it's the era of ugliness. People today would accept Opal."

WITH SHELLEY WINTERS
IN THE TV MOVIE,
A DEATH OF INNOCENCE (1971)

Opal of *Everybody Loves Opal* is a shabby frump who collects garbage and saves old tea bags, pegging them on an inside clothesline. Expressing a wish to film the play, Ann also mentioned in Dallas that she'd just completed a new movie, *Are You a Good Boy?* Visiting the set of this film, which was an old Hollywood mansion past its glory days, was Australian female impressionist Tracy Lee. A movie buff, his favorite actresses were Dorothy Lamour, Bette Davis, Ruby Keeler and Ann Sothern. We met through a mutual acquaintance, Sally Sherman, who was the No. 1 fan of, and is now secretary-companion to, Kathryn Grayson. Tracy knew of my admiration for Ann Sothern and mentioned he was about to visit Los Angeles. Kathryn had organized meetings for him with Bette and Dorothy and he asked me if I could arrange a meeting with Ann, which I did. The meeting took place at the old house where they were filming *Are You a Good Boy?* Upon his return to Australia, he telephoned and was "over the moon" about his trip and meeting his favorite stars. He told me, "Ann Sothern was very, very nice and asked about you. You really should make the trip to the U.S., as I'm positive she'd enjoy meeting you."

With Tracy's advice on my mind, I made arrangements for my first trip to the United States in 1973. Charleston, S.C., Denver, Colorado, New Orleans and Chicago were other cities visited on that first excursion, which turned out to be the trip of a lifetime. For not only did it open my eyes to a country of fabulous people and entertainment, it gave me the opportunity and privilege of meeting face to face the stars of stage and screen whose work filled me with the highest admiration.

The Killing Kind, as *Are You a Good Boy?* was now retitled, got a special feature layout in *After Dark* magazine. Ann received a rave review, and other publications hinted at an Oscar nomination. An independent production, its two producers from Texas would limit the release, which meant that voters at the Academy didn't get to assess Ann's remarkable performance for Oscar consideration. Playing the doting mother of homicidal John Savage, Ann's *tour-de-force* acting had her sister Marion say, "Those final moments when Ann has to kill her son had me in tears."

After being home for just a month, I was pleasantly surprised to find *The Killing Kind* was about to open in Australia on a double bill with *Madame Sin*, starring Bette Davis. It did good business and got great reviews, while *Madame Sin* did

AS AND DAUGHTER, TISHA STERLING, AT THE BALLET SOCIETY OF LOS ANGELES, 1972. [PHOTO BY FRANK EDWARDS]

not. *The Killing Kind* boasted a strong cast, with veteran Ruth Roman making a guest appearance. Director Curtis Harrington also extracted top performances from Luana Anders, Marjorie Eaton and newcomer Cindy Williams. The film was very well received in Los Angeles when it was released in 1974. Ann's reviews were outstanding. *The Los Angeles Times*: "Miss Sothern's mother is alternately shrewd, stupid, vexing and pathetic, valiant and lazy." *After Dark*: "…a smashing triumph for Ann Sothern. Gloriously slattern, ravishingly beauteous, she's every inch and every overweight ounce a terrific actress and an ever lustrous star." Curtis Harrington spoke of Ann Sothern, "Ann had been off the screen for about six years and this was a great comeback vehicle for her. She has done an excellent job in a dramatic role."

1973 PHOTO BY JOHN ENGSTEAD

Chapter Fifteen: "Opal"

A production of *Everybody Loves Opal* was planned for Jacksonville, Florida, to open on August 15, 1973, and she was looking forward to a second season in this role. *Everybody Loves Opal* is a play with a lot of heart. Opal, an eccentric bag lady-type who collects junk, is a character an audience must like for the play to succeed. Ann had that winning, personable warmth and charm required, which enabled the public to overlook the derelict surroundings and the frowsy appearance of the character. When I saw Abby Dalton as Opal it did not quite work, as she was too young at that time to be completely convincing. The character also has to be so trusting and optimistic that the three criminals she befriends are finally converted by her altruism before the final curtain falls. In the late 1970s I directed the Australian premiere of *Everybody Loves Opal* and, despite its large slice of sentimentality and lack of cynicism, it went over very well with audiences. Living in a shack with a collapsible ceiling full of used cans, debris and assorted antique pieces, Opal suffers an accident at the end of Act 1. There is a fake tree trunk supporting all the overhead junk and, at the first act conclusion, it is triggered to fall and release all the overhead debris onto the stage. On opening night in Jacksonville, the pole (tree trunk) was released a fraction too early, which did not allow Ann sufficient time to get out of the way. She suffered the full impact of the trunk hitting her back, across the spine. Trouper that she was, and despite severe pain, she continued on throughout Act 2 and, after medical treatment, managed to complete the season. The pain must have been excruciating and it is to her credit and valor that she was able to complete the show on that opening night.

During the run I had a card from Ann showing "The Fountain of Friend-ship" in Jacksonville. I'd written earlier to say that I would be returning to the U.S. in 1974. Her message was chirpy and upbeat. The card was postmarked September 3. Having had the accident on August 15, it seems the initial crushing of her back was thought to be a temporary incapacity. Ann said she felt that *Opal* was a really good play for her and would make a good picture.

At Christmas there arrived a charming greeting from Marion and Char-lie Tetley, as well as a warm friendly one from Ann. There was no mention of the accident or its aftermath. Then, on January 31, 1974, I received a hand-written letter from Ann: "Am so happy you liked *Killing Kind*. It's a super role - and I enjoyed it. It finally opens here March 13th! Well - you won't believe where I am going? Leaving February 11th for Hong Kong for a picture called *Golden Needles* for AIP. Joe Don Baker, Liz Ashley, Burgess Meredith and me. Have never been to the Orient so am looking forward to it. Will be at the Peninsula Hotel on Kowloon February 15-25th. Is that awfully far from Aus-tralia? Why don't you all fly over?...An accident in Jacks., Florida, threw my vertebrae way out and my back's been playing up ever since. That's one of the reasons I decided to make *Golden Needles* as I've heard Chinese acupuncture in Hong Kong will help my back. The other reason, I wanted to work and as well it'll be lovely to see Burgess Meredith again."

On February 18, a postcard arrived from Hong Kong: "Hi—this is a fas-cinating, unbelievable place. Saw Red China from the frontier yesterday. Liked Tokyo too. Suffering jet lag and jet puff—but hanging in there. Start work Wednesday. Have lost a whole day tho due to the trip—somewhere! Greetings from Sal [Grasso] who is with me." I did phone Ann at the Penin-sula Hotel and enjoyed a lengthy chat with both her and Sal.

April 28, 1974 brought a long letter from Ann: "My trip to Hong Kong was interesting, informative and practically a disaster as far as I am con-cerned. The working conditions there are completely primitive—no adequate toilet facilities, dressing rooms etc...The weather also dropped to 37 & 40 degrees, and we all froze to death on the set because there was no heat. I did have seven acupuncture treatments but they only helped a little. Still I got through the picture, though at times the back pain was very intense. Picked up a very strange oriental bug which has laid me low for 8 weeks, and I am finally entering St. Johns Hospital this Monday to stay there until they find out what's wrong with me. I really have been quite ill for just the second time in my life, so I guess, in the long run, I have been lucky..."

Ann hated nostalgia and in yet another 1974 communication she wrote me on that subject at length. "...I would be grateful if you corrected all the inadequacies in that ridiculous article by Ronald Bowers. He had no okay from me to do that article and really had no right to release it. However, we are all victims these days of writers who vicariously make a living on inaccuracies called nostalgia. I have given up even reading that nonsense." The article to which Ann referred was published in the now-defunct *Films in Review*.

PHOTO BY JOHN ENGSTEAD

Out of the hospital, she devoted her time to art—painting and sketching, including a large portrait of Tisha. Seeing her paintings, I was surprised at the vivid use of color as her personal style of dress was always pastel, subdued or the form-flattering navy blue or black. She was also one of the few star ladies who could wear brown successfully and in 1949 a full-page color cover of her in brown hat and gown, from *Shadow on the Wall*, looked fabulous in a New York supplement.

In 1974 Ann was invited to be Artist in Residence at Jacksonville University in Florida. The engagement, for three days, took place from September 17- 20. Ann's duties included running a series of workshops on Stanislavsky, The Moscow Art Theatre and Method Acting. On September 19, she was awarded the "Key to the City" by the University during a tea held in her honor by The Friends of the Fine Arts. Her final day was devoted to a lecture, to which members of the general public were admitted. Ann told me that she found this area truly stimulating and hoped there would be more of those bookings.

For Christmas, 1975, Ann sent a large card with a snowy background and a tiny bird resting on the handle of an old oaken bucket in the foreground. Inside was a particularly inspiring message by Fra Giovanni. Her personal message was uplifting too and she added, "as you can see I have moved. The landlord raised my rent by $465 per month, which I thought was a bit much! Have a divine little townhouse which suits me perfectly. Tisha has been working in 5 shows in a row—but I am very quiet yet. My case comes to trial December 13 in Jacksonville, Fla… "

Ann's new address was on Manning Avenue in Westwood. When I saw her in 1974, she was busy selling lots of stored items, including a complete set of stills from all her MGM films. The stay in the hospital had helped her lose weight, but mostly from her face and neck. A new restaurant chain had opened in Los Angeles called The House of Pies in 1974. Unfortunately, these delicious eateries only survived for about four years, but my first of many visits to their establishments was with Ann. She drove Gordon Hunter and myself to the Beverly Hills branch and spoke with knowledgeable "delight" of their gourmet offerings. Gordon selected Banana Cream and, on Ann's advice, I opted for Boston Chocolate. It must have been "hell" for her sitting there and not ordering anything for herself. However, she did ask for an extra fork and contented herself with just one small sampling from each of our plates. Marion had mentioned that year, "Thank God, she's begun to shed."

On our next visit the following year, Ann, resplendent behind the wheel of her Rolls-Royce, drove her neighbor Sarah Mitchell, Gordon Hunter and myself to a very popular "in" restaurant on the Marina called The Warehouse. An outdoor waterfront setting, it provided a perfect backdrop for a friendly informal luncheon. It was a time when Ann, truly relaxed, ate heartily and was warmly affectionate toward me. Telling Sarah about the length of my penmanship with her, Ann put her arm around me saying, "my dear, dear friend." Sarah, a nonprofessional, was excited when she began talking about a movie Ann had just done and how she had appeared as an extra. Upon returning to her home, Ann wistfully said she'd be putting the Rolls up for sale, as she now found it too heavy to drive. The outfit worn by Ann that day had a navy blue smock top and Sarah exclaimed, "That's one of Ann's costumes in *Crazy Ladies*." This was a film that Ann had agreed to do because she was friendly with the producer, Julie Corman, and thought the director, Jonathan Demme, a real talent. Tisha had a brief bit at the film's start playing Ann's character as a young woman. Likewise, Cloris Leachman, who had above-the-title billing, used her daughter, Dinah Englund, to play her younger self. Though Cloris would erroneously state, "Ann Sothern plays my sister," Ann, in actual fact, played her mother. Sarah, present when Ann read the clipping about them being sisters in the film, gallantly chirped, "She's got more wrinkles than you." Cast also in the satirical *Bonnie and Clyde*-type melodrama was Stuart Whitman, Linda Purl, Jim Backus and Cloris Leachman's son, Bryan Englund.

Golden Needles was now in release and was considered not worthy of its stars or of the location hike. Her character was Finzie, from New Jersey, whose bar also contained a Mahjong Parlor. Garbed in a multitude of feathers and a curly wig, she managed to disguise her girth to a certain extent. However, some critics were discerning enough to notice, sometimes with a little cruelty.

Ann's lawsuit for negligence was filed on February 18, 1975 against the Thunderbird Motor Hotel over the mishap when a heavy pole collapsed and hit her in the back during a performance of *Everybody Loves Opal*. She said she had not been able to perform since the date of her injury, August 15, 1973, declaring she did not realize the extent of her injuries until later. The defendants were the Thunderbird Corporation and Master-Host Thunderbird Incorporated, motel owners, who had filed for bankruptcy in December 1974.

During 1975 I received several communications from Ann and in all she expressed her inability to work and how the inactivity was driving her up the wall. In response to one of her letters, I mentioned how Bette Davis had scored a hit with a one-woman show in Australia. Bette had brought the house down when she strode onto the stage of the packed Sydney Opera House and, with legs akimbo, took in the entire auditorium with a huge sweeping stare and declared, "What a dump!" This line is probably more famous than the film, *Beyond the Forest*, where she first uttered it. Ann said she'd been asked to do a similar show with film clips plus a question-and-answer segment with the audience.

Ann always photographed Gordon Hunter and myself each year and would send a copy. Similarly, we would always take shots as a memento of each meeting with Ann and it was always such a nice surprise to see our pictures displayed in Ann's big photographic albums. Ann maintained an annual

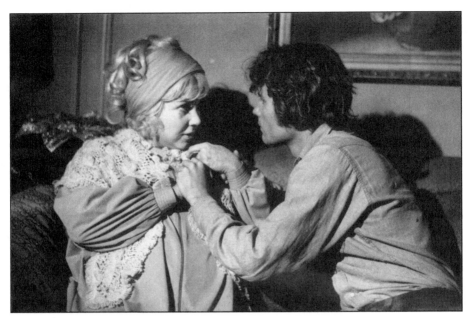

ANN DESERVEDLY RECEIVED SUPERLATIVE REVIEWS FOR HER ROLE
OF JOHN SAVAGE'S MOTHER IN THE ACCLAIMED BUT SPARSELY
RELEASED *THE KILLING KIND* (MEDIA TREND, 1973)

photographic record which included shots with family, co-stars and friends. *Crazy Ladies*, now retitled *Crazy Mama*, had been released and was almost unreservedly panned by the critics.

Medical Story, an hour-long TV drama series, utilized Ann as a guest star. Robert Forster was her co-star in the episode titled "The Moonlight Healers." Ann was the veteran nurse who has to explain the way the emergency hospital operates. Forster was a physician "moonlighting" overnight from his different day job. Unable to wear camouflaging stoles or drapes of any kind, Ann is at her heaviest here dressed in a stark white uniform and cap. Tisha was also a guest on the show, along with Rosemary DeCamp, Leif Erickson and Sam Jaffe.

At the end of 1975, Ann took off for Switzerland, and in December 1975 I received a letter and Christmas card telling me of the reason for the trip. "…just back from Switzerland. Was there to see a doctor about my health and my back…had several shots which are supposed to help. I do so hope it will eventually—and I'll be my old self again. 'Old' is right—that time goes so fast!"

A longer handwritten letter from Ann, dated January 10, 1976, was very endearing. I had once given her an opal pendant for luck and she later told me it had been stolen. Asking if she'd like another, Ann said, "I'm very much a green person, so if you come across a green opal, I'd love it." I did and it was in the form of a ring. Her letter read, "So many thanks for the darling ring with the opal which I wear on my middle finger. I think it's good luck and many people have commented on it. My trip to Switzerland has been a success so far—had 10 shots for my general health and back. From too many X-rays on my back—my blood level had really gone down. Am feeling better and I hope the New Year will be a joyous and happy one for you. I know having you as my friend has made me very happy—dear Colin!"

On February 2, 1976, another letter arrived: "…I have a furious cold at the moment—but am beginning to feel better from my shots in Switzerland. By March 1st I should be responding well. I am turning down the role of

WITH JOHN SAVAGE IN THE UNDERRATED *THE KILLING KIND*
(MEDIA TREND, 1973)

'Roberta' which they're reviving in New York. Just read it—it seems awfully dated—although there were some great songs in it." (Ann would have sung Jerome Kern's "Yesterdays.")

In 1976 Ann joined a cast of big name guest stars appearing in the TV mini-series *Captains and the Kings,* based on Taylor Caldwell's novel. She'd just finished making it when I arrived for my fourth vacation in the U.S. Meeting at the townhouse where she now resided, we lunched at Nieman Marcus in Beverly Hills. There was a particular item on the menu they specialized in that "had to be sampled." It turned out to be what my mother used to call "Puffed Balloons"; large savory pastry, shaped like a ball and then puffed up until they were "lighter than air." The three of us enjoyed this speciality, but the downside was that although they were light in texture, the ingredients were very fattening. Talking about *Captains and the Kings,* Ann raved about Patty Duke's work in it and also that of Joanna Pettet's. We asked what role she played and Ann said, "I play this old one-eyed Irish woman. It's just a cameo. I had wanted to play the nun in it, as I read the book and thought it a nice role. Celeste Holm got that, but it's small too—not like as in the book." The incredible cast of actors in this, the first adaptation of a series of novels for television, included Ray Bolger, Henry Fonda, Burl Ives, John Houseman, Jane Seymour, Barbara Parkins, Robert Vaughan and Pernell Roberts.

Tragedy struck Tisha in 1976 when, after having a mole removed from her neck, it was discovered she had a melanoma. Doctors gave her only a year to live. This was a devastating and unendurable period of uncertainty for both mother and daughter. Ann prayed diligently to St. Anthony for her daughter's life and, defying the doctors' predictions, Tisha totally recovered. A specialist from the University of California performed the removal of the melanoma and later a plastic surgeon removed all traces of scarring. When talking of Tisha's ordeal Ann said, "As soon as Tisha was well again, I had every spot, mole, pimple removed from my person."

On January 31, 1977, a long letter from Ann detailed the court case in Jacksonville, Florida: "First I fractured my damned right ankle—just before leaving for Jacksonville for my big trial on my back injury. That in itself was enough, but with Tisha's help (she went with me as a witness) I managed to survive not only the trial—but the inconveniences. We had a 5-day jury trial—6 people—and would you believe 5 of them had never heard of me.

That gives you a rough idea about Jacksonville! A friend of mine in Paris, called on my birthday—and said it was a big story in the *Paris Herald Tribune*—but in JACKS!!—Although I was always on the front page with this trial—there were 5 people who had never heard of me! They were generous in their decision however and we won a $200,000 settlement. God knows when they'll pay it—these things keep getting appealed. Had a lovely Xmas in Santa Barbara with Tisha and Heidi at the San Yordic Inn—Ronald Colman's old Rancho…we have a wonderful new President and every one here feels he will be a good leader. I received a charming letter from him signed "Jimmy" [Carter]…One day, I'm going to have tapes made of the live tapes I have of performances in *Gypsy* and *Mame*. I will see you get them as a present! And fondest regards, dear Colin."

The press covering the trial were rather brutal in their reporting. Generally the summary was this: "Actress, Ann Sothern, walking with a cane and complaining of being 40 lbs. overweight, broke into tears when a lawyer suggested that at 67 she was too old to act much anymore. The sobbing actress then heard the Judge say, 'Don't you feel that when a person reaches the age of 67, you should not expect to work as much as you did when you were younger.' 'Acting is my life,' she replied, 'I love it. I've been acting since I was 15. And I like to think I've given the public some pleasure through my acting.'"

Back in Los Angeles, Ann and Tisha attended an exhibition of paintings to raise funds for Animal Welfare. Lots of celebrity animal lovers were in attendance and Ann's portrait of Tisha was prominently on display.

AS and Joe Don Baker in Golden Needles (Sequoia, 1974)

Chapter Sixteen: "Ann, Tisha And Heidi"

In the late 1970s, Ann was still sufficiently in demand to be offered guest spots on *The Love Boat* and *Fantasy Island,* and in the mid-1980s for *Murder, She Wrote.* When I asked why she hadn't accepted any of them she said, "The scripts or the roles weren't suitable or good enough." She was signed to play the mother in the Rock Hudson/Mia Farrow starrer *Avalanche* (1978), but had to withdraw when the shooting schedule was brought forward and clashed with other commitments. Another role she turned down was replacing Simone Signoret as a grandmother who urges her daughter into prostitution. Being shot in Venezuela, she would have liked the trip but said, "I will not do things that are dirty. I just don't believe in that. I've never done anything that I think is in bad taste."

One film role she did accept was that of a participant in a seance for the horror flick *The Manitou* (1978). It is noticeable that in this film, for the most part, she is seated and when it is necessary for her to stand or move, a cane is used, indicating her back problem was returning.

A PORTRAIT FOR GOLDEN NEEDLES
(SEQUOIA, 1974)

COLIN BRIGGS

Ann knew Tony Curtis socially and there are pictures taken of them dancing together in the 1960s. She was also friendly with his ex-wife, Janet Leigh, who, like Ann, spent a lot of time skiing in Sun Valley. Tony Curtis was the star of *The Manitou* and, with Burgess Meredith also cast, she agreed to play, with star billing, a quite tiny cameo. Also cast were Susan Strasberg, Michael Ansara and Stella Stevens. Ann told me that she "liked Stella very much. A nice girl, a hard worker and very friendly with no star-like airs about her." The movie was released in 1978 and got mixed reviews, deservedly so. On the credit side was the spooky musical score by Lalo Schifrin and the grizzly special effects. On the debit side was the plot, which in the novel by Graham Masterson was passably plausible, but seemed absurd in the movie. Susan Strasberg must have needed the money badly to agree to portray a woman with a growth on her spine which turns out to be a 400-year-old Indian seeking rebirth. *TV Week* was indignant. "60 lashes with a wet boot lace for talented Burgess Meredith and Ann Sothern for appearing in this load of tripe."

In 1978 I got to attend a television program, *Over Easy,* in San Francisco. The host was Hugh Downs, whom Ann admired. Quite a number of veteran stars appeared on his program as talk show guests including Alice Faye, Janet Gaynor and Mary Martin. Ann guested in February 1978 and was accompanied by Tisha. She spoke at length about her desire to revive *The Glass Menagerie* with Tisha as Laura. Her exit from the shooting area and also the television station required her to negotiate a very high tiered set of steps. With Tisha's aid she managed this difficult feat and, catching my eye as she passed by, gave a hefty sigh of relief—I guess at having prevailed.

Another TV guest shot, and truly unworthy of her appearance, was on *Flying High* again in 1978. The series starred Connie Selecca, Pat Klous and Kathryn Witt as three airline stewardesses who share an apartment. Ann's segment was "High Rollers" and set in Las Vegas, and also guesting were Lew Ayres, Shelley Berman, Jack Carter, David Hedison and Jack Jones. As receptionist to a psychiatrist played by Hedison, Ann is quite mobile and handles her character of Miss Kirkeby with dexterity. Her interchanges with Kathryn Witt are sharp and have her usual impeccable timing. She regretted having no scenes with Lew Ayres, playing Hedison's father, who is about to commit himself to a retirement home. Despite having a regular list of big-name guest stars, *Flying High* was short lived.

Around this time Ann donated a complete collection of her two television series, *Private Secretary* and *The Ann Sothern Show,* to AT AS-UCLA
Television Archives. She also gave to UCLA-Radio Archives a complete collection of *The Adventures of Maisie.*

In view of the seemingly unending physical problems of the past decade
her most courageous undertaking so far was to make a return to live theatre.
Ruth Webb found the script of a new play by George Tibbles with the central
character being a Russian matriarch. Claudette Colbert was the artist Tibbles
had in mind when he wrote it. Ann liked the role and after a lot of revisions
thought it ready for production. Chicago audiences, who had always adored
her, were thought to be the best people to judge the merit of the play's worth.
The play was called *The Duchess of Pasadena* and Ann wrote a Russian ballad
to sing in the production. The Drury Lane Theatre South, in Chicago, was
where it was to make its bow on February 13, 1978, and the season was set
for four weeks. Very excited about the play, which she now considered to be
most amusing, she told me of her plans for her first entrance. "I'm going to
wear a big hat with a lot of veiling, and while I'm removing it and my wrap,
the audience has time to chatter and remark to one another on the way I
look." Singing for me "Das Vidanya," the Russian ballad she wrote, she added
that the title meant "Goodbye" and it had been translated into Russian for her
by Princess Nicoli Teumanoff. Vernon R. Schwartz was the executive producer of the play, and also directed.

During rehearsals in Chicago, Ann got to do radio interviews and I later
heard one of them in which she mentioned me. It came about when the in-
terviewer asked about a possible biography from Ann. She said she had tried
on a couple of occasions, once in collaboration with George Eels (who died
before proceeding with the project) and another with writer David Chandler,
but publishers wanted scandal and she did not have that in her life. My name
came up when Ann said, "There's a boy in Australia who knows all about me
and has all those quotes from Judy Garland and others…in fact he knows
more about me than I know about myself." During the course of the interview it was mentioned that Jane Powell was also in Chicago appearing with
Howard Keel in *South Pacific.* A fan of Jane's telephoned and they conversed
on radio with his hoping that the two former MGM leading ladies could have
a reunion. Ann said, "Jane is a darling girl."

The Duchess of Pasadena opened and "Ann got two separate standing ovations," as Oscar Gold reported in the *Chicago Tribune,* with him also lauding "her brilliant comedic performance. It was an emotional evening for Miss Sothern who broke down and cried. This was her first return to the theatre since a back injury in a stage accident. (She still needs to be helped up and down the long ramps at this theatre in the round.)"

In another interview, Ann remembered her last season in Chicago at the Ivanhoe Theatre in *Glad Tidings.* "That was during the worst blizzard in 1969. My limousine driver was frightened by the hazardous conditions. 'Move over,' I told him, 'I'm from Idaho and I can handle snow,' and I did, driving on to the Ivanhoe Theatre." Critical reception was fine for this first airing of the play. Reported the *Chicago Sun-Times,* "Miss Sothern seems to enjoy it all hugely…playing her Countess [Duchess] as a cross between Queen Victoria and Mae West…There's a roguish glint in those Siamese cat eyes, a chuckle playing about those lips and a tearful curtain speech in which she assures us that yes, she's been ill, but she's well on the mend."

Pleased with the good business Ann had attracted, the owner of the Drury Lane Theatres, Tony De Santis, contracted her to do a second season at Drury Lane East the following May. Richard Christiansen of the *Chicago Tribune* gave it a very condescending review: "Miss Sothern first played the 'Duchess' earlier this season at Drury Lane South and now she is back in a slightly revised version of the comedy, starring as a grande dame at the turn of the century who is both insufferable and indomitable. She is—and let's say it straight out—pushing 70…however, clad in nightgown, piano shawls and a feather or two, she can still muster an imperious pose…she can still master a nifty double take…alternately offensively coy and mildly amusing…with messages of brotherly love, a dose of divine intervention and a sprinkling of laughter it seems to afford Miss Sothern and her audiences some slight pleasure."

Extremely hurt by this attack, not only on her age but also on her weight and the use of stage hands to help her exit quickly, she retaliated. Rogers Worthington of the *Chicago Tribune* quoted a furious Ann: "How dare he say I had to be carried up the aisle. The only reason I had to be assisted is because I cannot make that long aisle, make the change and get down in time …that's all…for him to indict senior citizen actors is really unconscionable. Because now he's saying if actors have reached the status of Senior

CRAZY MAMA (NEW WORLD PICTURES, 1975)

Citizens...I imagine that we must put out to pasture Kate Hepburn, James Stewart, Henry Fonda, Bette Davis, Ginger Rogers, Lucille Ball, Gene Kelly, Ethel Merman...the list is endless...How dare he indict people simply because they're older."

In her defense, other reporters gave their opinions of Ann in the show. Phyllis Feuerstein: "Sothern dominates the stage dressed in stunning Victorian costumes and one wonders why this versatile actress so utterly in command of her performance has been off stage for three years. Sothern expressed initial concern about the way the play ends because it evokes pathos...But the final scene and her performance are two elements that make 'The Duchess' a royal show." Lorraine Hardt: "Miss Ann is back and giving snow weary northerners a real treat with her own soft 'Sothern' presence. And when she stood there opening night—her arms almost completely hidden by red roses—there was no doubt about it—the entire evening had been a love affair between 'The Duchess of Pasadena' and her audience...Superb, someone behind us was saying about Miss Sothern's timing and we have to

agree. Women in the audience especially, were also struck by the magnifi-
cence of the 1904ish wardrobe."

I first met Tisha Sterling at her mother's townhouse, following a luncheon to which Ann had invited Gordon Hunter and myself. Some years later I
met Heidi, Ann's granddaughter, who was even taller than her mother. Heidi
did not resemble Tisha either physically or in coloring. A spirited brunette,
she was very outgoing and sang a few vocal exercises. Ann was now coaching
her in singing and she obliged with a number Ann had written, then Ann
joined her in a duet. I got to warble too, for Ann produced "Memory" from
Cats and insisted I sing it. Having heard recordings of it many times, I was
able to manage a passable rendition. This fun-filled musical afternoon was an
absolute delight. Ann would have a series of portrait studies done of herself
with Tisha and Heidi. They were very glamorous shots and Ann was hoping
to get some television commercials showing the three generations using "a
product."

Phil Sinclair, a San Francisco showbiz personality, contacted Ann about
an "In Person" one-woman show. Scheduled for April 18, 1979, at the War-
field Theatre, it was to benefit The San Francisco Lung Association. On previous occasions Sinclair held similar tributes to Irene Manning, Alice Faye,
Lana Turner and others and the format was film clips, an onstage interview,
followed by a feature film from the "star" lady's career.

Ann's Christmas greeting that year told of her two seasons in Chicago.
"You would have loved 'The Duchess.' Marvelous period—1904—great
time—I play a Russian Grande Duchess—and is generally a very audience
satisfying piece. However, I'm never off the stage—so get frantically exhausted. Have been in the hospital with some strange ailment for the past 2
weeks. Not feeling too well…Will be in Frisco in April for a Personal Tribute."

Stanley Eichelbaum reported about Ann's San Francisco tribute: "When
she came on stage for a conversation with Gerri Lange, the actress diverted
attention from herself by introducing her attractive granddaughter, Heidi,
from the audience. The teenager's mother is Tisha Sterling and Ann Sothern
commented that the girl was ready to 'carry on the family tradition.' Unexpectedly she announced, 'I'm a method actress—a Stanislavsky student. I believe in finding out who you are and what you are for a role. I've given semi-
nars in colleges on Stanislavsky and the Moscow Art Theatre.' In an hour of
clips that started with 'Kid Millions'…in that movie musical she was teamed

with George Murphy...Sothern couldn't help standing up from her seat and shouting to the audience, 'He's the same one who was our senator.' There were scenes from 'Maisie' (1939), 'A Letter to Three Wives' (1949) and 'Lady in a Cage' (1963). For a grand finale Sothern brought with her a print of the Gothic thriller 'The Killing Kind' (1973)...the movie was made independently by Curtis Harrington and distribution has been held up by litigation...'It was a big departure,' she said. 'I'm always working to stretch myself. I'll never retire. As a matter of fact, I just hope I cool it in the middle of a line.' Phil Sinclair said, 'I love stars who can still hold their heads up high, like Elizabeth Taylor and Ann Sothern. Such courage. The stars have not been paid for their appearances. Profits, when there were any, have gone to charity. So far the Klieg light has burned for Jane Russell, Joan Fontaine, Mae West, Ann Sothern (she was the most fun), Alice Faye, Lana Turner, Sophia Loren, Irene Manning...and director, Josh Logan, my only man and nobody came.'"

Ann later told me that she enjoyed the night and the audience, though not as large as hoped, were "wonderfully appreciative." Irene Manning attended and she was amazed at Ann's lovely singing voice. Although she left before *The Killing Kind* was ¼ through, Irene also commented on the deafening applause Ann got after her interview. As another critic wrote, "Her ovation could not have been more enthusiastic."

In September of 1979 Ann was offered a season at the Cirque Dinner Theater in Seattle. *The Duchess of Pasadena* was again her choice of play and she had heard good reports about the Cirque and its treatment of veteran stars. Preceding Ann had been Lynn Bari in *The Gingerbread Lady*, followed by Ruth Roman and then Eve Arden. Eve did say negatively that there were still a lot of empty bottles left in the main dressing room by the former occupant or occupants. I was in the U.S. just before Ann's departure for Seattle and she generously offered to fly Gordon Hunter and myself up there for the opening. Once again lady luck was not on our side as our return flight tickets to Australia were for the same day and could not be changed at such short notice.

Seattle audiences embraced Ann's *Duchess* warmly and in an interview with Andrea Vogel Gilbert for *The Times*, she said of her MGM years, "It's an era that is gone forever." Continuing, she added, "Both the era of the play [1904] and a generation later are long gone. There is no old Hollywood left. I

WITH CLORIS LEACHMAN IN *CRAZY MAMA* (NEW WORLD PICTURES, 1975). ANN PLAYED THE MOTHER OF CLORIS, WITH THEIR REAL-LIFE DAUGHTERS PORTRAYING THEM AS YOUNGER WOMEN.

walked through Paramount studios recently, and outside of their television studio, you could have shot a cannon off down the halls." She remembers her own days at MGM, "If you'd go there now, you'd cry. It's just terrible. That was the Cartier of motion pictures." Talking of rejecting scripts, where she would be cast as Madams or whorehouse women, she said, "I've turned down two *Love Boats* already and a *Fantasy Island*. On *Love Boat*, you know, you'd think they'd rent the whole boat for filming! Well, they only own one little piece of it, and the rest of it is full of tourists."

Once again contradicting herself, she hedged when asked about her attending the University of Washington. In the interview she said, "I didn't really attend the University. I sort of took a class there - I was really too young to be a student." In conclusion, she said, "I think we all have a destiny. God has a plan for you and it works out that way. Evidently mine was to be an actress ..."

Returning to Los Angeles, Ann had an offer to play in a Disney-type movie, *The Little Dragons*. An independent production, it would be released in 1980. Ann accepted her role, as it was similar to one Shelley Winters had played in Disney's *Pete's Dragon*. Playing Angela, the mother of two yokel and none-too-bright sons, she's the brains behind a kidnapping. Ann was not pleased with the film when she saw the advertisements billing her second after Charles Lane. The color photography is excellent and Ann's make-up was as good as the best she'd had in the past. In close-ups she looks fine, but the director seemed unnecessarily cruel by having her photographed mostly full-length, which emphasized her plumpness. If half of her scenes had been shot "waist high" she would have been a lot happier.

Visiting her that year I mentioned having seen *The Little Dragons* and for the first time saw a perverse side of Ann. Denying she'd made the film at all, the subject was closed. This brought to mind a quote she'd given *The Seattle Times*, "I've always been sort of fearless. If I don't like something happening in my life I will walk away from it and it turns around." So blocking out the unpleasant memories, and *The Little Dragons* must have been one of them, was the secret of her survival. I did write her later, though, and mentioned the positive points of the film, but that part of my letter was not mentioned in her response.

AS and Tony Curtis dancing, 1968. Ten years later,
they were co-stars in *The Manitou* (Avco Embassy, 1978)

Chapter Seventeen "Ann S. Sterling"

With certain feelings of trepidation and apprehension Ann accepted and embraced the 1970s, which she called "a time of ugliness." But the even freer use of violence, gratuitous sex and four letter words in motion pictures of the 1980s, held little or no appeal whatsoever for her.

After a couple of TV appearances, Tisha's career also reached a stalemate. Ann and she went to New York in November of 1982 for Ann to be interviewed on *Good Morning America*. Although she most frequently stated, "I hate nostalgia," her interview by Joan Lunden revealed feelings to the contrary. She appeared to be more than pleased to be reunited with Don Porter and Jesse White on the show. A regular segment of *Good Morning America* back then was to have reunions with casts from TV shows of yesteryear. When Ann Tyrrell was contacted by telephone and joined in the conversation, Ann and her three co-players reveled in recalling happenings on the two TV series they'd made. As the last segment of the series had been filmed twenty-one years before, they had a lot to say to each other and the vast television audience. In a letter, dated February 27, 1983, Ann wrote me of her appearance. "Finally took my CPA's advice and did something he could write off on the income tax. Went on ABC's 'Good Morning America' for 2 interviews played at several times—took Tisha with me to N. Y.—and stayed at our old home, The Plaza, and we had a lovely week. Saw 'Cats' which is absolutely astounding! Just adored it. Tish could not get over that the fans follow me around as if I'm still a big star. They were crushing! I don't understand it—but I guess it's time, to get myself together—and do something in the way of acting.

"Tennessee Williams died this past Friday. A dear, dear man. He was so sweet about my performance in the 'The Glass Menagerie.' He choked on a plastic cap that fits on an eye dropper or spray. Poor darling. I'll pray for him!

"There's much excitement this week here—Her Majesty Queen Elizabeth and Prince Phillip are visiting California for the first time, on the 'Brittania'— and everyone is completely enchanted by her—and giving her a huge welcome! Tonight there was a great gala at 20th Century-Fox, given by our First Lady, Nancy R. Although every star, practically in Hollywood, was invited, I was not on the guest list. I'm sure I was blackballed because Ron and I used to go out after his divorce from Jane [Wyman]—who, naturally, was not there either. Incidentally, Jane has a big hit TV show called 'Falcon Crest.' Nancy doesn't like any competition whatsoever—and I think she's a ***** !!!

"I'm going to Europe early in April to the clinic in Switzerland for treatment on my back and legs. Probably be gone a few weeks. All is well with Tisha and Heidi. Heidi is a marvelous child—and Tish is working now—she is happier…"

I had begun writing articles for a periodical called *Hollywood Studio Magazine*. This came about when I met columnist Lee Graham at a party given by the marvelous, zany Betty Kean. Betty would throw a soiree (as she called them) for us on each of our visits to the U.S. She'd been in Australia with the musical *High Spirits*, and was always very hospitable to people from OZ. Through these "get-togethers," I met such luminaries as Patsy Kelly, Virginia O'Brien, Jane Ball, Elliott Reid, and, of course, Lee Graham.

Lee had a persuasive charm about him and, learning of my annual trips to the U.S. and the stars I met, suggested I write a career article which he would submit. Naturally, my immediate thought was one on Ann. Mentioning her name to Lee, he said, "She's been too long neglected and a story on her would be a plus." The article was published during my next visit to California and I sent a copy to Ann. Calling her, she said, "A columnist friend told me of your story and thanks for the copy. Don't be concerned about what you write, Colin. I thought the whole thing nice, but rather innocuous." Later, I would write articles on films in which Ann had appeared. Two of these were *Cry Havoc* and *Lady Be Good*, and in the meantime the magazine had undergone a name change, becoming *Hollywood—Then and Now*.

In May of 1983, Ann wrote that she was off to Hawaii for a month. This must have delayed her planned trip to Switzerland, which eventually took

AS AND SPIRITUALIST STELLA STEVENS PREPARE TO HOLD A SÉANCE IN
THIS SCENE FROM *THE MANITOU* (AVCO EMBASSY, 1978)

place in August 1984. Writing me on December 15, 1984, she said "…thought the 'Cry Havoc' story you wrote was fine—at least you used a good (today) picture…Was in Europe for 2 months. Home Oct. 15. Have been awfully busy—but not working. My legs are better—and I'm hoping they will finally decide to behave." The "awfully busy" Ann was referring to was her relocating to live permanently in Sun Valley, Idaho. A professionally printed card announced: "MY NEW ADDRESS AS OF OCTOBER 10, 1984. ANN SOTHERN STERLING, ANN S. STERLING, 333 TOPAZ AVENUE, KETCHUM, IDAHO."

Settling in quite well, Ann endeared herself to the people of Ketchum and Ketchum endeared itself to her. In another communication she spoke of "the wonderful, smog free unpolluted air" and, on September 26, 1985, "we're having the most exquisite fall! Leaves starting to turn into magnificent autumn hues—crystal clear air and snow on the mountains…My little hairdresser here, Sally Veroski, is arriving in Sydney to attend a Vidal Sassoon seminar there. I have given her your address—in case she needs any information. She's a sweet girl and very unsophisticated. She is staying at Bondi

Beach…telephone…Anyway I wanted you to know in case you should hear from Sally."

Indeed I did hear from Ann's hairdresser and made plans to meet her early on a Sunday morning for a drive into the countryside of New South Wales. Gordon Hunter and a singer friend, Beryl Pacey, joined us on this pleasant drive which took us over mountains, through the fresh green valleys under clear blue skies. We drove by rivers and got to see some of our beautiful cascading waterfalls. Sally was an attractive, modern young woman in her late twenties and very easy to talk with. The day was a full one and as this would be Sally's only opportunity to see anything of the Australian countryside, we covered an awful lot of territory. Before taking her back to Bondi I made her welcome at my home. She expressed interest in seeing my scrapbooks on Ann, as she confessed to not having seen any of her movies. Amazed at how beautiful she looked in photographs I'd amassed she said, "I never realized how stunning she was." Sally also said, "Ann's never had a face lift. Washing the hair, you can tell. She likes her hair set in those big rollers! Janet Leigh is another customer of mine - she's had a face lift or two." Driving Sally to her accommodation, she thanked Gordon and I for our company and the great day and said she'd keep in touch. Ann wrote again on December 10 and thanked me for the snapshots we'd taken of Sally and for being so hospitable.

Before moving to Sun Valley, Ann had completed the TV movie *A Letter to Three Wives*. Updating the 1949 version, this remake cast Ann in the Connie Gilchrist role of Ma Finney, with Michele Lee reprising Ann's original character; Loni Anderson and Stephanie Zimbalist played the other two wives. Ann was most excited to be working again, especially with Ben Gazzara, who played her son-in-law. Tisha accompanied her on location in Vancouver and was of great help to her mother, who was becoming more immobile. With her typical sense of humor she told me, "They wanted one of the original three wives to be in the remake. Poor Linda Darnell was gone and they offered me either the sassy maid played before by Thelma Ritter or the Connie Gilchrist part. I told them 'the maid is out, I can't lift a bloody tray'— why Jeanne Crain wasn't available for Ritter's role is a mystery."

Writing me in September 1985, Ann mentioned "going to Los Angeles in the middle of October to do some promos for NBC on 'A Letter to Three

Wives'…sold a little house here [Ketchum] I bought on spec…all goes well—and I have been feeling good."

In a December letter she said, "The TV version of 'A Letter to Three Wives' has received awfully good notices…I've been on 6 talk shows and also radio and in lots of print too. More shows tomorrow—December 16—also am on the Today Show some day…Honey, I'll be in LA March 11, 1986 at Westwood Marquis. Doing a seminar for American Museum of Broadcasting. Also they are doing a recollection of my work a week later…"

In an interview with Gary Collins in 1983 on the *Hour Magazine* show, they talked about her two TV shows and he admitted to being a fan of her work back then. She admired him very much and the following year did a second interview, mentioning a TV movie she'd made in Vancouver. Previously discussing her series she said, "As well as being the star, I was also the producer so I was able to arrange things to be more convenient. Hollywood today is Panicsville—they shot this latest movie in 31 days."

Ann also mentioned living in Sun Valley and compared it to Switzerland. Holding on to her cane and hitting the floor with it, she testily said, "I've got this thing here. I keep on losing it. I hate this cane, I hate it. I leave it everywhere." Gary relieved the moment by replying, "But, it's great for emphasis," and Ann lightened up. When he asked how her health was in the Sun Valley winters, she laughingly said, "You get a little creakier."

Ann Rutherford told me how much she enjoyed the TV remake of *Wives*. "I watched it because I wanted to see Ann and you know after all these years she still has that incredible lovely face." *The New York Times* review said Ann and Doris Roberts, who got the Thelma Ritter role, "do their best to work up some salt-of-the-earth humor but come nowhere near the deadpan sarcasm of the Thelma Ritter-Connie Gilchrist routines." Nancy Morris, of *Shreveport Journal*, commented, "Sothern is delightful in this role and seems to be having a grand time playing the feisty woman who does not apologize for who and what she is." Reported *TV Week*, "Ann Sothern was one of the stars of the 1949 original and she is the only reason for watching this feeble telemovie remake."

When I saw the telemovie in 1987, I found that I was in agreement with the criticism that the scene between Doris Roberts and Ann lacked "the sarcasm of the original." However, I guess both ladies wanted a fresh approach. Upon asking people who had not seen the original version what they thought of the new one, they all found both Doris and Ann "tops." Certainly the more dramatic scene Ann had with Ben Gazzara came off beautifully. Their rapport was magnetic and Loni Anderson also worked well with Ann, who used a cane for her walking scenes.

Talking of her new home, Ann told *Idaho Mountain Express* writer Karen L Crowell, "I returned to the Wood River Valley because this is where I want to retire. Things don't change as fast here. Driving back from Bailey looks the same as it did in 1948. After that first winter, I was hooked. Whenever I'd go skiing, the lift operators would say 'Morning Ann' and pat me on the behind as I got on the lift."

1978 PORTRAIT,
USED FOR PUBLICITY ON
The Duchess of Pasadena

In 1986 Max Factor cosmetics named Ann as one the ten great Hollywood beauties of all time. Along with the current Jaclyn Smith, she joined such celebrated lovelies as Rita Hayworth, Carole Lombard, Vivien Leigh and Marlene Dietrich on a beautifully presented advertising card titled "MAX FACTOR—The Heritage Collection." Max Factor TV commercials also made use of these ladies' lovely faces to promote their cosmetics.

TCM's Robert Osborne was always most complimentary about Ann when he wrote of her in his "Rambling Reporter" column in *The Hollywood Reporter*. His report, dated April 22, 1986, told all about the recent marriage of Heidi to Mark Bates: "Also over the weekend, Ann Sothern—one of the best assets the world of movie and TV has ever had—became the grandmother of the bride at the Westwood Wedding of Heidi Baum to Mark Bates…Ann looked great, as did daughter Tisha Sterling, the mother of the bride, who's back in town reviving her acting career (and indeed looking too young to be cast as anyone's mother except maybe, Drew Barrymore's)…Miss Sothern, in from her home base in Ketchum, Idaho, was surrounded by close

friends such as Loretta Young, the Jean Louis's, Mrs. Ray Milland, Oliver Fu-
selier, Rupert Allen and others, helping toast the new Mr. and Mrs. Bates after
the ceremony (unexpectedly minus music when both the organist and the
soloist failed to show up - *sans* notice) when the reception got under way at
the Bel Air Country Club. Tisha, Ann and the wedding party all handled the
unexpected music snafu at the church like champs. Like classy pros. But as
someone mentioned later...'Who's surprised? MGM knew what it was doing
when it made Ann Sothern a star.'"

"Turning Back the Clock." Ann is in the second front row of this CBS-TV network reunion celebration. Among the host of stars are George Burns, Lucille Ball, Art Carney, Roy Rogers, Dale Evans, Eva Gabor, Arlene Francis, Ray Walston, Telly Savalas, William Conrad, Nancy Walker, Jean Stapleton, Ellen Corby, Alfred Hitchcock, Sally Struthers, Dennis Weaver, Vivian Vance, Rob Reiner, Red Skelton, Jackie Cooper, Ed Asner, Buddy Ebsen, Mary Tyler Moore, Buddy White.

Chapter Eighteen: "Ann - Susie - Katy - Tisha"

Christmas greetings from Ann in 1986 were bright and very optimistic. She enclosed a long article with pictures from a Los Angeles Sunday supplement dated November 23, 1986. Titled, "Hollywood Royalty Roughs It" by Clarke Taylor, it detailed some of the hazards facing Bette Davis, Lillian Gish, Ann and Vincent Price. They were starring in a just-completed film, *The Whales of August,* with a location shoot on

1980 PORTRAIT

Cliff Island, Casco Bay, Maine. Ann wrote, "I'm enclosing this article which I know you'll love, Colin, because I'm working again…my character's name is Tisha…and I felt that was a good omen. Tisha has been with me in Maine and plays my part as a younger woman in a flashback."

After seeing Ann in the TV remake of *A Letter to Three Wives,* British director Lindsay Anderson, who helmed *The Whales of August,* thought her perfect for the role of Tisha Doughty. The film's producer, Mike Kaplan, wondered whether her slow movement and her use of a cane would prove too arduous for her. He talked it over with Ann, who wanted to do the part, and an agreement was reached with Ann being allowed to have Tisha accompany her. Kaplan said, "Ann guaranteed she could do anything but run." The Australian actress Coral Browne was married to Vincent Price and her

TELEVISION REMAKE OF
A LETTER TO THREE WIVES,
WITH DORIS ROBERTS, 1985

acerbic and often biting humor has become legendary. When her husband told her, at 75, he was going to star with Lillian Gish, 90, Bette Davis, 78, and Ann Sothern, 77, in *The Whales of August* for "Alive" productions, Coral burst out laughing, remarking, "May I suggest they change their name to 'Just Barely?'"

Ann took her own poker chips and on free evenings found plenty of opportunities to play with the young crew. They all liked her and before she returned home she made a point of thanking each and every one of them. She also bonded very well with Lillian Gish, who had a hearing problem and needed the use of aids. Ann called Lillian her "little Botticelli Angel." Bette Davis played Lillian's blind sister, while Ann was their chirpy neighbor and lifelong friend. Vincent Price was an impoverished Russian hoping to find a home at the sisters' place or with Ann. Gish and Davis did not find friendship together during the difficult shooting. Bette had been very ill for quite a while and was very testy, with Lillian's hearing difficulty adding fuel to the fire. Bette asked Ann, whom she'd known for many years, to go to bat for her with Lillian. Ann told me, "Bette and I go back a long way. We've always had a sort of mutual admiration society—so I could tell her to 'fight your own battles' and get away with it."

With four big-name stars on location together, there were leisure-time screenings organized of Ann's *Lady Be Good*, Vincent Price's *The Raven*, Lillian's *The Wind*, and Bette's *All About Eve*. Playing a supporting role of a handyman in *Whales* was veteran Western player, Harry Carey, Jr. To ensure that the genial Carey didn't feel left out, *Wagon Master* (1950) was also given a screening.

At our meeting at the Westwood Marquis in late 1987, Ann mentioned how much study she'd done to acquire the right accent for her role. "Tisha is around 75 years old and the film is set in 1950, which means I had to assume the accent of a Maine woman born around 1875. It's a very indigenous sound, so I listened to it today and asked people how their grandparents spoke." Bette Davis would congratulate Ann during the filming saying, "You got a hell of a good accent." Ann said that was indeed praise from "Caesar." Later, Bette would also call Ann, full of praise for her performance.

Making the producer very happy was that, despite the worries of using what many cruelly called a "geriatric" cast, the film wrapped well under its three-million-dollar-budget.

Ann was saddened when Lucille Ball's new show, *Life with Lucy*, was cancelled. "I told her not to do it, but Gary Morton, her husband, wanted her to. She was crying when she told me, 'ABC has fired me, my series has been cancelled after two months.'" Commiserating with her friend, Ann told her that "she was greatly loved and that something else will undoubtedly be on the horizon."

Ann was now a devotee of yoga, claiming its gentle therapeutic powers worked for her. She continued with her painting, and completed several canvasses in 1986, and the relaxation of fishing was still one of her favorite pastimes. The trap shooting at which she had become so expert was one sport she had to give up, blaming her loss of balance and general unsteadiness as the reasons.

In January 1987 it was announced that *The Ann Sothern Show* would be rerun on cable's Nickelodeon channel, as part of its "Nick at Nite" programming. Ann had sold

WITH COLIN BRIGGS, 1981

the rights originally of both *The Ann Sothern Show* and *Private Secretary* to Metromedia, but neither achieved much syndication exposure in the period 1961-1966. Lying on the shelf at Metromedia, the shows were dusted off when Fox TV acquired 194 of the shows in the spring of 1986. Beginning on January 5, 1987, the show was screened Monday through Friday in two timeslots. At the conclusion of *The Ann Sothern Show's* run, *Private Secretary/Susie* followed with the entire episodes of this also to be rerun. Proving

AT HOME WITH COLIN BRIGGS,
1983

popular with audiences of all ages, Nickelodeon then reran them again, but this time with both shows alternating on consecutive nights.

Having completed a new movie and with her TV series being rerun, Ann found herself inundated with fan mail. As she'd later tell *Entertainment This Week*'s Leonard Maltin, when talking about the re-running of her two TV series, "Those shows have brought me a whole new legion of fans and they're all youngsters." She also recalled a stewardess on a flight to New York waylaying her and saying, "'My six-year-old and my four-year-old are just mad about you,' and she went on and on…"

Her final remarks revealed the human side of Ann, which endeared her to so many. "People are wonderful to me. I can never thank the public enough for how wonderful they are to me. They have never deserted me."

This renewed popularity caused Ann to travel to New Orleans to talk with NATPE for an ATV network's conference. While there, she celebrated her 78th birthday.

After such a propitious start, the rest of 1987, in Ann's own words, was "the worst year of my life." In May she was rushed to the hospital with a blocked intestine. Meeting with her later that year she said, "They had to operate abdominally and what they did to me was literally like peeling the skin off a pineapple."

But heartbreaking tragedy lay ahead, with the untimely death of her granddaughter Heidi's young husband, Mark Bates. She said, "Delivering the eulogy at his funeral was the hardest thing I've ever had to do." Mark was killed in a motorcycle accident, making Heidi a widow just sixteen months after their idyllic marriage. His death occurred on October 11, 1987, and UCLA Medical Center received the young victim's donation of both liver and kidneys, thus enabling lifesaving surgery for patients waiting for a transplant of these organs. For Heidi, this unexpected tragedy must have been shockingly traumatic for, in addition to the loss of her husband, her father Lal Baum had died of cancer toward the end of the previous month.

Picking up the pieces of her shattered life, Heidi, according to Ann, went into training as a flight stewardess and eventually got her wings. Ann also did her bit toward nurturing the young widow and wrote two songs, "Peace and Love" and "Children All Are We," which she had Heidi record in December of 1987. I had the pleasure of hearing the two tracks and they were both melodically and lyrically fine compositions. Sadly, probably because of their altruistic leanings, the demonstration disc did not get a commercial release.

Two more recent deaths that made Ann aware of the clock catching up with her were the passings of Richard Egan, at 67, and, in March 1986, Ray Milland. Ann would have Mal, his widow and her best friend, as a guest at her Ketchum home. Now that Ray was gone Ann also revealed that she had written an anonymous letter to Grace Kelly. Prone to affairs with all her leading men, Ray was no exception. Grace fell in love, so much so that she and Ray were openly mentioned in the tabloids as an item. Protective of her friend Mal, Ann wrote to Grace emphasizing the happy family life of the Millands and to consider what she would be breaking up. Her epistle must have triggered Grace's conscience for at the conclusion of filming *Dial M for Murder*, the pair broke up.

Romance entered Tisha's life when she began dating Arthur Lake, Jr. The son of the original Dagwood, Arthur was a wealthy and accomplished man, who was also researching data on actress Marion Davies. The couple visited the home of film historian Bob Board, whose "Le Petit Cinema" housed a huge collection on the enigmatic Davies.

Tisha owned a house in Ketchum, but Ann rented her's still, keeping her grand piano which was topped with family photos. Also on display was a photograph of Ann as Queen Victoria, taken when she attended a costume party in New York in the 1970s. *The Whales of August* was released generally in October

AS AND GRANDDAUGHTER, HEIDI, 1982

WITH COLIN BRIGGS, 1979

1987. Reviews on the whole were complimentary to both the cast and film, but the consensus also was that it might have difficulty in attracting younger audiences. *The New York News* showed a radiant Ann alongside Lillian Gish at a special "March of Dimes" premiere performance on October 14. The event also honored Lillian, as it was her birthday and the black tie event had Helen Hayes as Chairman. Lindsay Anderson introduced Ann, who received tumultuous applause, Vincent Price and his wife Coral Browne, the screenwriter David Berry, co-producer Mike Kaplan and cinematographer Mike Fash. Also attending were Vivian Blaine, Arlene Dahl, Joseph L Mankiewiecz with his wife, and many other New York-based celebrities. A notable absentee was Bette Davis.

An official entry at the Cannes Film Festival, both the film and its stars received positive reviews. *The Chicago Sun-Times* thought Ann "sensible and cheery as a neighbor," while the *New Jersey Star Ledger* felt she "practically steals the movie." *Long Island* raved: "Ann Sothern as their childhood friend and neighbor is plump, vivacious jolly—good company, clever, a gossip who knows everybody's business. In her ringleted orange wig she looks like a large, cuddly stuffed Orphan Annie." *Boise, Idaho Statesman* said, "Ann

Sothern whose red wig gives the impression that fireworks are shooting from her head—as they are from her mouth—gives the film its energy. The sassy, heart-faced blonde is still evident in Sothern's easy skill with a wisecrack; she's been particularly missed from the screen." *The Enquirer* noticed that, "In just a few brief scenes she manages to convey the loneliness and fear beneath her outgoing nature." As *The New York Times* succulently put it, she was "wonderful."

Appearances on TV to help plug the film also came Ann's way and she was on *Showbiz Today* on CNN in October 1987 discussing her career and *The Whales of August.* In December, Gene Shalit did a similar interview on NBC's *Today. Variety* ran a full-page advertisement with a character shot of Ann from *The Whales of August* on December 21, 1987. Headlining "FOR YOUR CONSIDERATION. BEST SUPPORTING ACTRESS ANN SOTHERN," it also listed four glowing reviews of her work, including one from her always dependable friend and critic, Robert Osborne.

Ann claimed she thought she would be overlooked as far as a nomination went and thought little more about it. Awakened at 6 a.m. by her former neighbor and friend, Sarah Mitchell, telephoning from Los Angeles, she heard, "You've been nominated." Ann did tell me there had been a mix-up with the supporting nominees' ballot papers and she had to get the Academy to ensure they were all sent out.

With this nomination, Ann felt 1988 was getting off to a year of rejoicing. Asked to be guest-of-honor at a tribute for the Santa Barbara International Film Festival, she was persuaded to accept by Lindsay Anderson. The event took place on March 4, 1988 and a luncheon honoring Ann preceded the tribute. Excerpts were shown from her films *Lets Fall in Love, Kid Millions, Folies Bergere, Maisie, Lady Be Good, Panama Hattie, Words and Music, A Letter to Three Wives, Lady in a Cage, The Killing Kind, Crazy Mama,* and *The Whales of August,* and from her TV years, *Private Secretary* and *The Lucy Show.* After the excerpts, *A Letter to Three Wives* was shown in full. Other guests were Curtis Harrington and Mike Kaplan; Dennis Doph was the moderator. My friend actress Anabel Shaw was unable to attend, but her daughter, Anabel Ford, did and sent me the press picture of Ann and other items from the press coverage of the event. The audience was wonderfully responsive and Ann, in turn, delighted them with her graciousness, perennial charm and that quick sense of humor uniquely her own.

ANN AND COLIN BRIGGS, 1974

On March 7, 1988, Ann gave Leonard Maltin an interview on *Entertainment Tonight*. They discussed her Oscar nomination, the revived interest aroused by her television series being shown on cable and also her appearances in musical films. Maltin called her "a delightful musical performer" and Ann proclaimed it was her "RE period, the rediscovery, the resurgence, the reappearance; my RE period."

Although she was excited about the gown she would wear to the Academy Awards ceremony, the item that she was particularly thrilled about was the pretty pair of shoes she chose to wear. With the use of a cane, Ann managed to walk quite a distance from her car drop-off to her seat, which was down front in the auditorium. Pictures taken of her arrival at the Academy Awards telecast itself reveal a much slimmer Ann, who, in close-up, looked amazingly youthful.

Also nominated were Ann Ramsey, Anne Archer, Olympia Dukakis and Norma Aleandro. When Dukakis was announced as the winner, the TV cameras focused briefly on Ann, who was smiling complacently and applauding. I had spoken with her earlier and she said then, "I want to win!" Calling her after the ceremony, Tisha answered the telephone and we spoke briefly about Olivia de Havilland's appearance on the show. Upon taking up the receiver, Ann continued on about Olivia saying, "She's a marvel, the traffic, crowds and conditions were terrible, but Olivia ran almost all the way and it was like three blocks." She never mentioned her missing out on the Oscar, but did loudly object to the selection of *The Last Emperor* as Best Film. As she had done when her own nomination had been announced, she decried the fact that Lillian Gish had been overlooked.

Lee Graham told me that Ann looked "fabulous" and much, much slimmer when she attended the Warner Bros. Rededication Celebration. She always made the effort to look her best when she knew a lot of contemporary or younger actresses would be present. An earlier example of this was when she "turned back the clock" at a special celebrating television network CBS. With one hundred other performers who had appeared on CBS in a regular series, she looked no different than her 1960s' TV image.

Items began appearing in the press that Ann was the "dark horse" in the line-up of actresses wanting to play Daisy in *Driving Miss Daisy*. Jessica Tandy, whom Ann often referred to as a "powerhouse," got the role and deservedly won a Best Actress Academy Award.

For American Movie Classics, Ann did a couple of brief interviews shown on cable television. Garbed in a dark gown with a satin scarf, she looked much like her image in the early 1960s. She spoke about how "Harriet Arlene Lake became Ann Sothern," and how she found a secret exit (via a closet door) when Greta Garbo's old dressing room was assigned to her at MGM. This was in the stars' building which housed four dressing rooms. Ann said,

ANN, DAUGHTER TISHA AND COLIN BRIGGS, 1980

"There was Ava, Lana, Greer Garson and me." She also spoke at length of being a producer and hating bossy women, of hiring the best crew she could get and having had no trouble at all. She hesitated briefly and then smilingly said that her cameraman had approached her once and asked her various things and what she thought. Pointing to the director she said, "That's your director, ask him," and she found that that one incident cleared the air and let every crew member get on with their jobs with the knowledge of exactly where the point of command was. Leonard Maltin recalled her for another interview, on *Entertainment This Week* in April, and then she was not seen, but capably narrated, *Collecting America*, a documentary covering the Shelbourne Museum for PBS.

Having previously declared 1987 as the worst year of her life, Ann must have found 1988, as it progressed, no better. Following the Academy Award disappointment, Ann was upset when her beloved sister Marion became very ill. Marion was now widowed and a devoted grandmother and Ann felt sure Marion would survive. Her subsequent death shocked Ann and brought her face to face with her own mortality. Not knowing that Marion had passed away, I phoned her late in 1988 and my call was relayed to another number in the Midwest. A youngster, Marion's grandchild, answered the phone and I said, "Could I speak to Marion Tetley, please?," to which the child replied, "You can't, she's dead." Apologizing for my gaffe, I hung up and called Ann. Although she sounded very down, Ann was friendly and polite as always, so I told her of my call to Marion and asked if the child's statement was true. "Yes, Yes," Ann softly replied. "My beloved Marion has gone." As I recall Ann said, "Marion had brain surgery—I just can't talk about it." The grief in her voice was so profound, I did not prolong the conversation. Thinking about that call today caused me to wonder if Marion, to Ann, was "the wind beneath her wings."

Always sensitive about her age, one paper printed how her birth date had gone from 1909 to 1911, 1912, 1913 and 1923 in various publications. When making *The Whales of August*, she said she was the youngest in the cast being 69, making her birth date 1919. Later on, she refused to discuss her age.

Chapter Nineteen: "Ann"

My next communication from Ann arrived in April 1989, when she sent me a cassette of the songs from her LP *Sothern Exposure*, beautifully re-recorded in stereo. As an added bonus, her singing of "Baubles, Bangles and Beads," from *The Andy Williams Show*, was included on the tape. This parcel came from Ketchum, Idaho, and in a letter received a few days later she was very bitter about being idle. Calling to thank her for the tape she said, "I haven't had one film offer since *The Whales of August*." She was now devoting most of her time to painting and had completed a number of new canvasses. In a brief note, dated July 3, 1989, she said, "I've sold a lot of them already." This was at an exhibition held at A Matter of Taste in Trail Creek Village, Ketchum. Ann said, "I usually paint in the 20s genre and frontier women come to the fore in the twelve paintings I've put on display." Most of Ann's early art-works had been auctioned off for various charities, but a gallery in Seattle featured her paintings for sale on a regular basis.

AS and Don Porter at her art exhibition, 1990

AT HER ART EXHIBITION, 1990

On April 20, 1990, an invitation arrived for me to attend an "Exhibition of Paintings by Ann Sothern." The venue was Elizabeth's Staircase, 8645 Sunset Boulevard, Los Angeles. Tisha Sterling's name also appeared on the invitation as hostess. The invitation strikingly featured in bold color a copy of one of Ann's paintings. The scene was by the oceanside and there were three women looking out to sea. Set in the 1920s, birds, small animals and a picnic basket were also part of the vivid and nostalgic provoking scene.

The Art Exhibition was quite a success and it gave Ann a chance to catch up with so many of her best and oldest friends—Cesar Romero, Roddy McDowall, Robert Osborne, Marie Windsor, Elyse Knox and Don Porter. Lee Graham attended the affair on opening night when Tisha was the official host. He told me, "Ann looked wonderful in a green, full-length gown and has lost 40 lbs. since she did *The Whales of August*." Lee also liked a portrait Ann had done of herself as Maisie and he thought, as I did, how the 1920s' frontier women bore facial resemblances to Ann and her sister Marion.

In another oceanside painting, three girls are shown looking out to sea. The smaller girl could well be her sister Bonnie, as the age difference between her and the other two girls is parallel with the actual differential between Bonnie and her real-life sisters, Ann and Marion. Another painting, "Girl in White Hat," is simplistic in style but, again, the subject bears a resemblance to another member of Ann's family - in this instance her daughter, Tisha. Her work was described as a cross between Primitive and Impressionism. One critic said, "She lights up a canvas the way she lights up a screen."

Returning to Ketchum, Ann would make one more TV appearance in a special about her longtime friend and co-star, Bette Davis. Titled *If Looks*

Could Kill, it was shown on the Hallmark cable channel as part of their Biography series. Also appearing were Roddy McDowall, Robert Wagner, Leonard Maltin, writer James Spada, and Michael Merrill, Bette's adopted son. Ann said, "To me, a star is someone who brings people into the theatre and Bette was capable of doing that. She was kind to people that she had respect for but for people that she didn't have respect for, she was a hellion." In the summing up, Ann also said, "I liked her, I respected her and I enjoyed working with her." The special was filmed in 1994 and, to my knowledge, this was the last time Ann faced a professional camera.

Quite odd was a catalogue published in connection with an upcoming auction to be held in Dallas, Texas. The long inventory included Ann Sothern furniture, memorabilia and even silver-framed photographs. Ann never mentioned this event and I never got to question her about it.

For my part, I kept the communication line open and continued to write and send her birthday and Christmas greetings. One afternoon in 1998 the telephone rang and to my surprise it was Ann. The first thing I asked about was her health and she said, "I'm fine." One disturbing thing about the call was the way both our voices seemed to reverberate and the echo was decid-

AS and Vincent Price in *The Whales of August*
(Alive Films, 1987)

LILLIAN GISH AND AS IN *THE WHALES OF AUGUST* (ALIVE FILMS, 1987).
THEY FORMED A WONDERFUL FRIENDSHIP DURING THE FILM'S MAKING.

edly louder. It crossed my mind that Ann's hearing may have diminished. During our conversation she asked if I would consider doing a book on her career and, of course, I replied affirmatively. We chatted on for a few more minutes, during which she mentioned her half-sister Sally being close to her now. There was, however, a guarded quality in her voice, which made me think she was sneaking the call while her companion or housekeeper was out.

Ann had not responded to a letter I wrote her in 1998, nor to the flowers I sent for her 90th birthday, a year later. Thinking she may not now be capable of writing, I continued sending her regular greetings. Also, her telephone number had been changed so it was possible she had moved from her rented home in Ketchum and perhaps relocated to another in the area.

Ann was honored in 1999 with a retrospective at the Museum of Modern Art in New York City. This festival showcased her versatility by showing excerpts from many of her films, including *Folies Bergere, Lady Be Good, A Letter to Three Wives* and *Shadow on the Wall*. There was no mention of Ann

WITH COLIN BRIGGS, AT OUR LAST MEETING, 1990

being in attendance and no explanation was revealed as to why she was not there. It could have been ill health or it could have been a rekindling of her earlier feelings when she proclaimed, "I hate nostalgia," which precluded her from being present.

On January 15, 2001, I sent off a birthday greeting to Ann for her 92nd year. Just prior to this I'd written a career article on Ann for a U.S. periodical, *Films of the Golden Age*. This was at the request of another Sothern fan, the late Allan Herzer of Philadelphia. Allan mentioned there'd been a lot of requests for an article on Ann and, knowing how much regard I had for her as a person and an actress, he suggested I write one. I did and it was the first of many such career articles I would write for that publication and another from the same publishers, *Classic Images*.

Allan told me he had sent a copy of the *Films of the Golden Age* piece to Ann, so I hope she got to see it, for on March 22, 2001 our papers carried the sad news of her death. The obituary listed March 15 as the date of her passing and that the cause was heart failure. Also mentioned was that she died at home in Ketchum, Idaho and her survivors were her daughter Tisha, granddaughter Heidi, and half-sister Sally Adams from Boise, Idaho.

I was extremely saddened by the loss of the idol I'd long admired—but more importantly the friend I had loved for so many years.

Ann Sothern Filmography: 1929 - 1987

THE SHOW OF SHOWS, 1929 (Warner Bros.)
Technicolor
Director: John Adolfi; Photography: Bernard McGill

CAST: Monte Blue, Alice White, Molly O'Day, Frank Fay, Beatrice Lillie, Louise Fazenda, Richard Barthelmess, Dolores Costello, Loretta Young, Sally Blane, Winnie Lightner, Irene Bordoni, Myrna Loy, Douglas Fairbanks Jr., Ted Lewis and Band, John Barrymore, Harriette Lake (unbilled) and Marion Byron as Italian Sisters.

NOTES: From 1929: "Since their first startling introduction of Vitaphone, Warner Bros have gradually massed wonder upon wonder until it seemed their talking pictures progress had surely reached its peak. But now suddenly at a single stride Vitaphone comes forward with an achievement so immeasurably superior to any that have gone before, that the history of screen development must be completely revised. *The Show of Shows* is a connoisseur's collection of the supreme examples of almost every form of stage and screen entertainment."

HEARTS IN EXILE, 1929 (Warner Bros.)
Director: Michael Curtiz; Photography: Bill Rees; Story: John Oxenham, from the play by Owen Davis; Adaptation and Dialogue: Harvey Gates; Film Editor: Thomas Pratt

CAST: Dolores Costello, Grant Withers, James Kirkwood, Olive Tell, David Torrence, George Fawcett, William Irving, Tom Dugan, Rose Dione and Harriette Lake (unbilled)

HOLD EVERYTHING, 1930 (Warner Bros.)
Technicolor
Director: Roy Del Ruth; Screenplay: Robert Lord, based on the play by B.G. DeSylva and John McGowan; Film Editor: William Holmes; Photography: Dev Jennings

CAST: Joe E. Brown, Winnie Lightner, Georges Carpentier, Sally O'Neill, Edmund Breese, Bert Roach, Dorothy Revier, Jack Curtis, Tony Stabeneau, Lew Harvey, Jimmie Quinn and Harriette Lake (unbilled)

SONG OF THE WEST, 1930 (Warner Bros)
Technicolor
Director: Ray Enright; Screenplay: Harvey Thew, based on a play by Oscar Hammerstein II and Laurence Stallings (*Rainbow*); Photography: Dev Jennings; Film Editor: George Marks

CAST: John Boles, Vivienne Segal, Joe E. Brown, Edward Martindel, Harry Gribbon, Marie Wells, Sam Hardy, Marion Byron, Rudolph Cameron and Harriette Lake (unbilled)

DOUGHBOYS, 1930 (MGM)
Producer: Buster Keaton; Director: Edward Sedgwick; Screenplay: Al Boasberg, Sidney Lazarus & Richard Schayer, based on a story by Boasberg and Lazarus; Film Editor: William Le Vanway; Photography: Leonard Smith; Art Direction: Cedric Gibbons

CAST: Buster Keaton, Sally Eilers, Cliff Edwards, Edward Brophy, Victor Potel, Arnold Korff, Frank Mayo, Pitzy Katz, Sydney Bracy, William Steele and Harriette Lake (unbilled)

FREE AND EASY, 1930 (MGM)
Director: Edward Sedgwick; Screenplay: Richard Schayer, Al Boasberg & Paul Dickey; Story: Richard Schayer; Photography: Leonard Smith; Art Direction: Cedric Gibbons; Film Editor: William Le Vanway and George Todd

CAST: Buster Keaton, Anita Page, Robert Montgomery, Trixie Friganza, Edgar Dearing, Gwen Lee, John Miljan and Harriette Lake (unbilled). Guest Appearances: Lionel Barrymore, Cecil B DeMille, Jackie Coogan, William Haines and Fred Niblo.

WHOOPEE!, 1930 (United Artists)
Technicolor
Producer: Samuel Goldwyn; Co-producer: Florenz Ziegfeld; Director: Thornton Freeland; Photography: Lee Garmes, Ray Rennahan & Gregg Toland; Screenplay: William Conselman; Story: Owen Davis (*The Nervous Wreck*), and the musical by William Anthony McGuire, Walter Donaldson and Gus Kahn; Editor: Stuart Heisler

CAST: Eddie Cantor, Eleanor Hunt, Paul Gregory, Ethel Shutta, John Rutherford, Spencer Charters, Albert Hackett, Walter Law, Chief Caupolican, with Barbara Weeks, Virginia Bruce, Claire Dodd, Betty Grable and Harriette Lake (unbilled). Guest Appearance: George Morgan and His Orchestra

FOOTLIGHT PARADE, 1933 (Warner Bros)
Producer: Darryl F. Zanuck, Robert Lord, and Hal Wallis; Directors: Lloyd Bacon, William Keighley & Busby Berkeley; Screenplay: Manuel Seff and James Seymour; Photography: George Barnes; Film Editor: George Amy

CAST: James Cagney, Ruby Keeler, Joan Blondell, Dick Powell, Claire Dodd, Guy Kibbee, Ruth Donnelly, Hugh Herbert, Frank McHugh, Renee Whitney, Herman Bing; with Harriette Lake and Jean Rogers (unbilled)

BROADWAY THRU A KEYHOLE, 1933 (20th Century-United Artists)
Associate Producers: William Goetz & Raymond Griffith; Director: Lowell Sherman; Screenplay: Gene Towne and Graham Baker; Story: Walter Winchell; Photography: Barney McGill; Film Editor: Maurice Wright

CAST: Constance Cummings, Russ Columbo, Paul Kelly, Blossom Seeley, Gregory Ratoff, Texas Guinan, Hobart Cavanagh, C. Henry Gordon, with Harriette Lake and Lucille Ball (unbilled). Guest Appearances: Abe Lyman and His Orchestra, Frances Williams and Eddie Foy Jr.

LET'S FALL IN LOVE, 1934 (Columbia)
Running time - 64 minutes
Director: David Burton; Assistant Director: Arthur Black; Screenplay: Herbert Fields; Songs: Harold Arlen & Ted Koehler; Associate Producer: Felix Young; Sound: George Cooper; Musical Director: Constanin Bakaleinikoff; Photography: Benjamin Kline; Editor: Gene Milford

CAST:
Ken: Edmund Lowe
Jean (Sigrid Lund): Ann Sothern
Max: Gregory Ratoff
Gerry: Miriam Jordan
Lisa: Greta Meyer
Svente: John Qualen
Forsell: Tala Birell
Composer, Singer: Art (Arthur) Jarrett
Linda: Betty Furness
Allen: Anderson Lawler
Agatha: Marjorie Gateson
Nellie: Ruth Warren
and Kane Richmond, Selmer Jackson, Niles Welch, Sven Borg, Consuelo Baker

STORY: Temperamental Swedish movie star Tala Birell walks out on a movie, written and directed by Edmund Lowe. He persuades studio chief Gregory Ratoff to search for a Swedish newcomer to use as a replacement. Lowe's neglected fiancee, Miriam Jordan, insists he accompany her and friends, including Betty Furness, to the circus. While waiting for the main event to start, he is charmed by a "French" girl, Ann Sothern, working as a spruiker in an accompanying sideshow. Discovering she's really from Brooklyn, he returns later to offer her the star spot in his film. Initially declining, but attracted to him, she agrees after he explains she will live with a Swedish family for one month. Her tutors, Greta Meyer and John Qualen, not only teach her the language, but also the habits, likes, dislikes and manners of a Swedish girl. Their efforts prove successful enough for her to fool Ratoff who, after a screen test, gives her the vacant role. Lowe partners Jean (Sothern) in the test and their obvious chemistry is noticed by his fiancee. When Jean, now renamed Sigrid Lund, is the guest of honor at a party to meet the press, her vocalizing so enrages the jealous fiancee that she exposes her as a fraud. Lowe is fired, the fiancee storms out and Sothern disappears. The publicity over the hoax spreads nationwide and provides every reason for the production to continue. Ratoff rehires Lowe and tells him to finish the film with Sothern. Reluctantly, tutor Meyer tells him that Sothern has rejoined the circus and after tracking her down, Lowe declares his love for her.

NOTES: Ann told me that the Swedish accent was no hardship for her. Having lived for some years in Minnesota and with her mother's Danish background, it fell easily in place. She also mentioned that everyone on the film was supportive, especially Edmund Lowe. "Mr. Lowe was a gentleman and a really dedicated actor; I learned so much from him. We later did a second film (*Grand Exit*) and his amazing, quick delivery of dialogue was a lesson to be learned," she recalled. In another conversation with Ann she remarked that "his total preparation and complete knowledge of his lines rubbed off enough on me to try always to do the same." When she saw the film again on television some twenty-odd years later she did say, "I'm afraid my lines in the love scenes with him were perhaps too earnest, too overstated. He was so compelling and so ardent, I guess I tried to match that. Still, it was the early days of talkies and actors were florid and demonstrative back then." Ann sang "Love is Love Everywhere" and "Let's Fall in Love." The former is performed in Swedish and broken English and later there is a choir and folk dance sequence. "Let's Fall in Love" is sung to a backing track at the home of her tutors. To allow her to sing the verse and chorus in perfect English, she says, "This is the only place I can be myself." She reprises the chorus at the press party toward the film's conclusion, until she is interrupted by Miriam Jordan. Ensuring the two songs are given due treatment, Art Jarrett sings "Let's Fall in Love" at the start of the film and his version also includes a vocal chorus of lovely girls. At the press party he reprises "Love is Love Everywhere," giving it a more commercial American version as opposed to the early European musical-comedy style.

REVIEWS: *Film Daily* - "Ann Sothern ...emerges as a new screen find in this picture. She's got the goods to put her across big with the fans." *Evening Herald Examiner* - "Miss Sothern plays her role with a depth of feeling ... if her debut is a criterion for her future, she should make a name for herself. She has the ability to act, has a good voice and isn't a bit hard to look at."

MELODY IN SPRING, 1934 (Paramount)
Running time - 75 minutes
Producer: Douglas MacLean; Director: Norman Z. McLeod; Photography: Henry Sharp; Editor: Richard Currier; Screenplay: Benn W. Levy, based on a story by Frank Leon Smith; Songs by Harlan Thompson and Lewis Gensler

CAST:

Warren Blodgett: Charles Ruggles	Suzanna: Jane Gale
Mary Blodgett: Mary Boland	Mrs. Shorter: Norma Mitchell
John Craddock: Lanny Ross	Anton: Wade Boteler
Jane Blodgett: Ann Sothern	House Detective: Thomas Jackson
Wesley: George Meeker	Blonde: Helen Lynd
Wirt: Herman Bing	Second Guide: William J. Irving
Suzette: June Gale	Suzuki: Wilfred Hari
Suzan: Joan Gale	

STORY: Charlie Ruggles is the sponsor of a popular radio program. He is also a collector of bells of all descriptions. Ann is his daughter, engaged to George Meeker but finding herself in love with singer Lanny Ross. When Ross fails to impress the sponsor and Ann breaks her engagement, Ruggles takes the family, including wife Mary Boland, to Switzerland. His intention is that she forget Ross. Fortunately, it doesn't deter Ross, who follows the family. In order to ingratiate himself with Ruggles, he steals some cowbells, which the sponsor greatly covets. More hindrances occur when Meeker arrives and Ross is arrested and jailed for the theft of the bells. Ultimately, Ruggles relents to his daughter marrying Ross and Ann purposely gets herself arrested to enable her to join Ross in jail.

NOTES: Ann moved over to Paramount for this musical. An attempt by the studio to make radio singer Lanny Ross a movie personality didn't quite come off. His voice is pleasant enough and, in the style of Dick Powell and Kenny Baker, he sings the title song and "Ending With a Kiss." Ann did mention to me that she liked Mary Boland, and that Mr. Ross was okay, but she did not elaborate when I asked why she didn't sing in the film. June Gale would later be under contract to 20th Century-Fox and eventually marry Oscar Levant. She also appeared in *Folies Bergere* with Ann. Her sister, Joan Gale, would be in the cast of *Blind Date* due to a friendship with Ann.

THE HELL CAT, 1934 (Columbia)
Running time - 70 minutes
Director: Albert Rogell; Screenplay: Fred Niblo, Jr., based on a story by Adele Buffington; Photography: Benjamin Kling; Editors: John Rawlins and Joel Sayre

CAST:

Dan Collins: Robert Armstrong	Regan: Irving Bacon
Geraldine Sloane: Ann Sothern	Butler: Purnell Pratt
Snapper Dugan: Benny Baker	Graham: Henry Kolker
Pauline McCoy: Minna Gombell	Gillette: Guy Usher
Joe Morgan: J. Carrol Naish	Captain Barnett: Joseph Crehan

STORY: Ann plays the title role, a brunette socialite with an explosive nature. When reporter Robert Armstrong arrives to photograph her, a fight develops during which she socks him and he socks her back. Donning a blonde wig, she wangles a job on his newspaper and intends to get even. The couple eventually pool their resources, fall in love, and uncover a smuggling racket. It, also, by coincidence turns out to be her father's yacht that is being used to bring illegal Chinese into the United States.

REVIEWS: *Motion Picture Herald* - "Miss Sothern is reasonably effective in her role of the spoiled young woman of wealth. This is a mighty good entertaining newspaper story. Ann Sothern is fine and Robert Armstrong is always good." *Film Daily* - "Miss Sothern handles her dual role in fine fashion and Robert Armstrong gives plenty of pep."

BLIND DATE, 1934 (Columbia)
Running time - 71 minutes
Director: Roy William Neill; Screenplay: Ethel Hill, based on a story by Vida Hurst and Art Black

CAST:

Kitty Taylor: Ann Sothern
Bob Hartwell: Neil Hamilton
Bill: Paul Kelly
Freddy: Mickey Rooney
Pa Taylor: Spencer Charters
Ma Taylor: Jane Darwell
Flora: Joan Gale

Dot: Geneva Mitchell
Tom: Theodore Newton
Emy: Tyler Brooke
Hartwell Senior: Henry Kolker
Mrs. Hartwell: Billie Seward
Burt Stearns: Ben Hendriks, Jr.

STORY: Ann, top billed, plays Kitty, the sole support of a large slothful family. Engaged to a car repair shop proprietor, Paul Kelly, her fortune changes when she becomes a model in a department store. A meeting with the owner's son, Neil Hamilton, leads to her falling for him. Torn between the rough but amiable fiancé, who takes her loyalty for granted, and the wealthy employer's son, she temporarily chooses Kelly. Suspecting that she still loves Hamilton, Kelly deliberately quarrels with her, thus paving the way for her return to Hamilton.

REVIEWS: *Film Daily* - "Particularly good work by Ann Sothern, Neil Hamilton and Paul Kelly."

THE PARTY'S OVER, 1934 (Columbia)
Running time - 63 minutes
Director: Walter Lang; Screenplay: S. K. Lauren, based on a story by Daniel Kussell; Editor: Viola Lawrence; Photography: Benjamin Kline

CAST:

Bruce: Stuart Erwin
Ruth: Ann Sothern
Phyllis: Arline Judge
Martin: Chick Chandler
Mabel: Patsy Kelly
Sarah: Catherine Doucet

Betty: Marjorie Lytell
Theodore: Henry Travers
Fred: Rollo Lloyd
Clay: William Bakewell
Tillie: Esther Muir

STORY: Stuart Erwin is a certified Public Accountant who is supporting a family of spongers. Ann is a co-worker with whom he falls in love. When his lazy family causes trouble between them, he instigates a few changes and moves out to let them earn their own living.

NOTES: Ann replaced Elissa Landi in the lead role.

REVIEWS: *Film Daily* - "Fairly amusing and interesting comedy drama of domestic life with good cast. Ann Sothern as his secretary aids... characters are cleverly handled throughout." *Los Angeles Examiner* - "In a few scenes Miss Sothern is so beautiful it takes your breath away, in the rest of the picture she is just beautiful."

KID MILLIONS, 1934 (United Artists)
Running time - 90 minutes
Producer: Samuel Goldwyn; Director: Roy Del Ruth (black & white) and Willy Pogany (Technicolor); Screenplay: Arthur Sheekman, Nat Perrin and Nunnally Johnson; Photography: Ray June (black & white) and Ray Rennehan (Technicolor); Editor: Stuart Heisler; Musical Director: Alfred Newman; Art Director: Richard Day; Costumes: Omar Kiam; Songs: Walter Donaldson, Gus Kahn, Irving Berlin, Harold Adamson and Burton Lane; Choreography by Seymour Felix

CAST:

Eddie Wilson, Jr.: Eddie Cantor	Shiek Mulhulla: Paul Harvey
Joan Larrabee: Ann Sothern	Khoot: Otto Hoffman
Dot Clark: Ethel Merman	Herman: Edgar Kennedy
Jerry Lane: George Murphy	Specialty: Nicholas Brothers
Ben Ali: Jesse Block	William Slade: Guy Usher
Fanya: Eve Sully	Adolph: John Kelly
Toots: Doris Davenport	Pop: Jack Kennedy
Colonel Larrabee: Berton Churchill	Oscar: Stanley Fields
Louie the Lug: Warren Hymer	Attorney: Henry Kolker

and the Goldwyn Girls, included Lucille Ball, Irene Bentley, Helen Ferguson, Barbara Pepper, Lynne Carver (Virginia Reid) and Helen Wood

STORY: Social misfit Eddie Cantor inherits a million dollar treasure and heads for Egypt to claim it. His archeologist father, whom he never knew, has left it to him. On board ship, he meets Ann (who is accompanying her con-man uncle), Ethel Merman, posing as Cantor's long-lost stepmother, and her boyfriend, Warren Hymer, a thug. These phoneys are also after the treasure. Also on board is George Murphy. Ann and he spat initially, but get romantic in song. Cantor, after an amusing dalliance with an amorous Eve Sully, escapes with the treasure. Back in America, he opens an ice cream factory for all the poor kids of his neighborhood. None of the other principals, with the exception of Merman, reappear in this lavish Technicolor finale.

NOTES: Ann duetted "Your Head on My Shoulder" with George Murphy and had the first line to sing of "Mandy," a big production number with Eddie Cantor, Ethel Merman, Murphy, The Nicholas Brothers, and the whole company.

REVIEWS: *Los Angeles Examiner* - "Ann Sothern and George Murphy added a necessary note of attractive youth." *Los Angeles Illustrated Daily News* - "Ann Sothern ... a pleasant acquisition to the plot... when she and George Murphy sing 'Your Head on

My Shoulder,' they come through with a swell hit."

FOLIES BERGERE, 1935 (20th Century/United Artists)
Running time - 83 minutes
Producer: Darryl F. Zanuck; Associate Producers: William Goetz and Raymond Griffith; Director: Roy Del Ruth; Screenplay - Bess Meredyth & Hal Long, based on the play *The Red Cat* by Hans Adler and Rudolph Lothar; Photography: Barney McGill and Peverell Marley; Editors: Allen McGill and Sherman Todd; Musical Director: Alfred Newman; Art Director: William Darling; Choreographer: Dave Gould; Songs: Jack Meskill, Jack Stern, Harold Adamson, Burton Lane, Victor Young, Ned Washington, Bing Crosby, Andre Christian, Albert Willemetz and Herbert Reynolds; Costumes: Omar Kiam and Albert M. Levy

CAST:
Baron Cassini/Eugene Charlier: Maurice Chevalier
Baroness Cassini: Merle Oberon   Palet: Halliwell Hobbes
Mimi: Ann Sothern   Josephine: Barbara Leonard
Rene: Walter Byron   Stage Manager: Olin Howland
Gustav: Lumsden Hare   Joseph: Francis McGlynn, Sr.
Henri: Robert Grieg   Victor: Philip Dare
Francois: Eric Blore   Premier: Georges Renaveat
Also: Irene Bentley, Lucille Lund, Bernadene Hayes, Joan Woodbury and June Gale

STORY: Maurice Chevalier plays a dual role, an entertainer at the Folies Bergere and a Baron. Ann is the entertainer's tempestuous partner and mistress, while Merle Oberon is the Baron's neglected wife. When the Baron is called away to London, the entertainer, who has been doing an impersonation of him in his act, is called on to fill in for the Baron for real. Ann flirts with who she thinks is the Baron while Merle Oberon is pleased with her supposed husband's revived interest in her. Then the real Baron returns, and his wife isn't sure just who spent the night with her. The spectacular "Singing a Happy Song" concludes the proceedings with Ann and Chevalier on stage and Merle and Chevalier in the audience.

NOTES: Shot concurrently with a French version, Sim Viva and Natalie Paley played the roles enacted in English by Ann and Merle Oberon. Ann sang in the two big production numbers opposite Chevalier, "Rhythm of the Rain" and "Singing a Happy Song." There was another duet featuring the two stars, "I Was Lucky," but it was not in the final print; it can be heard on an LP recording, "Personalities on Parade" (Vol.1 PP-1). A rumored romance between Chevalier and Ann took fire when her family expressed exuberance over it. He delayed his return to Paris several times because of Ann and contrary to the stories of his legendary meanness he presented her with a piece of jewelry and a bouquet of roses for her birthday.

REVIEWS: *Los Angeles Examiner* - "Ann Sothern is a vivacious alive young miss as

Chevalier's jealous sweetheart. She is much becurled and most exciting." *Evening Herald Examiner* - "Ann Sothern as the Revue singer's jealous sweetie gives a nice performance."

EIGHT BELLS, 1935 (Columbia)
Running time - 69 minutes
Producer: J.G. Bachman; Director: Roy William Neill; Screenplay: Ethel Hill and Bruce Manning, based on the play by Percy C. Mandley; Photography: Joseph August; Editor: Gene Havlick

CAST:

Marg Walker: Ann Sothern	Williams: Arthur Hohl
Steve Andrews: Ralph Bellamy	MacIntyre: David Clyde
Roy Dale: John Buckler	Grayson: Charley Grapewin
Walker: Spencer Charters	Finch: Franklin Pangborn
Aunt Susan: Catherine Doucet	Carl: John Darrow

STORY: Ann is a wealthy gal engaged to John Buckler, the first mate of a freighter owned by her father who disapproves of the match. To break the engagement, he appoints Buckler captain of another vessel sailing immediately. The fiery girl, with her aunt in tow, stows away on the ship and is discovered by Ralph Bellamy, formerly captain of the ship. Encountering a typhoon, Buckler wants to flee in the only lifeboat, taking Ann and her aunt with him. She declines to go and Bellamy and crew safely bring the ship to port in Shanghai on time. Having switched her affection to Bellamy, she and Buckler part amiably.

REVIEWS: *Los Angeles Examiner* - "*Eight Bells*, however, is not primarily a woman's story, and therefore not a very good introductory starring vehicle for a girl with the versatile talents of Ann Sothern. Ann is lovely and convincing."

HOORAY FOR LOVE, 1935 (RKO)
Running time - 75 minutes
Associate Producer: Felix Young; Director: Walter Lang; Screenplay: Lawrence Hazard and Ray Harris, based on a story by Marc Lachmann; Photography: Lucien Andriot; Editor: George Crone; Musical Director: Alberto Colombo; Songs: Dorothy Fields and Jimmy McHugh; Choreographer: Sammy Lee

CAST:

Pat: Ann Sothern	The Duchess: Georgia Caine
Doug: Gene Raymond	Judge: Etienne Giradot
Commodore: Thurston Hall	Regan: Harry Kernell
Chowsky: Lionel Stander	Ganz: Sam Hardy
Trixie: Pert Kelton	Grady: Eddie Kane

Specialties: Bill Robinson, Jeni Le Gon, Maria Gambarelli and "Fats" Waller

STORY: College graduate Gene Raymond, along with a lot of noisy celebrating friends, attends a club where the singer is Ann. When the revelry brings in the police, he helps her escape through a window. Now working as a guide at a radio station, once again he causes chaos during a live broadcast which features Ann's singing. Fired, he encounters Thurston Hall, who persuades him to invest his money and the family home in a Broadway show. Finding that Ann is Hall's daughter and the star of the show, he succumbs in more ways than one. All is going well with the show until the phoney producers scram with the funds and Raymond, left holding the empty bag, is jailed. Hall, who has been pursued throughout by a lusty Duchess, "sacrifices his all" and marries her after getting her guarantee to back the show.

NOTES: For her first film at RKO, Ann was top billed and got on very well with leading man Gene Raymond. When I asked her about an alleged feud between the two she said, "I don't feud with anybody. Gene was a talented man, he composed songs and we dated for a while. Maybe he was more serious than I, but Roger [Pryor] was still very much in my life and Gene also seemed too close to his mother. Later, after he and I had both married, our film partnership became a bit tiresome for us both, but this was due to what we both thought was inferior material." Virginia Reid (whom Ann had befriended when she was a Goldwyn Girl in *Kid Millions*), also has a bit in the film's opening. Like Marion Byron, Joan Gale and other co-workers she'd become friendly with, Ann would try to find work for Virginia. Later she would end up at MGM and, changing her name to Lynn Carver, she would work with Ann again when her staunch supporter suggested her for a role in *Dulcy*. Ann sang "I'm in Love all Over Again," duetted "You're an Angel" with Gene, and sang "Palsie Walsie" with the chorus. The finale had her singing solo, part of "Hooray for Love," which was featured by the entire company with the exception of Raymond and Etienne Giradot.

REVIEWS: *Los Angeles Examiner* - "Meanwhile we are treated to some very fine crooning by Miss Sothern, whose voice is a match for her blonde beauty." *Motion Picture Herald* - "There is also a pleasing theme song, 'I'm in Love All Over Again,' which is engagingly sung by Ann Sothern. This is fine entertainment."

THE GIRL FRIEND, 1935 (Columbia)
Running time - 67 minutes
Producer: Samuel Briskin; Director: Edward Buzzell; Editor: John Rawlins; Screenplay: Gertrude Purcell and Benny Rubin, based on a story by Gene Towne and Graham Baker; Photography: Joseph Walker; Sound: Glen Rominger; Musical Sequences Staged by Seymour Felix; Songs: Arthur Johnson and Gus Kahn; Costumes: Murray Meyer; Musical Director: Louis Silvers

CAST:
Linda: Ann Sothern   Harmon: Thurston Hall
Henry: Jack Haley   Sunshine: Victor Kilian
George: Roger Pryor   Doc: Ray Walker

Hilda: Inez Courtney   Grandma: Margaret Seddon
Also: Lee Kohlman, Geneva Mitchell, John T. Murray and Victor Potel

STORY: Roger Pryor plays an actor whose musical satire on Napoleon is rejected by
Broadway producer Thurston Hall. Another script, by farmer Jack Haley, is a serious
look at Bonaparte and by error Pryor gets a copy of this as well. Journeying with two
hungry cronies, Ray Walker and Victor Kilian, to Haley's farm, the trio pretend to be
producers. Moving in with the family in order to be fed, they announce they will
stage the play in the barn. Ann is Haley's sister and she becomes the play's leading
lady, with Pryor falling for her. Learning that Ann's grandmother is paying for the
show by mortgaging the farm, Pryor and his two friends have a change of heart.
They combine the two plays, with Haley as Napoleon, and, despite heavy rain creating havoc, the show starts to take good shape. Pryor then pulls a final trick and sub-
stitutes his show for one Thurston Hall has arranged at a Playhouse. After threatening Pryor with the law for kidnaping his cast, Hall sees the show and deems it a success. Ann forgives Pryor for his deception and all ends fine and dandy.

NOTES: While watching the film one is aware of the genuine deep emotions shared
by Ann and Roger Pryor. Their love, previously daunted by his wife's backing out of a
divorce at the last moment, is on open display here. The 34-year-old Pryor has the
ardor of a 19-year-old discovering his first love. Ann, looking unbelievably beautiful,
glows with a special radiance in her love scenes with him. The songs are good, as is
the sound, but the staging of the musical numbers is restricted to mostly formation
walking. Admittedly, the stage in the barn is small and the dancing is supposed to be
clumsy, but the finale needed much more movement and pep. Ann and Roger duetted "Two Together," Jack Haley and chorus performed "That's How I Got to be Napoleon," Ann and Jack sang "More Power to You," and, in the finale, Pryor sang a reprise
with Ann.

GRAND EXIT, 1935 (Columbia)
Running time - 68 minutes
Director: Erle C. Kenton; Screenplay by Bruce Manning & Lionel Hauser, based on a
story by Gene Towne and Graham Baker; Photography: Henry Freulich; Consultant:
Murray Mayer; Editor: Gene Milford

CAST:
Tom Fletcher: Edmund Lowe   Drake: Russell Hicks
Adrienne Martin: Ann Sothern   Warden: Wyley Birch
John Grayson: Onslow Stevens   Noah: Miki Morita
Fire Chief Mulligan: Robert Middlemass   1st Secretary: Iris Adrian
District Attorney Cope: Selmer Jackson   Klover: Edward Van Sloan
Police Chief Roberts: Guy Usher   Dave: Arthur Rankin

STORY: Described by Clive Hirschorn, in his book *The Columbia Story*, as one of the year's better 'B' films, *Grand Exit* indeed was. The script was full of surprises and kept one guessing until almost the end. An insurance company, plagued by a series of fires, reluctantly rehires an investigator, Edmund Lowe. The previous holder of this job is Onslow Stevens, whom Lowe keeps on to assist him. Adrienne Martin (Ann Sothern) is the mysterious gal who is always at the scene of each fire. Both Lowe and Stevens fall for her, but a suspicious Lowe breaks into her apartment and finds a passport bearing her real name, Adeline Maxwell. Further investigation finds that her father, whose business dealings with the insurance company had caused his bankruptcy, is the firebug. Ann has been purposely framed by Lowe and is imprisoned. When her father starts a fire in prison as a ruse to free his daughter, he is killed. Lowe explains the case to the parties concerned and leaves Stevens and Sothern with the comment of making a "grand exit" and of going to Rome. Ann surprises him by leaving Stevens behind and announcing she is also going to Rome.

NOTES: Over a period of eight years Iris Adrian and I discussed her work in films many times. Of *Grand Exit* she said: "I played a glamour girl secretary to Edmund Lowe. He puts a lot of demands on the insurance company he worked for and one of them was to have a secretary who had to be all things to him and for him. The joke of the script was that each time he returned to his office, the secretary would be a different girl. My immediate replacement was a platinum blonde with a bad dye job and strident voice. Things really got bad as the third secretary was a prudish spinster in her fifties. Edmund Lowe was a debonair guy and fun to work with. I shared no scenes with Miss Sothern, but did see her in wardrobe trying on her prison garb. She was so tiny it surprised me, a bit like Mae West too, for they had her in the highest heels even in the prison scenes. All the extras were in the lowest, regulation shoes so as not to dwarf Ann, who seemed to take all this in the best of humor."

YOU MAY BE NEXT!, 1936 (Columbia)
Running time - 67 minutes
Associate Producer/Director: Albert S. Rogell; Editor: John Rawlins; Screenplay: Fred Niblo, Jr. and Ferdinand Reyher, based on a story by Henry Wales and Ferdinand Reyher; Photography: Allen G. Seigler; Costumes: Samuel Lange

CAST:

Fay Stevens: Ann Sothern	Miss Abbott: Nana Bryant
Neil Bennett: Lloyd Nolan	Dan McMahon: Robert Middlemass
Beau Gardner: Douglass Dumbrille	Mitch Cook: George McKay
Eddie House: John Arledge	Ted Lane: Gene Morgan
J.J. Held: Berton Churchill	Nick Barrow: Clyde Dilson

STORY: Ann plays a singer employed at a roadhouse run by Douglass Dumbrille. Escaping from pursuing police, after committing a bank robbery, Dumbrille's capture is foiled when the police radios are jammed. Radio engineer Lloyd Nolan's invention has accidentally caused the jam. Introduced to Ann by Dumbrille, Nolan is attracted not only by her beauty, but also her voice and he arranges a radio audition for her. In the meantime, Dumbrille has discovered Nolan's invention and uses it by blackmailing the radio station. His scheme is to jam their broadcasts unless $150,000 is paid. Covering himself, Dumbrille has kidnaped Nolan and makes it appear that he is the mastermind behind the blackmail. Ann believes him innocent and eventually finds him hidden in another part of the roadhouse. Nolan is released long enough to contact authorities, before he and Ann are bound and gagged by Dumbrille and his henchmen. With the help of the Navy, the gang is rounded up and Ann and Nolan are off on a Parisian honeymoon.

NOTES:In an uncredited musical score, Ann sang "In My Dreams," "When I'm With You Sweetheart" and "Without You." Also featured were snatches of "Two Together," "Love Me Forever" and "I'm Just a Vagabond Lover."

DON'T GAMBLE WITH LOVE, 1936 (Columbia)
Running time - 65 minutes
Associate Producer: Irving Briskin; Director: Dudley Murphy; Screenplay: Lee Loeb and Harold Buchman; Editor: James Sweeney; Photography: Henry Freulich; Costumes: Samuel Lange

CAST:

Ann Edwards: Ann Sothern	Grace: Elisabeth Risdon
Jerry Edwards: Bruce Cabot	Dan: George McKay
Rock Collins: Irving Pichel	Bob: Clifford Jones
John Crane: Ian Keith	Salesman: Franklin Pangborn
Martin Gage: Thurston Hall	Baby: Richard Livernoin

STORY: Former partners in an honest gambling club, Ann and Bruce Cabot, disagree when she leaves the business with the birth of their baby. He won't give up the club, despite her urging him to do so, especially when he is swindled. When he opens a new gambling house, which is crooked, she leaves him and finds success in a dress business. Meanwhile, Cabot's crooked gaming house is so successful that rival racketeers become menacing and threaten his life. At the opening of his new club, in a desperate effort to save her husband's life, Ann exposes to the customers the tricks of her husband's trade, including a fixed roulette wheel, thereby indicating to "the mob" who are present that her husband's club no longer poses any threat to their livelihood. This leads to an exciting climax with frenzied customers wrecking the club. Ann's ruse has worked, the racketeers no longer feel he is a risk and the "hit" is called off. A remorseful Cabot then returns to wife Ann and their baby in happy surroundings far away from the world of gambling.

REVIEWS: *Film Daily* - "Good performances from Ann Sothern and Bruce Cabot ... plus a story that holds interest fairly well."

HELL-SHIP MORGAN, 1936 (Columbia)
Running time - 64 minutes
Producer: Irving Briskin; Director: D. Ross Lederman; Story/Screenplay: Harold Shumate; Photography: Henry Freulich; Editor: Otto Meyer; Costumes: Samuel Lange; Special Camera Effects: E. Roy Davidson

CAST:

Mary: Ann Sothern	Cabot: Howard Hickman
Morgan: George Bancroft	Dale: Ralph Byrd
Jim: Victor Jory	Hawkins: Rollo Lloyd
Covanci: George Regas	Pittsburgh (The Cook): Snowflake

STORY: Ann, daughter of a drowned sea captain, unable to find work, throws herself in front of a taxi so she can collect damages. Morgan (George Bancroft), the cab's passenger, has always been unlucky in love. Captain of a small schooner, who supplies fish to a San Francisco cannery, he finds her work there. She meets Victor Jory, the first mate, and he assumes she is just one of Bancroft's usual one night stands. Making a pass at her, Jory is surprised by her furious rejection. Gratitude toward Bancroft leads to a marriage between them and a honeymoon on his boat. Unable to hide her true feelings, Bancroft discovers his wife's love for Jory. During a hurricane, Jory's life is saved by Bancroft, whose back is broken in the attempt. Writing in his log book, he asks Ann and Jory to leave him alone. Returning later, they find his cabin empty. The self-sacrificing Bancroft has paved the way for the happiness of the couple by crawling from his bed and throwing himself overboard.

NOTES: This was Ann's last Columbia feature. Sam Briskin, who had been that studio's general manager, moved over to RKO where he was the vice-president in charge of production. He signed Jean Arthur and Herbert Marshall for pictures at RKO and then he signed Ann. Sam Briskin said, "I had worked with her at Columbia. I wanted her because she is adaptable and easy to cast. As a leading lady she can fit into many pictures. She wasn't happy with her parts at Columbia so after she got a release I was able to convince her to sign with RKO."

REVIEWS: *Film Daily* - "Fair drama with good work by players, but handicapped in the way of story."

MY AMERICAN WIFE, 1936 (Paramount)
Running time - 65 minutes
Producer: Albert Lewis; Director: Harold Young; Screenplay: Virginia Van Upp and Edith Fitzgerald, based on story by Elmer Davis; Photography: Harry Fischbeck; Editor: Paul Weatherwax; Costumes: Travis Banton; Musical Director: Boris Morros; Art Direction by Hans Dreir and Robert Odell; Sound Recording: Earl Hayman and Louis Messenkep

CAST:

Count Ferdinand: Francis Lederer

Mary Cantillon: Ann Sothern

Lafe Cantillon: Fred Stone

Mrs. Robert Cantillon: Billie Burke

Adolph: Ernest Cossart

Robert Cantillon: Grant Mitchell

Vincent: Hal K. Dawson

Stephen: Adrian Morris

Agnes: Dora Clement

Butler: Montague Shaw

STORY: Ann plays the granddaughter of Arizona rancher Fred Stone. Conflict occurs in this comedy about snobbery when his daughter-in-law, Billie Burke, orchestrates the marriage of Ann to a foreign Count, Francis Lederer. With Lederer's arrival at the family spread, Stone is initially appalled at his unsuitability for ranch life. He wins the approval of Stone when he demonstrates that he is "macho" enough for brawls and bronco busting. Ann, on her way to get a divorce, hears that Lederer is living with a red-haired woman and changes her mind upon discovering the redhead is a bespectacled spinster and the daughter of Ernest Cossart. She and Lederer reconcile on a tractor.

NOTES: This was a remake of a 1923 silent Paramount feature which had starred Gloria Swanson in Sothern's role.

REVIEWS: *Hollywood Citizen News* - "Miss Sothern is good too...Lederer is the Count, Stone is Grandpa Cantillon and Miss Sothern the heiress. All three play their roles in top notch fashion." *Film Daily* - "Ann Sothern, Ernest Cossart, Billie Burke and Grant Mitchell are splendid in their parts."

WALKING ON AIR, 1936 (RKO)

Running Time - 70 minutes

Producer: Edward Kaufman; Director: Joseph Santley; Screenplay: Bert Kalmar, Harry Ruby, Viola Brothers Shore and Rian James, based on a story by Francis M. Cockrell; Photography: J. Roy Hunt; Editor: George Hively; Photographic Effects: Vernon Walker; Songs: Bert Kalmar, Harry Ruby & Sid Silver; Costumes: Bernard Newman; Set Dressing: Darrell Silvers

CAST:

Pete Quinlan: Gene Raymond

Kit Bennett: Ann Sothern

Aunt Evelyn Bennett: Jessie Ralph

Mr. Bennett: Henry Stephenson

Joe: Gordon Jones

Tom Quinlan: George Meeker

Flo Quinlan: Maxine Jennings

Fred Randolph: Alan Curtis

Mrs. Randolph: Anita Colby

Radio Receptionist: Patricia Wilder

Butler: Charles Coleman

Albert: George Andrew Beranger

and Frank Jenks, Arthur Hoyt, Robert Graves, Fred Stanley, A. S. Byron, Manny Harmon

STORY: Ann is a spoiled heiress who is in love with a gold digger, Alan Curtis. Henry Stephenson, her father, disapproves of the match and has her locked in her room. She eventually meets Gene Raymond. He is hired to pretend to be her fiancé, a French count, and to be as obnoxious as possible to her father and aunt (Jessie Ralph). They recognize he is a phoney and play along with the charade. Raymond gets a singing job on the radio and Ann, now in love with him, misconstrues the radio switchboard operator who mentions that Raymond is married. The operator was actually referring to Raymond's brother, but Ann, in a rage, takes off to elope with Curtis. Eventually, she learns the truth. However, Raymond now is in jail because of the fracas he created during his broadcast in trying to get the message through to Ann. Wishing to be with him, she smashes a courthouse window with her shoe and the happy couple go to the lock-up together.

NOTES: This was the leads' second teaming and was so successful that RKO executives, delighted with the receipts, continued the partnership. Ann sang "Let's Make A Wish" as a duet with Raymond.

REVIEWS: *The Los Angeles Examiner* - "Gene and Ann make a swell romantic team … while Ann continues to look more interestingly lovely in each succeeding picture, as well as to reveal increased power as a performer." *Hollywood Citizen News* - " This is not the first time, as I recall it, that Raymond has sung on the screen. For Raymond's sake, I cannot forbear hoping, however, that it will be the last. His vocal enterprises are distinctly unsuccessful. Ann Sothern… sings also…but her sweet, small voice is as least heard to advantage in comparison with Raymond's. Both Raymond and Miss Sothern do well in their acting assignments."

SMARTEST GIRL IN TOWN, 1936 (RKO)
Running time - 58 minutes
Producer: Edward Kaufman; Director: Joseph Santley; Photography: J. Roy Hunt; Editor: Jack Hively; Screenplay: Viola Brothers Shore, based on a story by Muriel Scheck and H. S. Kraft; Special Effects: Vernon Walker; Art Director: Van Nest Polglase; Associate: Al Herman; Musical Director: Nathaniel Shilkret; Song "Will You" by Gene Raymond; Gowns by Bernard Newman; Set Dressing: Darrell Silvera; Recorded by Clem Portman

CAST:

Dick Smith: Gene Raymond	Torine: Erik Rhodes
Frances Cooke: Ann Sothern	Terry: Harry Jans
Gwen: Helen Broderick	Opening Escort/model: Alan Curtis
Philbean: Eric Blore	Photographer: Frank Jenks

STORY: Ann is a photographic model. Her sister, Helen Broderick, married to a no-hoper, Harry Jans, insists that Ann find a wealthy husband. On an assignment she mistakes yacht owner Gene Raymond for a male model. Actually very rich, Raymond has his valet, Eric Blore, pose as an advertising head so he can hire Ann for modeling work. Erik Rhodes is the Baron, targeted by Ann and Helen as a more likely prospective spouse for Ann. There are some incredible events, including a fake suicide by Raymond, ending with an unbelievable hotel sequence where Ann admits her love for him. Their wedding is at his supposed deathbed - with Ann discovering that the "blood" on his cheeks is actually ketchup.

NOTES: Ann did not sing in this one, but Raymond sang his own composition, "Will You," to her, in what seems like a proposal. In real life, she chose Roger Pryor instead. Again garnering good notices and a positive public response, the film scored a hit with Joseph Santley's direction constantly injecting the script with added vitality. Raymond suffered, though, when in a hair washing scene, the director insisted the suds fall on a specific spot. This necessitated countless retakes involving shampooing and hair drying for Mr. Raymond.

REVIEWS: *Film Daily* - "A very attractive sweetheart team, this Gene Raymond and Ann Sothern." *Los Angeles Examiner* - "Ann Sothern has never looked prettier...and she's particularly delightful in a scene...with Gene while she's shampooing his hair."

DANGEROUS NUMBER, 1937 (MGM)
Running time - 71 minutes
Director: Richard Thorpe; Producer: Lou Ostrow; Photography: Leonard Smith; Editor: Blanche Sewell; Screenplay: Carey Wilson, based on a story by Leona Dalrymple; Musical Score by David Snell; Wardrobe by Dolly Tree; Recording by Douglas Shearer; Art Director: Cedric Gibbons

CAST:
Hank: Robert Young
Elinor: Ann Sothern
Cousin William: Reginald Owen
Gypsy: Cora Witherspoon
Dillman: Dean Jagger
and Spencer Charters and Clem Bevans

Vera: Marla Shelton
Minehardi: Barnett Parker
Hotel Manager: Charles Trowbridge
Desk Clerk: Franklin Pangborn

STORY: Showgirl Ann marries wealthy Robert Young. When her show business relatives and friends constantly interfere with their marriage, he wants a way out. Misunderstandings abound as their totally disparate backgrounds produce conflict leaving the rather staid Young dumbfounded. Finally he learns his marriage may not be legal when an acrobat, Dean Jagger, arrives claiming *he* is Ann's husband. This reprieve is short lived, and Young resigns himself to a wacky marriage. Young is assured by Ann that all will be well now, for she'll quit showbiz. They drive off for a second honeymoon.

NOTES:The legality surrounding the marriage between Ann and Dean Jagger was a replica of the circumstances of her real-life wedding to Roger Pryor. The plot utilized the three-day waiting period in Los Angeles after a license is obtained.

FIFTY ROADS TO TOWN, 1937 (20th Century-Fox)
Running time - 80 minutes
Associate Producer: Raymond Griffith; Director: Norman Taurog; Photography: Joseph H. August; Editor: Hanson Fritch; Screenplay: George Marion, Jr. & William Conselman, based on a story by Louis Frederick Nebel; Costumes by Royer; Musical Director: David Buttolph; Songs: Mack Gordon & Harry Revel; Art Director: Rudolph Sternad; Assistant Director: Ad Schaumer; Sound: Bernard Freericks and Roger Heman

CAST:

Peter Nostrand: Don Ameche	Percy: Stepin Fetchit
Millicent Kendall: Ann Sothern	Tom: Paul Hurst
Edwin Henry: Slim Summerville	George Hession: Spencer Charters
Mrs. Henry: Jane Darwell	Captain Galloway: Dewitt Jennings
Sheriff Daw: John Qualen	Pinelli: Bradley Page
Dutch Nelson: Douglas Fowley	Smorgen: Oscar Apfel
Leroy Smedley: Allan Lane	Carroll: John Hamilton
Jerome Q. Kendall: Alan Dinehart	Police Officer: Russell Hicks
and Arthur Aylesworth and Jim Toney	

STORY: Ann is a runaway heiress and Don Ameche is on the run to avoid being a witness in a friend's divorce. Douglas Fowley is a public enemy, escaping the law. When they are snowbound together in a deserted cabin, she thinks Ameche is the gangster while he mistakes her for a process server. All is sorted out with Fowley's subsequent arrest by John Qualen. Ann forgets her fiancé, Allan Lane, and admits she's attracted to Ameche.

NOTES: Ann and Ameche duetted "Never in a Million Years," which was first sung in *Wake Up and Live* (1937) with Jack Haley and Alice Faye.

REVIEWS: *Film Daily* - "Ably directed by Norman Taurog, a veteran in the comedy field...Don Ameche and Ann Sothern romp through their roles, with Ann being especially decorative."

THERE GOES MY GIRL, 1937 (RKO)
Running time - 74 minutes
Producer: William Sistrom; Director: Ben Holmes; Screenplay: Harry Segall, based on the story *Women in Prison* by George Beck; Photography: Joseph H. August; Editor: Desmond Marquette; Special Effects: Vernon L. Walker; Recorded by Earl A. Wollcott; Art Director: Van Nest Polglase; Gowns by Edward Stevenson

CAST:

Jerry Martin: Gene Raymond	Dunn: Gordon Jones
Connie Taylor: Ann Sothern	Tate: Frank Jenks
Tim (T.J.) Whalen: Richard Lane	Joe Rethburn: Bradley Page

Margot Whitney: Joan Woodbury
Grace Andrews: Marla Shelton
Bum: Alec Craig
Sergeant Wood: Joseph Crehan
Actress: Maxine Jennings
Dan Curtis: William Corson
and Roy James, Harry Worth and Dorothy Vaughn

Actor: Clyde Dilson
Faraday: Charles Coleman
Waiter: George Davis
Police Officers: Irving Bacon and
Edgar Dearing
Ideas Man: Chester Clute

STORY: Lovebirds Ann and Gene Raymond are reporters on rival newspapers. Her managing editor, Richard Lane, does not want his "star" reporter to marry and does everything in his power to prevent a ceremony taking place. One of his ruses is a fake murder case, which has Ann abandoning her groom at the altar to pursue the story. There are two real murders, though, which she solves - but she gets herself shot in the process. The couple do get married at the finish with Raymond knocking Lane out and Frank Jenks sitting on him while the Justice of the Peace conducts the frenzied service.

REVIEWS: *Hollywood Citizen News* - "Most of it is derived from the tantrums of Miss Sothern, who does this thing rather well."

SUPER-SLEUTH, 1937 (RKO)
Running time - 75 minutes
Producer: Edward Small; Director: Ben Stoloff; Screenplay: Gertrude Purcell & Ernest Pagano, based on a play by Harry Segall; Photography: Joseph H. August; Editor: William Hamilton; Gowns: Edward Stevenson; Art Director: Van Nest Polglase; Associate: Al Herman; Special Effects - Vernon L. Walker; Recorded by Earl A. Wolcott

CAST:

Willard (Bill) Martin: Jack Oakie
Mary Strand: Ann Sothern
Professor Horman: Eduardo Ciannelli
Larry Frank: Alan Bruce
Lieutenant Garrison: Edgar Kennedy
Doris Dunne: Joan Woodbury
Ralph Waring: Bradley Page
Gibbons: Paul Guilfoyle
Warts: Willie Best
Beckett: William Corson

Barker: Richard Lane
Eddie: Alec Craig
Motorcycle Cop: Paul Hurst
Jailer: Fred Kelsey
Policeman: George Rosener
Grimes: Dick Rush
Casey: Robert E. O'Connor
Sullivan: Phillip Morris
Movie Gangster: Dewey Robinson

STORY: Jack Oakie is a movie detective with a swollen head. Ann plays the studio publicity chief who tries to keep him out of trouble. His latest scrape finds him trying to solve a real-life murder case masterminded by Eduardo Ciannelli, known as the "Poison Pen." With the aid of a valet, Willie Best, and a movie-struck police lieutenant, Edgar Kennedy, he captures the killer. Ann is on hand at the finish, showing her admiration and eventually closing the mouth of the egocentric Oakie with a kiss.

DANGER – LOVE AT WORK, 1937 (20th Century-Fox)
Running time - 81 minutes
Associate Producer: Harold Wilson; Director: Otto Preminger; Screenplay: James
Edward Grant and Ben Markson; Photography: Virgil Miller; Associate Director:
Gordon Cooper; Musical Director: David Buttolph; Songs: Mack Gordon & Harry
Revel; Art Director: Duncan Cramer; Costumes: Gwen Wakeling; Sound: Joseph
Aiken & Roger Heman; Set Decoration: Thomas Little

CAST:

Toni Pemberton: Ann Sothern	Chemist: Elisha Cook, Jr.
Henry MacMorrow: Jack Haley	Maid: Hilda Vaughn
Alice Pemberton: Mary Boland	Butler: Charles Coleman
Howard Rogers: Edward Everett Horton	Attendant: George Chandler
Herbert Pemberton: John Carradine	Hick: Spencer Charters
Uncle Alan: Walter Catlett	Chauffeur: Hal K. Dawson
Junior Pemberton: Bennie Bartlett	Thug: Stanley Fields
Uncle Goliath: Maurice Cass	Cop: Paul Hurst
Allan Duncan: Alan Dinehart	Salesman: Claude Allister
Albert Pemberton: Etienne Giradot	Parsons: Jonathan Hale
Wilbur: E. E. Clive	Gilroy: Charles Lane
Aunt Patty: Margaret McWade	Hilton: Paul Stanton
Aunt Pitty: Margaret Seddon	

STORY: Ann plays the daughter from a crazy family, the Pembertons. Enter lawyer
Jack Haley, who needs their signatures on a document involving the sale of their deceased grandfather's farm. Edward Everett Horton is the rather dumb heavy of the
piece who, believing there to be oil on the property, attempts a scam. When the lawyer departs without the family's signatures, they follow him to New York. Ann, now
in love with him, gets the paper signed and Haley forgives all the chaos the family
has caused and becomes one of them by marrying Ann.

NOTES: Ann and Jack Haley duetted on "Danger - Love at Work."

REVIEWS: *Film Daily* - "Ann Sothern and Jack Haley do some of their best acting
yet." *Los Angeles Evening Herald* - "Ann Sothern, Jack Haley, Edward Everett Horton,
Bennie Bartlett, John Carradine, Mary Boland and others perform in the best insane
manner in a long, long time."

ALI BABA GOES TO TOWN, 1937 (20th Century-Fox)
Running time - 80 minutes
Producer: Darryl F. Zanuck; Director: David Butler; Screenplay: Harry Tugend and
Jack Yellen, based on a story by Gene Towne, Gene Fowler and Graham Baker; Pho-
tography: Ernest Palmer; Editor: Irene Morra; Costumes: Gwen Wakeley; Songs:

Mack Gordon, Harry Revel & Raymond Scott; Art Director: Bernard Herzburn; Settings: Thomas Little

CAST:

Aloysius Babson/Ali Baba: Eddie Cantor

Yusuf: Tony Martin

Sultan Abdullah: Roland Young

Princess Miriam: June Lang

Sultana: Gypsy Rose Lee (Louise Hovick)

Ishak: John Carradine

Dinah: Virginia Field

Boland: Alan Dinehart

Prince Musah: Douglass Dumbrille

Captain: Paul Hurst

Doctor: Charles Lane

Arab, Wife Beater: Eddie Collins

Arab Wife: Marjorie Weaver

Guest Artists: Raymond Scott Quintet, Pearl Twins, Peters Sisters, Jeni Le Gon
Premiere Celebrities: Lady Sylvia Ashley, Phyllis Brooks, Eddie Cantor, Dolores Del Rio, Douglas Fairbanks, Sonja Henie, Victor McLaglen, Tyrone Power, the Ritz Brothers, Cesar Romero, Ann Sothern, Shirley Temple and Michael Whalen.

STORY: Ann and Cesar Romero are seen as themselves in a brief flash as celebrities attending a premiere. Eddie Cantor is a movie fan and autograph collector. Falling asleep on a movie set where he is working as an extra, his dream transports him back to the year 937 A.D., the place Baghdad. His identity is Ali Baba and he helps Tony Martin in his romance with June Lang, the Sultan's daughter. A political campaign, run by the Sultan to discredit Ali Baba, fails and Ali Baba is elected President. When the Sultan's henchmen attempt to kill him, Cantor escapes by way of a magic carpet which leads to his awakening.

THERE GOES THE GROOM, 1937 (RKO)

Running time - 64 minutes

Producer - Albert Lewis; Director - Joseph Santley; Screenplay - S.K. Lauren, Dorothy Yost & Harold Kussell, based on a story by David Garth; Photography - Milton Krasner; Editor - Jack Hively; Costumes - Edward Stevenson; Recorded by Denzil A. Cutler; Set Dressing - Darrell Silvera; Art Director - Van Nest Polglase; Special Effects - Vernon L. Walker

CAST:

Betty Russell: Ann Sothern

Dick Mathews: Burgess Meredith

Mrs. Russell: Mary Boland

Dr. Becker: . Onslow Stevens

Potter Russell: William Brisbane

Janet Russell: Louise Henry

Hank: Roger Imhof

Billy Rapp: Sumner Getchell

Yacht Captain: George Irving

Martha: Leona Roberts

Eddie: Adrian Morris

STORY: Ann is the younger sister of to soon-to-be-wed Louise Henry. Burgess Meredith, her fiancé now wealthy, arrives on the scene unexpectedly. Ann is secretly in love with him and, knowing her sister is really in love with Onslow Stevens, goes all out to win him for herself. Her family is broke and wants his money, whichever daughter he marries. A compromising situation with Ann has him choosing her, but, discovering that the family only wants his money, he does not go through with a wedding. Feigning amnesia, he ends up in a clinic where Ann convinces him she's not a gold digger – and so they get hitched.

NOTES: Ann was reunited with Mary Boland once again, and was glad to work with Onslow Stevens again too. Burgess Meredith would many years later work with her in *Golden Needles* and *The Manitou*. The background music consists of "Let's Make a Wish" and other themes from *Walking on Air*. Roger Pryor approved of Meredith as one of Ann's escorts during his absence in Chicago. Originally cast in Meredith's role was John Boles, who quit over a billing dispute.

REVIEWS: *Film Daily* - "Ann Sothern enters fully into the spirit of the script as a pretty young thing with limited intelligence and a flighty conscience." *The Motion Picture Herald* - " This was very good. All enjoyed it and heard many good remarks about it."

SHE'S GOT EVERYTHING, 1938 (RKO)
Running time - 72 minutes
Producer: Albert Lewis; Director: Joseph Santley; Screenplay: Joseph Hoffman and Monroe Shaff, based on a story by Harry Segall and Maxwell Shane; Photography: Jack McKenzie; Editor: Frederic Knudson; Song by Leon and Otis Rene: "It's Sleepy Time in Hawaii."

CAST:

Fuller Partridge: Gene Raymond	Corrio: Sally Ward
Carol Rogers: Ann Sothern	Justice of Peace: Alec Craig
Aunt Jane: Helen Broderick	Reporter: Fred Santley
Waldo Eddington: Victor Moore	Dr. Bricker: Richard Tucker
Nick: Parkyakarkus	Doctor: George Irving
Chaffee: Billy Gilbert	Ransome: Jack Carson
Roger: William Brisbane	Hotel Manager: Paul Guilfoyle
Courtland: Alan Bruce	Cab Driver: Hill
Watkins: Herbert Clifton	Van Driver: Pat Flaherty

STORY: Former rich gal Ann, now penniless, is loaded with debts. Pursued by creditors, she becomes a secretary in a coffee company owned by Gene Raymond. They fall in love and become engaged, but he breaks it off when he discovers she is broke and has so many creditors. Victor Moore, one of the creditors, convinces Raymond that Ann loves him and that she is not just after his money. Their wedding, involving a lot of traffic chaos, finally takes place on a coffee truck.

NOTES: Following the completion of this movie, Ann resigned from her RKO contract and misleading press items, which appeared saying she was dropped, were retracted. This was the last teaming of Ann with Gene Raymond, although 25 years later they would be in the cast of *The Best Man*. Like Ann, Gene took time off from films and composed some songs. He made a movie, *Stolen Heaven,* at Paramount in 1938, but it was not until *Cross Country Romance* (1940) that he resumed his film career, back at RKO. It was not well received nor was his work in *Mr. & Mrs. Smith* (1941), but this was an improvement. His wife, Jeanette MacDonald, whom he'd wed in June 1937, got him the second lead in *Smilin' Through* at MGM. After this, he joined the air force and excelled as a pilot during World War II.

REVIEWS: *Film Daily* - "The fans who enjoy the highly decorative Miss Sothern and the blonde Mr. Raymond…will be pleased with this new RKO pix…Miss Sothern sings one song pleasingly." *Motion Picture Herald* - "Of all the Sothern-Raymond vehicles…it's the best to date. There's one pleasing song that deserves special mention, 'It's Sleepy Time in Hawaii.'" Dorothy Manners later reported, "If Gene Raymond and Ann Sothern had been better personal friends they might still be co-starring in the amusing romances they made at RKO. Raymond's wife and her film partner Nelson Eddy were also reported to be a feuding twosome with 'dividing the best songs and close-ups' as two reasons."

TRADE WINDS, 1938 (United Artists)
Running time - 93 minutes
Producer: Walter Wanger; Director: Tay Garnett; Screenplay: Dorothy Parker, Alan Campbell and Frank R. Adams, based on a story by Tay Garnett; Photography: Rudolph Mate; Editors: Dorothy Spencer, Otho Lovering and Walt Reynolds; Costumes: Irene and Helen Taylor; Foreign Exterior Photography: James B. Shackelford; Musical Director: Alfred Newman; Art Directors: Alexander Toluboff and Alexander Golitzen

CAST:

Sam Wye: Fredric March	Peggy: Patricia Farr
Kay Kerrigan: Joan Bennett	Ruth: Phyllis Barry
Ben Blodgett: Ralph Bellamy	Judy: Wilma Francis
Jean Livingstone: Ann Sothern	Clara: Dorothy Tree
Thomas Bruhm II: Sidney Blackmer	Grace: Kay Linaker
Chief of Detectives: Thomas Mitchell	Ann: Dorothy Comingore
Faulkner: Robert Elliott	Bob: Walter Byron
John Johnson: Richard Tucker	Martin, the Butler: Wilson Benge
Mrs. Johnson: Joyce Compton	Captain: Harry Paine

STORY: Ann plays private eye Fredric March's secretary. March is engaged to find Joan Bennett, an innocent suspect in a murder case. This search takes him halfway around the world. Also on Bennett's trail is dumb cop Ralph Bellamy, and eventually Ann is on the trail too as she wants the $100,000 reward. March and Bennett fall in love, but he turns her over to the police. Thought to be a heel, he redeems himself by hosting a party to which he invites all the suspects, and reveals the real murderer. Bennett and March are reconciled while Bellamy and Ann also become a romantic team.

NOTES: The film reunited Ann with Ralph Bellamy, her romantic interest in *Eight Bells*. They would team romantically for a third time in *Brother Orchid*. Her decision to hold out for an "A" film had her say, "After five years of being in so many 'B' pictures, I thought they'd begin to swarm." After an intimate kissing scene with Bellamy, Ann introduced him to her husband, Roger Pryor. Wiping off Ann's lipstick, he said to Roger, "If there was a window around here, I'd probably jump."

MAISIE, 1939 (MGM)
Running time - 72 minutes
Producer: J. Walter Ruben; Director: Edwin L. Marin; Screenplay: Mary C. McCall, Jr., based on the novel *Dark Dame* by Wilson Collison; Photographer: Leonard Smith; Editor: Frederick Y. Smith; Art Directors: Cedric Gibbons and Malcolm Brown; Costumes: Dolly Tree; Set Design: Edwin B. Willis; Musical Score: Edward Ward; Sound Recording: Douglas Shearer

CAST:

Maisie Ravier: Ann Sothern	Prosecutor: Minor Watson
Slim Martin: Robert Young	Deputy: Harlan Briggs
Sybil Ames: Ruth Hussey	Judge: Paul Everton
Clifford Ames: Ian Hunter	Wilcox: Joseph Crehan
Shorty: Cliff Edwards	Ernie: Frank Puglia
Richard Raymond: Anthony Allan	Lee: Willie Rung
(John Hubbard)	Court Clerk: Emmett Vogan
"Red": Art Mix	Sheriff's Wife: Mary Foy
Rico: George Tobias	Drunk: C. L. Sherwood
Roger Bannerman: Richard Carle	and Robert Middlemass

STORY: Ann is adventurous showgirl Maisie who, down on her uppers, seeks a job on a ranch managed by woman-hating Robert Young. He refuses to employ her but the ranch's owner, Ian Hunter, hires her as a maid for his wife Ruth Hussey. Hunter grows very fond of Ann, so much so that Young mistakes their friendship for love. Meanwhile, Ruth has been secretly meeting her lover, John Hubbard, and Maisie discovers her infidelity. Trying to reunite the husband and his errant wife leads to her leaving the ranch. Reading later that Young is being tried for Hunter's murder, she returns to clear him. Hunter, having found out about his wife's betrayal, had committed suicide, but before doing so made a will leaving the ranch to Maisie. She and Young are set for a happy ending.

REVIEWS: *The New York Times* - "Sothern, hitherto a reasonably restrained actress, throws left hooks, gags and fits of temperament with surprising abandon." *Silver*

Screen - "Ann Sothern as Maisie gives a performance you'll never forget. She's that good." *Screenland* - "Sothern does a grand job of sincere emoting in her 'big scene' – and in fact all through the film she gives adequate evidence that she possesses all the necessary equipment to step right into a big-star spot any time now." *Los Angeles Examiner* - "... that Miss Sothern is a wow ... all in all it's a swell performance that should open a new career for her."

HOTEL FOR WOMEN, 1939 (20th Century-Fox)
Running time - 83 minutes
Producer: Darryl F. Zanuck; Director: Gregory Ratoff; Associate Producer: Raymond Griffith; Screenplay: Kathryn Scola & Darrell Ware, based on a story by Elsa Maxwell and Kathryn Scola; Editor: Louis Loeffler; Photography: Peverell Marley; Art Direction: Richard Day and Joseph C. Wright; Musical Director: David Buttolph; Songs: Elsa Maxwell; Sound: Arthur Van Kirbach and Roger Heman; Costumes: Gwen Wakeling; Set Decorations: Thomas Little

CAST:

Marcia Bromley: Linda Darnell	Galdos: Ivan Lebedoff
Jeff Buchanan: James Ellison	Miss Collins: Helen Ericson
Eileen Connolly: Ann Sothern	Miss Wilson: Dorothy Dearing
Nancy Prescott: Jean Rogers	Receptionists: Amanda Duff
Barbara Hunter: Lynn Bari	and Ruth Terry
Joan Mitchell: June Gale	Photographers: Arthur Rankin
Emeline Thomas: Joyce Compton	and Barnett Parker
Herself (Mrs. Tilford): Elsa Maxwell	Woman: Virginia Brissac
John Craig: John Halliday	Van Ellis: Russell Hicks
Melinda Craig: Katherine Aldridge	Man: Edward Earle
Stephen Gates: Alan Dinehart	Elevator Boy: Russell Lee
McNeil: Sydney Blackmer	Model: Kay Griffith
Ben Ritchie: Chick Chandler	Taxi Driver: Allen Wood
Fernando Manfredi: Gregory Gaye	Jane: Kay Linaker
Albert: Charles Wilson	Irene: Helen Brown
Butch: Herbert Ashley	Extra: Bess Flowers

STORY: Wise and witty model Ann helps newcomer Linda Darnell pursue a successful career. She also gets her to double-date with wealthy businessmen. Linda's former boyfriend, James Ellison, is dating his boss's daughter while Linda is pursued by his boss, John Halliday. This irks Halliday's former lover, Lynn Bari, another model living at the same hotel as Linda. Lynn truly loves the lecherous Halliday and, in a struggle, shoots him. He recovers but Linda, now reconciled with Ellison, decides to marry and quit their turbulent lifestyle.

REVIEWS: *Los Angeles Evening Herald Express* - "Lynn Bari is excellent as the frantic jealous girl while Ann Sothern packs a wallop with her portrayal as the wise girl who knows her way around. *Hotel for Women* owes a lot of its smartness and pace to the performance of Miss Sothern."

FAST AND FURIOUS, 1939 (MGM)
Running time - 73 minutes
Producer: Frederick Stephani; Director: Busby Berkeley; Screenplay: Harry Kurnitz; Photography: Ray June; Editor: Elmo Veron; Recording Director: Douglas Shearer; Art Director: Cedric Gibbons; Associate: David B. Cathcart; Set Decoration: Edwin B. Willis; Music Score: C. Bakaleinikoff and D. Amfitheatrof

CAST:

Joel Sloane: Franchot Tone	Jenny Lawrence: Mary Beth Hughes
Gerda Sloane: Ann Sothern	Sam Travers: Cliff Clark
Lily Cole: Ruth Hussey	Clancy: James Burke
Mike Stevens: Lee Bowman	Captain Joe Bunke: Frank Orth
Ted Bentley: Allyn Joslyn	Emmy Lou: Margaret Roach
Eric Bartell: John Miljan	Miss Brooklyn: Gladys Blake
Ed Connors: Bernard Nedell	Chief Miller: Granville Bates

STORY: Franchot Tone and Ann play antique book dealers who are also amateur detectives. A friend, Lee Bowman, asks Tone to be a judge in a beauty pageant. When John Miljan is murdered, Bowman is arrested and Ann and Tone try to solve the crime. Mary Beth Hughes is the next victim and Ann and Tone narrowly escape death also. Lion tamer Frank Orth leaves a couple of big cats in their hotel suite and this far fetched sequence is played to the hilt by Tone. Ann has her moments too, one of the best having her swim underwater and bite Tone on the leg when he is cavorting with the beauty queens. They eventfully solve the murders.

NOTES: This marked the second time Ann worked with Busby Berkeley and the fact that she was one of his chorus girls in his *Footlight Parade* did not worry her at all. She also caught up with Bert Roach, who was in her earlier Warner Bros. film *Hold Everything* and she made a point of him being photographed with her. *Fast and Furious* was the third and final film in the trilogy of mysteries with rare bookshop owners, Joel and Gerda Sloane. Melvyn Douglas and Florence Rice had the roles first in *Fast Company* (1938) and they were succeeded by Robert Montgomery and Rosalind Russell in *Fast and Loose* (1939).

REVIEWS: *Motion Picture Herald* - Franchot Tone at his best and that gal Ann Sothern is a wow."

JOE AND ETHEL TURP CALL ON THE PRESIDENT, 1939 (MGM)
Running time - 70 minutes
Producer: Edgar Selwyn; Director: Robert B. Sinclair; Screenplay: Melville Baker, based on the story *A Call on the President* by Damon Runyon; Photography: Leonard

Smith; Editor: Gene Ruggiero; Make-up: Jack Dawn; Recording Director: Douglas Shearer; Associate: Gabriel Scogna Millo; Musical Score: Edward Ward & David Snell; Set Decorator: Edwin B. Willis

CAST:

Ethel Turp: Ann Sothern	Pat Donegan: Robert Emmett
The President: Lewis Stone	O'Connor
Jim: Walter Brennan	Garage Owner: Cliff Clark
Joe Turp: William Gargan	Mr. Graves: Russell Hicks
Kitty Crusper: Marsha Hunt	Senator: Paul Everton
Johnny Crusper: Tom Neal	Cabinet Member: Charles
Henry Crusper: James Bush	Trowbridge
Fred: Don Costello	Dr. Standish: Louis Jean Heydt
Francine La Vaughn: Muriel Hutchinson	Mrs. Standish: Ann Teeman
Parker: Jack Norton	Mrs. O'Leary: Mary Gordon
Mike O'Brien: Aldrich Bowker	Young Johnny: Lon McCallister
Bishop Bannon: Frederick Burton	Neighbor: Verna Felton
Father Reicher: Al Shean	

STORY: Ann and William Gargan have the title roles of the Turps, a Flatbush couple who go to Washington to see the President, Lewis Stone. Their reason for the journey is to have Walter Brennan, a postman dismissed for destroying a letter, reinstated. Brennan's reason for not delivering the letter is that it contains bad news for his ailing former sweetheart, Marsha Hunt. Her missing son, Tom Neal, has become a criminal and Brennan has always been protective of her. Hearing the reason, the President reinstates Brennan and the Turps return home, mission accomplished.

REVIEWS: *Motion Picture Herald* - "They love this girl Sothern. She's perfect in these 'Maisie' type roles.

CONGO MAISIE, 1940 (MGM)
Running time - 70 minutes
Producer: J. Walter Ruben; Director: Henry C. Potter; Screenplay: Mary C. McCall, Jr., based on the book *Congo Landing* by Wilson Collison; Photography: Charles Lawton; Editor: Frederick Y. Smith; Art Director: Cedric Gibbons; Associate: Gabriel Scognamillo; Music: Edward Ward; Wardrobe: Dolly Tree; Technical Adviser: Ralph F. Donaldson; Recording Director: Douglas Shearer

CAST:

Maisie Ravier: Ann Sothern	Horace Snell: E. E. Clive
Dr. Michael Shane: John Carroll	Jallah: Everett Brown
Kay McWade: Rita Johnson	Nelson: Tom Fadden
Dr. John McWade: Sheppard Strudwick	British Consul: Lionel Pape
Captain Finch: J. M. Kerrigan	Luemba: Nathan Curry

Farley: Leonard Mudie   Varnai: Ernest Whitman
Zia: Martin Wilkins

STORY: Maisie (Ann) is stranded in a West African settlement. Stowing away on a steamer, she ends up with an ex-doctor, John Carroll, at a rubber plantation in the interior. The hospital there is headed by Sheppard Strudwick, whose wife Rita Johnson is tempted to have an affair with Carroll. Ann prevents this from happening and when Strudwick is accidentally shot, Carroll and she save his life. After Ann saves the group from an attack by hostile natives, Carroll switches his attentions to her.

NOTES: This was John Carroll's first film at MGM. It was a remake of *Red Dust* (1932), with Ann in the Jean Harlow role and Carroll and Rita Johnson substituting for Clark Gable and Mary Astor. MGM would remake it again as *Mogambo* (1953), with Gable reprising his original role, this time in authentic African locations. Ava Gardner had the Harlow/Sothern role, while Grace Kelly filled in for Mary Astor and Rita Johnson.

REVIEWS: *L.A. Evening Herald Express* - "Little Ann Sothern, always in there pitching, comes through in fine fashion." *Film Daily* - "… and will make many more fans for Ann Sothern. She is nigh perfect in the role…"

BROTHER ORCHID, 1940 (Warner Bros.)
Running time - 91 minutes
Producers: Hal Wallis & Mark Hellinger; Director: Lloyd Bacon; Screenplay: Earl Baldwin, based on *Collier's* magazine article by Richard Connell; Photography: Tony Gaudio; Editor: William Holmes; Music: Heinz Roemheld; Art Direction: Max Parker; Costumes: Howard Shoup; Special Effects: Byron Haskin

CAST:
Little John Sarto: Edward G. Robinson
Flo Addams: Ann Sothern
Jack Buck: Humphrey Bogart
Brother Superior: Donald Crisp
Clarence Fletcher: Ralph Bellamy
Willie, the Knife: Allen Jenkins
Brother Wren: Charles D. Brown
Brother Goodwin: Cecil Kellaway
Philadelphia Powell: Morgan Conway
Mugsy O'Day: Richard Lane
Red Martin: Paul Guilfoyle
Texas Pearson: John Ridgely
Brother McEwen: Joseph Crehan

Brother MacDonald: Wilfred Lucas
Curley Matthews: Tom Tyler
Buffalo Burns: Dick Wessell
Pattonsville Superintendent: Granville Bates
French Frank: Paul Phillips
Al Muller: Don Rowan
Turkey Malone: Tim Ryan
Fifi: Nanette Valon
Handsome Harry: Joe Caites
Dopey Perkins: Pat Gleason
Joseph: Tommy Baker

STORY: Edward G. Robinson is King of the Rackets; Ann is his girl. He quits the rackets to seek culture in Europe only to lose money which necessitates his wanting to resume his former career once more. Humphrey Bogart is now the King, and not about to be deposed. When Robinson tries to muscle back in, Bogart has him shot. Ann, believing him dead, finds wealthy country hick Ralph Bellamy willing to marry her. Robinson, however, is rescued by a group of Brothers who work tirelessly for the poor. After his recuperation, he is put in charge of the flower gardens, earning the name of Brother Orchid. When the Brothers try to sell their flowers, they find that Bogart has taken over the markets. Robinson, with the aid of Ann, and Bellamy with a group of his rancher pals, disrupts the gang and Bogart is killed. Wishing Ann and Bellamy luck with their wedding, Robinson returns to the monastery and his life with the Brothers.

DULCY, 1940 (MGM)
Running time - 73 minutes
Producer: Edwin Selwyn; Director: S. Sylvan Simon; Screenplay: Albert Mannheimer, Jerome Chodorov and Joseph A. Fields, based on a story by George S. Kaufman and Marc Connelly; Photography: Charles Lawton; Editor: Frank E. Hull; Music: Bronislau Kaper; Gowns by Adrian; Art Direction: Cedric Gibbons; Associate: Howard Campbell; Hairstyles for Miss Sothern by Sydney Guilaroff; Recording Director: Douglas Shearer; Set Decorations: Edwin B. Willis

CAST:

Dulcy Ward: Ann Sothern	Bill Ward: Dan Dailey
Gordon Daly: Ian Hunter	Homer Patterson: Jonathan Hale
Roger Forbes: Roland Young	"Sneezy": Donald Hule
Eleanor Forbes: Billie Burke	Henry: Guinn "Big Boy" Williams
Schuyler Van Dyke: Reginald Gardiner	Vincent Leech: Hans Conried
Angela Forbes: Lynne Carver	and Mary Treen

STORY: Scatterbrained Dulcy (Ann), falls for inventor Ian Hunter. Hoping to sell his patent, Dulcy suggests her brother Dan Dailey's future father-in-law, Roland Young, would be the ideal purchaser. Young, his wife Billie Burke and daughter Lynne Carver, are all invited to spend the weekend in a mountain cabin, with speedboat and lake to create chaos. Eccentric Reginald Gardiner, who is also visiting, spots Hunter's invention and wants to purchase it himself, but Young manages to outbid his competitor and secures the patent for himself. Ann and Hunter get set for a happy ending.

REVIEWS: *Film Daily* - "Spirited comedy with fine cast…Ann Sothern's characterization of Dulcy will find favor with any audience."

GOLD RUSH MAISIE, 1940 (MGM)
Running time - 84 minutes
Producer: J. Walter Ruben; Director: Edwin L. Marin; Screenplay: Betty Reinhardt

and Mary McCall, Jr., based on a story by Wilson Collison; Photography: Charles Lawton; Editor: Frederick Y. Smith; Musical Score: David Snell; Wardrobe by Dolly Tree; Set Decorations: Edwin B. Willis; Art Director: Cedric Gibbons; Associate: Gabriel Scognamillo; Recording Director: Douglas Shearer

CAST:

Maisie Ravier: Ann Sothern	Matt Sullivan: Wallace Reid, Jr.
Bill Anders: Lee Bowman	Graybeard: Clem Bevans
Jubie Davis: Virginia Weidler	Drunk: John Sheehan
Sarah Davis: Mary Nash	Greek Café Owner: Charles Judels
Bert Davis: John F. Hamilton	Mrs. Gilpin: Virginia Sale
Fred Gubbine: Slim Summerville	Ben Hartley: Eldy Waller
Harold Davis: Scotty Beckett	Mrs. Sullivan: Kathryn Sheldon
Harry Gilpin: Irving Bacon	Harris: Frank Orth
Elmo Beecher: Louis Mason	Davis Baby: Baby Quintanillo
Ned Sullivan: Victor Kilian, Jr.	

STORY: Ann's Maisie has car trouble and asking for help from wealthy woman-hating Lee Bowman is almost fruitless. Befriending Virginia Weidler, she gets to meet her poor family, headed by stoic mother Mary Nash. They are prospecting for gold along with many other former farmers, all of whom are practically destitute. When the gold they mine proves to be worthless, all of the families start to move out for fresh destinations. Ann finally gets the hard-hearted Bowman to soften up and allow the families to stay. They will work his land as farmers and he will accept them as friends. There is no romantic finale in this episode as Maisie drives off at its conclusion.

REVIEWS: *Film Daily* - "Miss Sothern does all that could be expected of her… carrying off one drunk scene with hilarious results." *L.A. Daily News* - "Miss Sothern, as usual does a bang-up job as the wisecracking heart of gold chorine."

MAISIE WAS A LADY, 1941 (MGM)
Running Time - 76 minutes
Producer: J. Walter Ruben; Director: Edward L. Marin; Screenplay by Betty Reinhardt and Mary C. McCall, Jr., based on a story by Reinhardt and Myles Connolly from a character created by Wilson Collison; Photography: Charles Lawton; Editor: Frederick Y. Smith; Wardrobe: Dolly Tree; Art Director: Cedric Gibbons; Associate: Stan Rogers; Set Decorations: Edwin B. Willis; Musical Score: David Snell; Recording Director: Douglas Shearer

CAST:

Maisie Ravier: Ann Sothern	Link Phillips: Edward Ashley
Bob Rawlston: Lew Ayres	Diana Webley: Joan Perry
Abigail Rawlston: Maureen O'Sullivan	"Cap" Rawlston: Paul Cavanagh
Walpole: C. Aubrey Smith	Judge: William Wright

Cop: Edgar Dearing
Doctor: Charles D. Brown
Barker: Joe Yule

Guest: Hans Conried
Guest: Hillary Brooke
Bearded Lady: Jody Gilbert

STORY: Maisie is working in a carnival when drunken playboy Lew Ayres causes her to lose her job. A judge makes Ayres responsible for her employment and she ends up being the maid under the stern guidance of head butler C. Aubrey Smith. Ann resolves all the family's problems by leading Ayres to the path of sobriety and protecting his sister, Maureen O'Sullivan. She is engaged to a two-timing fortune hunter, Edward Ashley, until his former lover, Joan Perry, arrives and Maureen learns the truth. Attempting suicide because of loneliness, Maureen is rescued by Ann who also brings home the siblings' errant father. At the film's conclusion it looks like wedding bells for Ann and Lew.

NOTES: Maureen O'Sullivan and Ann became good friends during this shoot and years later Tisha would be a close friend of Maureen's daughter, Mia Farrow.

REVIEWS: *L.A. Evening Herald Express* - "Miss Sothern makes a better impression than ever in this role. She gives it glamour and heart quality." *Hollywood Citizen News* - "Its principal asset is Miss Sothern herself, whose Maisie is all the more provocatively sexy for the fact that she is so incredibly pure."

RINGSIDE MAISIE, 1941 (MGM)

Running time - 96 minutes
Producer: J. Walter Ruben; Director: Edward L. Ruben; Screenplay: Mary C. McCall, Jr., based on a character created by Wilson Collison; Photography: Charles Lawton; Editor: Frederick Y. Smith; Music: David Snell; Set Decorations: Edwin B. Willis; Costumes: Robert Kalloch; Art Director: Cedric Gibbons; Assistant: Stan Rogers; Recording Director: Douglas Shearer

CAST:

Maisie Ravier: Ann Sothern
Skeets Maguire: George Murphy
Terry Dugan: Robert Sterling
Cecilia Reardon: Natalie Thompson
Chotsie: Maxie Rosenbloom
Mrs. Dolan: Margaret Moffat
Peaches: John Indrisano
Specialty: Virginia O'Brien
Jacky-boy Duffy: Eddie Simms

Rick du Prez: Jack LaRue
Taylor: Purnell Pratt
Day Nurse: Mary McAvoy
Checker: Tom Dugan
Dr. Kramer: Jonathan Hale
Jitterbug: Roy Lester
Conductor: Oscar O'Shea
Vic: Rags Ragland
Landlady: Almira Sessions

STORY: Ann, again Maisie, loses two jobs before wandering into a training camp for boxer Robert Sterling and his woman-hating manager, George Murphy. She meets Sterling's mother, Margaret Moffat, and his ever-eating, selfish fiancee Natalie

Thompson. Learning he wants to quit boxing, she tries to intervene for him with Murphy, earning his enmity by so doing. Going through with a fight, Sterling is blinded and his fiancee deserts him. Ann and Murphy have fallen in love but split when he insists on Sterling continuing in the fight game. They reconcile when Murphy pays for an operation which restores Sterling's sight.

NOTES: When Ann was shown photographs of jitterbug dancers, she selected Roy Lester to be her partner. Calling him on the phone out of the blue, the boy thought he was being ribbed when Ann asked him if he would like to dance with her in the movie. They rehearsed with Lester throwing her over his shoulder and around his neck. Ann thought the lad terrific and so did producer Ruben, until the second day when he threw her too far and knocked her out. Finally coming to, she saw all those anxious, scared executive faces. Quick with a quip she said, "Why can't I do Noel Coward drawing room comedies?"

REVIEWS: *L.A. Evening Herald Express* - "Ann Sothern in another well-rounded series of adventures in which the stout-hearted gal overcomes the bad breaks and softens up a few more hard-boiled fronts."

LADY BE GOOD, 1941 (MGM)
Running Time - 110 minutes
Producer: Arthur Freed; Director: Norman Z. McLeod; Screenplay: Jack McGowan, Kay Van Riper & John McClain; Original Story by McGowan; Photography: George Folsey and Oliver T. Marsh; Editor: Frederick Y. Smith; Choreography: Busby Berkeley; Musical Director: George Stoll; Songs: Naciio Herb Brown, Roger Edens, Arthur Freed, George and Ira Gershwin, Oscar Hammerstein II and Jerome Kern; Costumes: Adrian; Sets: Edwin B. Willis; Art Director: Cedric Gibbons; Associate: John S. Detlie; Recording Director: Douglas Shearer

CAST:

Marilyn Marsh: Eleanor Powell	Bill Pattison: Dan Dailey
Dixie Donegan: Ann Sothern	Max Milton: Reginald Owen
Eddie Crane: Robert Young	Mrs. Wardley: Rose Hobart
Judge Murdoch: Lionel Barrymore	Announcer: Phil Silvers
Buddy Crawford: John Carroll	Policeman: Edward Gargan
Red Willet: Red Skelton	Singer: Connie Russell
Lull: Virginia O'Brien	Themselves: The Berry Brothers
Mr. Blanton: Tom Conway	

STORY: Songwriters Ann and Robert Young marry and divorce when success goes to his head. Rose Hobart is the society woman out to get him while John Carroll is enamored of Eleanor Powell, who plays Ann's best friend. By making Young jealous over a supposed interest in Carroll herself, she brings him down to earth and they remarry. Judge Lionel Barrymore refuses to grant a second divorce when the couple parts again. Young is unaware that they are still married and Ann, knowing they work together best when he thinks they're divorced, won't tell him otherwise.

NOTES: Also involved in the scriptwriting were the uncredited Arnold Auerbach, Robert McGunigle, Vincente Minnelli, Ralph Spence and Herman Wouk. After viewing the rushes, Louis B. Mayer announced that Ann and Kathryn Grayson would star in the Jerome Kern musical *Very Warm for May*. This was not filmed until two years later, as *Broadway Rhythm,* with Ginny Simms and Gloria DeHaven playing the roles announced for Ann and Kathryn. Ann did mention that "All The Things You Are" and "The Song is You" were two songs Kern wanted to hear her sing.
REVIEWS: Ann's singing of "The Last Time I Saw Paris" got its share of praise: *Hollywood Citizen News* - "Miss Sothern's singing of 'The Last Time I Saw Paris' had preview audiences weeping." *Los Angeles Evening Herald Express* - "Miss Sothern sings the nostalgic Kern number with unusual feeling." *Los Angeles Examiner* - "There's Ann Sothern, looking very smart in her Adrian finery... singing 'The Last Time I Saw Paris' as it has seldom been sung before." *Liberty* - "... her singing of 'The Last Time I Saw Paris'...is a gem." *Photoplay* - "... delightful, especially Ann Sothern's singing of 'The Last Time I Saw Paris.' *Time* - "Her singing of 'The Last Time I Saw Paris' is a model of how to put across that over-bleated dirge and her version of 'Lady Be Good' should please even a Prime Minister."

MAISIE GETS HER MAN, 1942 (MGM)
Running time - 85 minutes
Producer: .J. Walter Ruben; Director: Roy Del Ruth; Screenplay: Betty Reinhardt and Mary C. McCall, Jr., based on a story by Reinhardt and Ethel Hill, from a character created by Wilson Collison; Photography: Harry Stradling; Editor: Frederick Y. Smith; Music: Lennie Hayton; Choreographer: Danny Dare; Song: Roger Edens and Lennie Hayton; Art Director: Cedric Gibbons; Associate: William Ferrari; Gowns by Kalloch; Set Decorations: Edwin B. Willis; Recording Director: Douglas Shearer

CAST:

Maisie Ravier: Ann Sothern	Jasper: Walter Catlett
Hap Hixby: Red Skelton	Cecil: Leo Gorcey
Pappy Goodring: Allen Jenkins	Percy Podd: Ben Weldon
Mr. Stickwell: Donald Meek	Ears Cofflin: Rags Ragland
Mr. Denningham: Lloyd Corrigan	Mrs. Taylor: Florence Shirley
Professor Orco: Fritz Feld	Elsie: Pamela Blake

and Frank Jenks, Willie Best, Esther Dale, William Tannen, Inez Cooper, Kay Medford and Karin Booth

STORY: Ann, as Maisie, is the stooge in a knife-throwing act with Fritz Feld. Quitting her job, she then works for Red Skelton, who is the innocent front man for con artist Lloyd Corrigan. Red is engaged to Pamela Blake, but she runs out on him when he is arrested and jailed. Ann tracks down Corrigan and is able to have him arrested and

Skelton released. Time passes and Ann is entertaining at a USO show, where Skelton is in the audience. He accepts the invitation to join her in a reprise of her song and dance, indicating there could be a future for the pair.

NOTES: With a much more glamorous wardrobe to display, Ann was surrounded by some of Hollywood's finest character actors in this "Maisie" adventure. Rags Ragland, Frank Jenks and Allen Jenkins were special favorites of hers and she welcomed the chance to work with Walter Catlett, Donald Meek and Fritz Feld. This would be the last of the "Maisie" series to be produced by J. Walter Ruben, who died on September 5, 1942. Very much aware how much his faith in her had advanced her career, Ann was deeply saddened by his passing. Although they were never close friends, Ann commiserated with Virginia Bruce, Ruben's wife and mother of his son.

REVIEWS: *The Motion Picture Herald* roasted the movie, and in particular Red Skelton: "This is the weakest picture of the series. Miss Sothern clicked as usual. Perhaps the children enjoyed the part assigned to Skelton as they cannot tell the difference when a performer is cast as a moron instead of a comedian. This star is not a favorite with my audience anyway. Just a fair picture."

PANAMA HATTIE, 1942 (MGM)
Running time - 79 minutes
Producer: Arthur Freed; Directors: Norman Z. McLeod and (uncredited) Roy Del Ruth; Screenplay; Jack McGowan and Wilkie Mahoney, based on the Broadway musical by Cole Porter, Herbert Fields and Buddy DeSylva; Musical Adaptation: Roger Edens; Photography: George Folsey; Editor: Blanche Sewell; Musical Director: George Stoll; Dance Director: Danny Dare; Costumes: Kalloch; Art Director: Cedric Gibbons; Hairstyles: Sydney Guilaroff; Songs by Cole Porter, Roger Edens, Walter Donaldson, Burton Lane, E. Y. Harburg, Phil Moore, Alex Hyde, Jeni Le Gon, Theodore F. Morse and Sir Arthur Sullivan; Sets: Edwin B. Willis & Hugh Hunt; Musical numbers staged by Vincente Minnelli; Recording Director: Douglas Shearer

CAST:

Red: Red Skelton	Lucas Kefler: Carl Esmond
Hattie Maloney: Ann Sothern	Geraldine Bulliett: Jackie Horner
Rags: Rags Ragland	Admiral Tree: Pierre Watkin
Rowdy: Ben Blue	Colonel Briggs: Stanley Andrews
Leila Tree: Marsha Hunt	Waiter: Joe Yule
Dick Bulliett: Dan Dailey	Shore Patrol: Grant Withers
Flo Foster: Virginia O'Brien	Specialties: The Berry Brothers
Jay Jeakins: Alan Mowbray	and Lena Horne

STORY: Ann and Dan Dailey fall in love but she, an overdressed entertainer, doesn't feel his social equal. Meeting his daughter, Jackie Horner, really discourages her as does a meeting with the Admiral's niece, Marsha Hunt. Ann's three sailor pals, Red

Skelton, Rags Ragland and Ben Blue, help to restore her confidence and they trap some Nazi spies led by Carl Esmond in the process. In a rousing finale - Ann, Dan, Marsha and the whole cast sing the stirring "The Son of a Gun Who Picks on Uncle Sam."

NOTES: Ann liked working with Rags Ragland and of the ex-burlesque comic she said, "He is one of the most gentlemanly persons I have worked in pictures with." The "I'll Do Anything for You" number, which was cut from the final print, had a night shooting. Ann waited off camera covering her flimsy evening gown with a fur coat, for it was quite chilly. Called to perform the song, she dropped the fur, got on the set and said, "I'm cold." Director Norman McLeod said, "It's supposed to be a hot night in Panama so Ann is bundled back into her fur and given a steaming hot cup of coffee. Tossing the coat to the assistant director she plays the scene and sings the song with the trio of Red, Rags and Ben Blue." According to columnist Sidney Skolsky, "Ann drank more coffee that night than Damon Runyon." Along with the uncredited second director, Roy Del Ruth, the names of Vincente Minnelli, Lillian Messinger, Mary C. McCall, Jr., Fred Finklehoff and Joseph Schrank would not appear in acknowledgment of their contributions to the screenplay. Ann sang "I've Got My Health" and "Let's Be Buddies."

REVIEWS: *Motion Picture Herald* - "Ann Sothern is pretty and convincing." *Hollywood Citizen News* - "It is a hit, for example when Miss Sothern sings 'I've Got My Health' but it is a miss whenever she tries to deal with the story situation."

THREE HEARTS FOR JULIA, 1943 (MGM)
Running Time - 89 minutes
Producer: John W. Considine, Jr.; Director: Richard Thorpe; Story/Screenplay: Lionel Houser; Photography: George Folsey; Editor: Irvine Warburton; Costumes: Irene; Music: Herbert Stothart; Art Director: Cedric Gibbons & Howard Campbell; Set Decorations: Edwin B. Willis; Associate: Helen Conway; Recording Director: Douglas Shearer

CAST:

Julia Seabrook: Ann Sothern	Clara: Ann Richards
Jeff Seabrook: Melvyn Douglas	Miss Stickney: Elvia Allman
David Torrance: Lee Bowman	Mattie: Mariette Canty
Anton Ottoway: Felix Bressart	Gateman: Frank Faylen
John Gerard: Reginald Owen	Cabbie: Joe Yule
Phillip Barrows: Richard Ainley	Jones: Russell Gleason
May Elton: Marta Linden	Colonel Martin: Russell Hicks
Thelma: Kay Medford	Program Seller: James Warren
Kay: Jaqueline White	

and Marie Windsor, Eve Whitney, Mary Field, Mary Benoit

STORY: Ann is the neglected wife of war correspondent Melvyn Douglas, who is constantly abroad on assignments. Becoming first violinist in a symphony orchestra, she is sought after by both Lee Bowman and Richard Ainley. Unable to decide which one she should choose, she asks her now returned husband who should become her husband when their divorce is final. Still in love with her himself, Douglas sabotages the plans of his rivals and regains the affections of his wife. The final sequence with Ann and the orchestra playing "I'll Be Working on the Railroad" gives the frothy comedy a meaty and topical conclusion.

THOUSANDS CHEER, 1943 (MGM)

Technicolor; Running Time - 126 minutes

Producer: Joe Pasternak; Director: George Sidney; Screenplay: Paul Jarrico and Richard Collins, based on their story, *Private Miss Jones*; Photographer: George Folsey; Editor: George Boemler; Music: Herbert Stothart; Art Directors: Cedric Gibbons and Daniel B Cathcart; Set: Edwin B Willis and Jacques Mesereau; Costumes: Irene; Songs: Earl Brent, Roger Edens, Lew Brown, George R. Brown, Nacio Herb Brown, Ralph Freed, Arthur Freed, Ralph Blane, Hugh Martin, Ferde Grofe, Leo Friedman, Walter Jurmann, Zequinnha Abreu, Fats Waller, Sam M Lewis, Harold Adamson, E. Y. Harburg, Burton Lane, E.H. Meacham, Andy Razaf, Harold Rome, Walter Ruick, Dimitri Shostakovich, Herbert Stothart, Beth S. Whitson, Guiseppe Verdi, Mabel Wayne, Paul Francis Webster and Joe Young; Technicolor Director: Natalie Kalmus; Associate: Henri Jaffa; Make-up: Jack Dawn; Recording Director: Douglas Shearer

CAST:

Kathryn Jones: Kathryn Grayson	Captain Avery: Dick Simmons
Eddy Marsh: Gene Kelly	Jack: Wally Cassell
Hillary Jones: Mary Astor	Chuck Polansky: Ben Blue
Colonel W Jones: John Boles	Sergeant Koslack: Frank Jenks
Mama Corbino: Odette Myrtil	Silent Monk: Ben Lessy
Marie Corbino: Frances Rafferty	Ringmaster: Ray Teal
Sisi Corbino: Mary Elliott	Alex: Pierre Watkin
Papa Corbino: Will Kaufman	Sgt.carrington Major: James Millican
Uncle Algy: Sig Arno	Prison Sergeant: William Tannen
Cab Driver: Connie Gilchrist	

and Frank Morgan, John Conte, Sara Haden, Don Loper, Maxine Barratt, Paul Speer, Marta Linden, Benny Carter & His Orchestra, Eve Whitney, Natalie Draper, Myron Healey, James Warren and Don Taylor

GUEST STARS: June Allyson, Lucille Ball, Lionel Barrymore, Bob Crosby & His Orchestra, Gloria DeHaven, Judy Garland, Lena Horne, Marsha Hunt, Kay Kyser & His Orchestra with Georgia Carroll, Marilyn Maxwell, Margaret O'Brien, Virginia O'Brien, Eleanor Powell, Donna Reed, Mickey Rooney, Red Skelton, Ann Sothern and Introducing Jose Itburbi.

STORY: Ann, Lucille Ball and Marsha Hunt play recruits for the WAVES in a skit with Frank Morgan as a barber pretending to be a doctor. This comedy item was part of a show with MGM's guest star roster involved in an army concert organized by

Kathryn Grayson. The slight plot had Kathryn reuniting her estranged parents and falling in love with soldier Gene Kelly, an ex-circus performer.

SWING SHIFT MAISIE, 1943 (MGM)
Running Time - 87 minutes
Producer: George Haight; Director: Norman Z. McLeod; Screenplay: Mary C. McCall, Jr. and Robert Halff, based on the character created by Wilson Collison; Photography: Harry Stradling; Editor: Elmo Veron; Art Director: Cedric Gibbons; Associate: Howard Campbell; Musical Score: Lennie Hayton; Costume Supervision: Irene; Set Decorations: Edwin B. Willis; Associate: Glen Barner; Recording Engineer: Douglas Shearer

CAST:

Maisie Ravier: Ann Sothern	Billie: Pamela Blake
Breezy McLaughlin: James Craig	Lead Woman: Rose Hobart
Iris Reid: Jean Rogers	Grace: Jaqueline White
Ma Lustvogel: Connie Gilchrist	Ruth: Betty Jaynes
Horation Curley: John Qualen	Ann: Kay Medford
Judd Evans: Fred Brady	Louise: Karin (Katherine) Booth
Emmy Lou Grogan: Marta Linden	Clerk: John Hodiak
Joe Peterson: Donald Curtis	Flyer: William Bishop
Helen Johnson: Celia Travers	Doctor: Jack Mulhall
Judge: Pierre Watkin	Detective: James Davis
Myrtle Lee: Lillian Yarbo	Messenger: Frances Rafferty
Schmitt Brothers: Wiere Brothers	

STORY: Ann plays Maisie, now working in an aircraft defense plant. Unable to find a birth certificate, which is needed to acquire work in this high-security factory, she has a co-worker friend, John Qualen, vouch for her. Saving Jean Rogers from a suicide attempt, she is miffed when Jean wins the affections of test pilot James Craig, whom Ann loves. Jean is only using Craig, but, when a better offer falls through, she agrees to marry him. Ann confronts Jean with the truth and tries to stop their wedding, but Jean retaliates, using the knowledge of Ann's lack of a birth certificate as evidence that she is a saboteur. A hectic car chase follows after Ann is released from internment and the wedding is stopped. Grateful to Ann, when the truth about Jean is made known to him, Craig's gratitude turns to love.

NOTES: This was the first "Maisie" adventure not produced by J. Walter Ruben. Ann remembered, "Jack Ruben asked me to do *Maisie*. Not until after *Maisie* had been previewed, and even Leo the Lion lay down and made with bleats like a lamb, did Jack tell me by what a hairline margin Maisie and I had missed getting together. 'If you had ever known,' he said, 'what I had to do to get you for the part!' They wanted to use one of their contract players for Maisie and did not want an outsider to do it. 'I fought tooth and nail to get you, fought tooth and nail not to have anyone but you do it. Finally in desperation they let you have it. But my neck was out to there,' he said with a reflex shudder. I will always be grateful for the faith Jack showed in me. Apparently he thought of me as the right candidate for Maisie, when he saw me in *Folies Bergere* with Maurice Chevalier." Ann was elated to have a small pooch called Butch to work with in this film. The dog rehearsed well, but as shooting commenced, he suddenly reached up and gave Ann one of his best dog kisses. Turning to the animal's trainer, director Norman Z. McLeod said, "I thought we had a dog, not a wolf." Ann and some other female cast members, including Betty Jaynes and Jean Rogers, sang "The Girl Behind the Boy Behind the Gun."

CRY HAVOC, 1943 (MGM)

Running time - 96 minutes
Producer: Edwin Knoph; Director: Richard Thorpe; Screenplay: Paul Osborne, based on the play *Cry Havoc* by Allen R. Kenward, later produced on Broadway as *Proof Through the Night;* Photography: Karl Freund; Editor: Ralph E. Winters; Music: Daniele Amfitheatrof; Costumes: Irene; Art Directors: Cedric Gibbons and Stephen Goosson; Make Up: Jack Dawn; Recording Director: Douglas Shearer; Set Decoration: Edwin B. Willis and Glen Barner.

CAST:
Lieutenant Mary Smith (Smitty): Margaret Sullavan

Pat Conlon: Ann Sothern	Andra West: Heather Angel
Grace Lambert: Joan Blondell	Sue West: Dorothy Morris
Captain Alice Marsh: Fay Bainter	Sadie: Connie Gilchrist
Flo Norris: Marsha Hunt	Steve Polden: Gloria Grafton
Constance Booth: Ella Raines	Luisita: Fely Franquelli
Helen Domerat: Frances Gifford	Dying Soldier: Robert Mitchum
Nydia Joyce: Diana Lewis	

STORY: Ann played an ex-waitress, one of nine volunteers who are recruited by Margaret Sullavan for nursing duty in war-torn Manila. Margaret and Ann are at loggerheads right from the start as the latter objects to taking orders. Adding fuel to the fire are Ann's constant visits to a male officer, who is also close to Margaret. Marsha Hunt played the friend of all the girls and, when the man in question is killed, she tells Ann that Margaret has malignant malaria. Marsha also reveals that she refused treatment in order to stay close to the officer, as they were secretly married. The Japanese invade their area and order all the women to leave their dug-out. Ann has told Margaret that her infatuation with Margaret's husband was not returned. "He never gave me a tumble," she says. The last scene has the two women gallantly vacating their shelter together, moving on to a fate unknown.

NOTES: The original Hollywood stage version had the audience in hysteria at the final curtain with the predominately female attendance in tears. Richard Thorpe blamed the play's Broadway failure on its being presented in too large a theatre; the Hollywood debut season had an intimacy and involvement. With its single setting in a large fox hole, it made the audience feel the claustrophobia that the actors were experiencing. On Broadway this was lost as there was too much distance between the play and its viewers. Ann told reporter Ruth Waterbury about young Dorothy Morris, "She's such a good actress." Ruth, in return, said of Ann, "She doesn't know the meaning of the word jealousy. She's really one mighty swell gal."

MAISIE GOES TO RENO, 1944 (MGM)

Running time - 90 minutes
Producer: George Haight; Director: Harry Beaumont; Screenplay: Mary C. McCall, Jr., based on a story by Harry Ruby and James O'Hanlon, from a character created by Wilson Collison; Photography: Robert Planck; Editor: Frank E. Hull; Music: David Snell; Song by Sammy Fain and Ralph Freed; Art Directors: Cedric Gibbons and Howard Campbell; Set: Edwin B Willis and Helen Conway

CAST:

Maisie Ravier: Ann Sothern
Flip Hennahan: John Hodiak
Bill Fullerton: Tom Drake
Winifred Ashbourne: Marta Linden
Roger Pelham: Paul Cavanagh
Gloria Fullerton: Ava Gardner
J. E. Clave: Bernard Nedell
Jerry: Roland Dupree
Tommy Cutter: Chick Chandler

Parsons: Donald Meek
Elaine: Bunny Waters
Dr. Cummings: Byron Foulger
Lead Man: William Tannen
Dr. Fleeson: James Warren
M. C. : Douglas Morrow
Clerk: Edward Earle
Boy: Leon Tyler

and Noreen Nash, Lynn Arlen, Karin Booth, Elizabeth Dailey, Ethel Tobin

STORY: Ann is back in the defense plant, but collapses and is ordered by the doctor to take a rest. The aftermath of her breakdown is a twitch which causes her to involuntarily wink. Chick Chandler invites her to sing with his band in Reno. Serviceman Tom Drake is being divorced by heiress Ava Gardner, who is living in Reno. Meeting Ann at the bus station, he entrusts her with a letter for Ava, hoping it will stop the divorce proceedings. Delivering the letter, Ava's secretary Marta Linden accepts it, pretending to be Ava. Marta and Paul Cavanagh, along with Bernard Nedell, are criminals intent on collecting Ava's money one way or another. Ann's winking has endeared her to bellboy Roland Dupree and dealer John Hodiak. With their assistance, Ann eventually stops the divorce, exposes the crooks and their scheme and reunites Ava and Tom. There is also a clinch at the finale between Ann and Hodiak, to consolidate the happy ending.

NOTES: Ann sang "Panhandle Pete."

UP GOES MAISIE, 1946 (MGM)

Running time - 89 minutes
Producer: George Haight; Director: Harry Beaumont; Screenplay: Thelma Robinson,

based on the character created by Wilson Collison; Photography; Robert Pianck; Editor: Irvine Warburton; Special Effects: A. Arnold Gillespie; Music: David Snell; Art Directors: Cedric Gibbons and Richard Duce; Costumes: Irene; Recording Director: Douglas Shearer

CAST:

Maisie Ravier: Ann Sothern	Miss Wolfe: Gloria Grafton
Joseph Morton: George Murphy	Benson: John Eldredge
Barbara Nuboult: Hillary Brooke	1st Cop: Lee Phelps
Kim Kingby: Stephen (Horace) McNally	2nd Cop: Glenn Strange
Mr. Henderickson: Ray Collins	Businessman: Jim Davis
Elmer Saunders: Jeff York	Cleaner in Window: Connie
J. G. Nuboult: Paul Harvey	Gilchrist
Mitch: Murray Alper	Barbara's Friends: Barbara
Bill Stuart: Lewis Howard	Billingsley, Karin Booth
Jonathan Marby: Jack Davis	

STORY: Ann, as Maisie, lands a job as secretary to George Murphy, inventor of a helicopter. George's girlfriend, Hillary Brooke, is two-timing him with his friend and co-inventor Stephen McNally. Unknown to George a second copter has been secretly built by McNally, who, in cahoots with Hillary and her father, is out to undermine Murphy's credibility and his invention. McNally sets fire to the building housing Murphy's copter. Ann discovers the second machine and flies it successfully to Pasadena's Rose Bowl, where George and an industrialist, who will finance more copters, are waiting.

NOTES: Ann got to demonstrate her unique comic style in a sequence where Hillary Brooke hands teetotaler Ann a drugged drink to embarrass her publicly; Ann ends up diving into a swimming pool fully clothed. Ann, in her final sequence with Hillary, takes her revenge by dousing her thoroughly in a trough.

UNDERCOVER MAISIE, 1947 (MGM)
Running time - 90 minutes
Producer: George Haight; Director: Harry Beaumont; Screenplay: Thelma Robinson, based on a character created by Wilson Collison; Photography: Charles Salernod; Editor: Ben Lewis; Set Decorations: Edwin B. Willis; Music: David Snell; Art Directors: Cedric Gibbons and Gabriel Scognamillo; Make-up: Jack Dawn; Recording Director: Douglas Shearer

CAST:

Maisie Ravier: Ann Sothern	Gilfred I. Rogers: Dick Simmons
Lieutenant Paul Scott: Barry Nelson	Mrs. Guy Canford: Gloria Holden
Chip Dolan: Mark Daniels	Captain Mead: Charles D. Brown
Amor Willis Farnes: Leon Ames	Daniels: Douglas Fowley
Guy Canford: Clinton Sundberg	Georgia Lorrison: Nella Walker

Viola Trengnam: Gene Roberts   Parker: Morris Ankrum
Isabelle: Celia Travers   and Minverva Urecal, Meg Randall

STORY: After being ripped off by phoney society con-woman Nella Walker, Maisie (Ann) reports the theft to the police. Police lieutenant Barry Nelson persuades her to join the police force as an undercover agent. Undergoing the rigorous training involved, she graduates, winning the admiration of both Nelson and Mark Daniels. Her first assignment is to get the goods on a phoney mystic, Leon Ames, who is in partnership with Clinton Sundberg and Gloria Holden. When Ann discovers their racket, they kidnap her. Nelson and the police arrive in the nick of time to save our heroine. Daniels and Nelson are still rivals for her affection, but it is Nelson who wins Ann in the final film of the series.

APRIL SHOWERS, 1948 (Warner Bros)
Running time - 93 minutes
Producer: William Jacobs; Director: James V. Kern; Screenplay: Peter Milne, based on the story *Barbary Coast* by Joe Laurie, Jr.; Music Arranged & Adapted by Ray Heindorf; Musical numbers created and staged by LeRoy Prinz; Photography: Carl Guthrie; Editor: Thomas Reilly; Sound: Stanley Jones; Songs by Walter Donaldson, Ted Fetter, Kim Gannon, Ray Heindorf, Gus Kahn, Walter Kent, Dave Radford, Jack Scholl, Louis Silvers, Buddy DeSylva and Richard Whiting; Art Director: Hugh Reticker; Montages by James Leicester; Wardrobe: Travilla; Make-up: Perc Westmore; Musical Director: Leo F. Forbstein; Special Effects: William McGann, Director, and Wesley Anderson

CAST:
Joe Tyme: Jack Carson   Mr. Barnes: Joseph Crehan
June Tyme: Ann Sothern   Mr. Barclay: Ray Walker
Buster Tyme: Robert Ellis   Mr. Swift: Phillip Van Zandt
Billy Shay: Robert Alda   Mr. Gordon: John Gallaudet
Mr. Curly: S. Z. Sakall   Vanderhouten: Billy Curtis
Al Wilson: Richard Rober   New York Secretary: Barbara Bates

STORY: Ann and Jack Carson are a married couple with a dying vaudeville act called The Happy Tymes. Almost broke, their act becomes successful when their young son, Robert Ellis, joins it. Because of his age, the Gerry Society forbids him to remain in the act and Carson turns to alcohol. Missing a performance, he is fired and Robert Alda steps in to take his place. With romantic designs on Ann, Alda is rebuffed and later takes it out on young Ellis by hitting him. Learning of this, Carson comes to his senses, sobers up and knocks Alda out. The show ends happily with Carson back in the act and The Three Happy Tymes look set for more success.

NOTES: Seeing this film on television in London, Ann proclaimed, "Sometimes I'll watch an old movie on television and once in a while one of mine – such as *April Showers* - will come on and I'll watch it. And you know something? I'm always amazed at what a lousy actress I was." Later, she told Frank Forster of *The Enquirer*, "I guess in the old days we just got by on glamour. Hollywood sold its stars on good looks and personality build ups. We weren't really actresses in the true sense. We were just big names – the product of a good publicity department."

WORDS AND MUSIC, 1948 (MGM)
Technicolor; Running time - 119 minutes
Producer: Arthur Freed; Director: Norman Taurog; Screenplay by Fred Finklehoff, from a story by Guy Bolton & Jean Holloway; Adaptation by Ben Feiner, Jr.; Orchestration: Conrad Salinger; Vocal Arrangements: Robert Tucker; Photographer: Charles Rosher and Harry Stradling; Musical Director: Lennie Hayton; Costumes: Helen Rose & Valles; Songs by Richard Rodgers & Lorenz Hart; Special Effects: Warren Newcombe; Editors: Albert Akst & Ferris Webster; Set: Edwin B Willis & Richard A. Pefferle; Make Up: Jack Dawn; Art Directors: Cedric Gibbons and Jack Martin Smith; Musical Numbers staged and directed by Robert Alton; Technicolor Color Director: Natalie Kalmus; Associate: James Gooch; Recording Director: Douglas Shearer; Hairstyles: Sydney Guilaroff

CAST:

Richard Rodgers: Tom Drake
Lorenz Hart: Mickey Rooney
Eddie Anders: Perry Como
Herbert Fields: Marshall Thompson
Dorothy Rodgers: Janet Leigh
Joyce Harmon: Ann Sothern
Peggy McNeill: Betty Garrett
Margo Grant: Cyd Charisse

Mrs. Hart: Jeanette Nolan
Ben Feiner Jr.: Richard Quine
Shoe Clerk: Clinton Sundberg
Dr. Rodgers: Harry Antrim
Mr. Feiner: Emory Parnell
Mrs. Feiner: Helen Spring
Thomas Fernby Kelly: Edward Earle

Guest Stars: June Allyson, the Blackburn Twins, Judy Garland, Lena Horne, Gene Kelly, Allyn Ann McLerie, Mel Torme, Dee Turnell and Vera-Ellen

STORY: In this highly fictionalized biographical film, loosely based on the lives of composer Richard Rodgers and lyricist Lorenz Hart, Ann plays a Broadway musical comedy star. Tom Drake, as Rodgers, develops a crush on Ann, his leading lady, who gently points that she is 34 and he is 24. He then suffers a similar fate with Janet Leigh, who turns his offer of a date down as she doesn't go out with "older men." Mickey Rooney plays Lorenz (Larry) Hart, whose continual worry and obsession about his lack of physical stature become paranoid eccentricity. Falling for singer Betty Garrett, her rejection has him descend into the world of alcoholism. Drake, in the meantime, has married Leigh and during the run of *A Connecticut Yankee*, Rooney collapses. Gene Kelly, as himself, closes the film with an address telling of the lyricist's death, which leads into Perry Como's rendering of "With a Song in My Heart" for an emotional conclusion.

THE JUDGE STEPS OUT, 1949 (RKO)

Running time - 91 minutes

Producer: Michel Kraike; Director: Boris Ingster; Assistant Director: Harry D'Arcy; Screenplay: Alexander Knox and Boris Ingster, based on a story by Ingster; Photography: Robert De Grasse; Editor: Les Millbrook; Music Director: Constanin Bakaleinikoff; Music: Leigh Harling; Art Directors: Albert S. D'Agostine and Field Gray; Executive Producer: Sid Rogell; Special Effects: Russell A. Cully; Make Up: Gordon Bau; Set Decorations: Darrell Silvera & Jack Hills; Gowns: Edward Stevenson

CAST:

Judge Thomas Bailey: Alexander Knox	Catherine Bailey: Martha Hyer
Peggy: Ann Sothern	John Struthers III: James Warren
Evelyn Bailey: Freida Inescourt	Mrs. Winthrop: Myrna Dell
Mike: George Tobias	Dr. Boyd: Whitford Kane
Nan: Sharyn Moffett	Judge Davis: Harry Hayden
Chita: Florence Bates	Martha: Anita Bolster
Hector Brown: Ian Wolfe	Birthday Guest: Ellen Corby
Chief Justice Haynes: H. B. Warner	Bridge Player: Mary Forbes

STORY: Alexander Knox is a Boston judge with a mid-life crisis. His socially ambitious wife wants him to accept a position he doesn't want and his daughter, about to be wed, overspends his income. A shock illness causes him to leave home without explanation. Freida Inescourt, his wife, believes him dead, but he has become a vagabond, firstly selling books and then ending up as a cook in a California diner. Ann plays the diner's owner who, because she is single, cannot adopt a little girl she has grown to love. Eventually, Ann and Knox fall in love and he decides to return to Boston to obtain a divorce to enable him to marry Ann. Discovering he is now a grandfather and that his wife really loves him causes him to have second thoughts. A custody case he makes a decision on results in a law being revised. This law also provides for single women, like Ann, to adopt children. Ann journeys to Boston to see him and, in a touching sequence similar to the famed *Brief Encounter*, realizes his place is with his family. She takes the train back to California and he is last seen on the steps of his family home.

NOTES: Held up for two years before its American release and given a new title, *The Judge Steps Out*, it was filmed in 1947 as *Indian Summer*. Under this name it was released in both Great Britain and Australia in 1947. RKO recalled Ann and Alexander Knox to shoot new publicity stills for the film; photos of a blonder Ann, with fringed hairstyle, sexily posed in a hammock or in an intimate pose with Knox, were featured in all the advertisements.

A LETTER TO THREE WIVES, 1949 (20th Century-Fox)

Running time - 103 minutes

Producer: Sol C. Siegel; Director: Joseph L. Mankiewicz; Screenplay: Joseph L Mankiewicz and Vera Caspary, based on the novel *A Letter to Five Wives* by John

Klempner; Photography: Arthur Miller; Editor: J. Watson Webb; Music: Alfred New-man; Costumes: Kay Nelson; Make-up: Ben Nye; Art Directors: Lyle Wheeler and J. Russell Spencer; Special Effects: Fred Sersen; Set: Thomas Little and Walter M. Scott

CAST:

Deborah Bishop: Jeanne Crain
Lora May Finney (Hollingsway):
    Linda Darnell
Rita Phipps: Ann Sothern
George Phipps: Kirk Douglas
Porter Hollingsway: Paul Douglas
Babe Finney: Barbara Lawrence
Brad Bishop: Jeffrey Lynn
Mrs Finney: Connie Gilchrist

Mrs Manleigh: Florence Bates
Mr Manleigh: Hobart Cavanagh
Sadie: Thelma Ritter
Kathleen: Patti Brady
Miss Hawkins: Ruth Vivian
Elderly Man: Stuart Holmes
Nick: George Offerman, Jr.
The voice of Addie Ross: Celeste Holm

STORY: Ann plays a soap opera writer who earns more than her husband, Kirk Doug-las, an English professor. They quarrel before she departs on a charity picnic with two other housewives, Linda Darnell and Jeanne Crain. A letter arrives from their "friend" Addie Ross, in which she apologizes for not making the picnic and claims to have left town with one of their husbands. Each wife then reflects on her marriage and the reasons there might be an estrangement. Crain met her husband, Jeffrey Lynn, while he was in the service and her small-town background and lack of style makes her feel his social inferior. Linda Darnell is a gold digger, who trapped her wealthy employer, Paul Douglas, into marriage. She genuinely falls in love with him, but is unable to express her feelings. Kirk Douglas upsets his wife's employers, Flor-ence Bates and Hobart Cavanagh, by criticizing the worth of the soap operas they produce. At a dance that night the only husband missing is Lynn and all assume that he is the one who has run off with Addie. Crain, visibly upset, is comforted by Paul Douglas, who tells all he was the one who Addie left with. Realizing he loved his wife, he returned home, and this revelation prompts Darnell to admit she loves him too.

SHADOW ON THE WALL, 1950 (MGM)
Running time - 84 minutes
Producer: Robert Sisk; Director: Patrick Jackson; Screenplay: William Ludwig, based on the story *Death in the Doll's House* by Hannah Lees & Lawrence F. Bachmann; Photography: Ray June; Editor: Irvine Warburton; Art Directors: Cedric Gibbons and Eddie Imazu

CAST:

Dell Faring: Ann Sothern
David Starrling: Zachary Scott
Susan Starrling: Gigi Perreau
Dr. Canford: Nancy Davis

Celia Starrling: Kristine Miller
Pike Ludwell: John McIntyre
Crane Weymouth: Tom Helmore
Miss Burke: Helen Brown

Olga: Barbara Billingsley
Secretary: Marcia Van Dyke

Bobby: Anthony Sydes
Boy: Jimmy Hunt

STORY: Ann plays the elder sister of Kristine Miller who is married to Zachary Scott. Discovering that Kristine has been having an affair with her fiancé, Ann breaks her engagement. Scott and Kristine quarrel over this and in the argument he is knocked unconscious. Awakening, he finds Kristine murdered and their daughter, Gigi Perreau, in a traumatic state of shock. Believing her to be a witness to the killing, Scott, who has been arrested for the crime, relies on psychiatrist Nancy Davis to unlock the child's mind. It is eventually revealed that Ann is the killer, but not before her foiled attempt to poison Gigi and to gain custody of the child. When Gigi is delivered to Ann's home, a bow in Ann's hair throws the same shadow on the wall which, when seen by the child, provides the key to her memory of the same shadow as that of the killer. Breaking down, Ann confesses and Scott is freed to care for his daughter.

NOTES: In response to a letter I wrote to Kristine Miller about this film she replied: "She (Ann) was well liked by everyone and I have pleasant memories of her and this, my only film made at MGM."

NANCY GOES TO RIO, 1950 (MGM)
Technicolor; Running time - 99 minutes
Producer: Joe Pasternak; Director: Robert Z. Leonard; Screenplay: Sidney Sheldon, based on a story by Jane Hall, Frederick Kohner and Ralph Block; Photography: Ray June; Editor: Adrienne Fazan; Musical Director: Georgie Stoll; Costumes: Helen Rose; Songs: Earl Brent, Nora Bayes, Jack Norworth, Fred Spielman, Ray Gilbert, Charles Pasquale, Maria Grever, Giacomo Puccini, and Georgie Stoll; Art Directors: Cedric Gibbons and Jack Martin Smith

CAST:
Frances Elliott: Ann Sothern
Nancy Barklay: Jane Powell
Paul Berton: Barry Sullivan
Marina Rodriguez: Carmen Miranda
Gregory Elliott: Louis Calhern
Scotty Sheldon: Scotty Beckett
Ricardo Domingos: Fortunio Bonanova
Arthur Barrett: Glenn Anders
Mrs. Harrison: Nella Walker
Alfredo: Hans Conried

Drunk: Frank Fontaine
Professor Gama: Leon Belasco
Ivan Putroff: Leonid Kinsky
Duettist Singer: Danny Scholl
Captain of Waiters: Sig Arno
Doctor Ballard: Ransom Sherman
Kenneth: Pierre Watkin
Party Guest: Bess Flowers
Party Guest: Forbes Murray
Dancer in Finale: Geary Steffen

STORY: Ann is the actress mother of Jane Powell. Offered a role in a musical written by Fortunio Bonanova, she leaves for Rio with her father, Louis Calhern, to study the role. Meanwhile, a trial-run of the show is successful in summer stock with Powell in Ann's role. Not privy to the fact that her mother is learning the same part, she also goes to Rio. On board ship she meets Barry Sullivan, who, hearing her rehearse lines from the play, mistakenly believes her to be pregnant. News of this "baby" reaches Ann's ears and she arranges to meet Sullivan, believing he is the prospective father of her daughter's child. Sullivan, a longtime admirer of Ann's work in the theatre, falls in love with her and she with him. The complications are finally sorted out satisfactorily with Jane taking the role in the play and Ann winning Sullivan, with whom Jane had previously been smitten.

NOTES: Ann sang "Time and Time Again," with Danny Scholl, "Magic is the Moonlight," with Jane Powell, and "Shine on Harvest Moon," with Jane Powell & Louis Calhern. Powell's then-husband Geary Steffen appeared in the film's closing song sequence, "Love is Like This," sung by his wife.

THE BLUE GARDENIA, 1953 (Warner Bros)
Running time - 90 minutes
Producer: Alex Gottlieb; Director: Fritz Lang; Screenplay: Charles Hoffman, based on the short story *Gardenia* by Vera Caspary; Photography: Nicholas Musuraca; Editor: Edward Mann; Song by Bob Russell & Lester Lee; Arrangement: Nelson Riddle; Music: Raoul Kraushaar; Art Director: Daniel Hall; Make-up: Gene Hibbs and James Parker; Women's Costumes: Maria Donovan; Sound: Ben Winkler

CAST:

Norah Larkin: Anne Baxter	Rose: Ruth Storey
Casey Mayo: Richard Conte	Homer: Ray Walker
Crystal Carpenter: Ann Sothern	Exchange Supervisor: Fay Baker
Harry Prebble: Raymond Burr	Flower Seller: Celia Lovsky
Sally Ellis: Jeff Donnell	Cleaner: Almira Sessions
Al: Richard Erdman	Himself: Nat King Cole
Captain Haynes: George Reeves	

STORY: Ann, Jeff & Anne are roommates who work on a telephone exchange. Wolf Raymond Burr obtains Ann's phone number with a view to arranging a date. However, she goes on a date with her ex-husband, Ray Walker. When Burr rings, Anne Baxter takes the call and, despondent over a broken engagement, accepts his invitation. Getting her drunk, the would-be seducer is knocked out as Anne passes out. Awakening, she finds him dead. Reporter Richard Conte writes open letters to the killer in his column and Ann and Anne meet with him. After Anne is arrested by the police, Conte seeks out the real killer, who turns out to be Ruth Storey, who is pregnant with Burr's child. She has killed him in desperation. Attempting suicide, she makes a confession.

NOTES: This film marked the first meeting and working relationship between Ann and make-up artist Gene Hibbs. An expert at beautifying older actresses, he would be hired by Ann for her TV series.

LADY IN A CAGE, 1964 (Paramount)
Running time - 94 minutes
Producer: Luther Davis; Director: Walter Grauman; Screenplay: Luther Davis; Photographer: Lee Garmes; Editor: Leon Barsha; Music: Paul Glass; Art Director: Hal Pereira; Set: Joseph Kish; Special Effects: Paul K. Lerpac; Make-up: Wally Westmore & Gene Hibbs; Production Design: Rudolph Sternad

CAST:

Mrs. Hilyard: Olivia de Havilland
Sade: Ann Sothern
Randall: James Caan
Essie: Rafael Campos
George Brady (Wino): Jeff Corey

Elaine: Jennifer Billingsley
Malcolm Hilyard: William Swan
Mr. Paull: Charles Seel
Paull's Assistant: Scatman Crothers

STORY: Sade (Ann) is a prostitute on skid row. When wino Jeff Corey shows her property stolen from the home of Olivia de Havilland, she joins him in a plan to rob the place. Olivia is trapped in an elevator and helpless as she watches them plunder her home. The two thieves had been observed by three less-than-pillars of society at the pawnshop of Mr. Paull and followed to the scene of the crime. These three, led by James Caan, are totally immoral, vicious dropouts, who murder Corey and terrify Ann before locking her in a closet. When Caan climbs up to the elevator, in an attempt to murder Olivia, she blinds him by gouging his eyes with two metal pieces she's managed to pry from the elevator. Falling to the ground, she crawls to the busy street for help, with the blinded Caan in pursuit. Attempting to strangle her, he falls into incoming traffic instead, while his two partners in crime flee.

THE BEST MAN, 1964 (United Artists)
Running time - 102 minutes
Producers: Stuart Miller and Lawrence Turman; Director: Franklin Schaffner; Screenplay: Gore Vidal, based on his play; Photographer: Haskell Wexler; Music: Mort Lindsey; Art Director: Lyle R. Wheeler; Costumes: Dorothy Jeakins; Set Decorator: Richard Mansfield; Film Director: Robert E. Swink; Sound Mixer: Jack Solomon

CAST:

William Russell: Henry Fonda
Joe Cantwell: Cliff Robertson
Sheldon Bascomb: Shelley Berman
Art Hockstader: Lee Tracy
Mrs. Cantwell: Edie Adams
Mrs. Russell: Margaret Leighton
Mrs. Gamadge: Ann Sothern
Dick Jensen: Kevin McCarthy
Don Cantwell: Gene Raymond
Oscar Anderson: Richard Arlen

Mahalia Jackson: Mahalia Jackson
Mrs. Claypoole: Penny Singleton
Howard K. Smith: Howard K. Smith
T. T. Claypoole: John Henry Faulk
Tom: George Furth
Janet: Anne Newman
Mrs. Merwin: Mary Laurence
Speech Writer: George Kirgo
Mrs. Anderson: Natalie Masters
Senator Lazarus: H. E. West

Cleaning Lady: Blossom Rock (Marie Blake)   Bill Stout: Bill Stout
Zealot: Michael MacDonald   Chairman: Tyler McVey
Governor Merwin: William R. Eberson   Doctor: Sherwood Keith

STORY: Ann plays a manipulator of the women's vote in this political drama. Prime contenders in the race for president are Henry Fonda and Cliff Robertson. The latter is unscrupulous in his campaign, never hesitating in revealing that in the past Fonda had suffered a nervous breakdown. When Fonda is given information that Robertson had a homosexual relationship with Shelley Berman, his sense of ethics prevails and he chooses not to reveal his opponent's secret. Fonda resigns but gives his support to a third contender, ultimately defeating Robertson.

SYLVIA, 1965 (Paramount)

Running time - 115 minutes
Producer: Martin H. Poll; Director: Gordon Douglas; Screenplay: Sydney Boehm, based on the novel by E.V. Cunningham; Photographer: Joseph Ruttenberg; Editor: Frank Bracht; Costumes: Edith Head; Make-up: Wally Westmore; Music: David Raksin and Walter Scharf; Special Effects: Paul K. Lerpae; Art Direction: Hal Pereira and Roland Anderson; Set Decoration: Sam Corner and Arthur Krams; Title song sung by Paul Anka

CAST:

Sylvia Karoki West: Carroll Baker   Peter Hemel: Paul Wexler
Alan Macklin: George Maharis   Father Gonzales: Jay Novello
Jane Phillips: Joanne Dru   Molly Baxter: Connie Gilchrist
Frederick Summers: Peter Lawford   Gus: Alan Carney
Irma Olanski: Viveca Lindfors   Muscles: Anthony Caruso
Oscar Stewart: Edmond O'Brien   Mrs. Karoki: Shirley O'Hara
Jonas Karoki: Aldo Ray   Gavin Cullen: Gene Lyons
Grace Argona: Ann Sothern   Pudgey: Val Avery
Bruce Stanford III: Lloyd Bochner   Pancho: Manuel Padilla
Lola Diamond: Paul Gilbert   Anne: Majel Barrett
Big Shirley: Nancy Kovack   and Bob Random

STORY: Ann plays a former roommate of mystery woman Sylvia (Carroll Baker). Baker is engaged to marry wealthy Peter Lawford. He hires private investigator George Maharis to find out the past history of his fiancée. This leads him to Pittsburgh and librarian Viveca Lindfors, who reveals Sylvia was raped by her stepfather, Aldo Ray, at age 14. Edmond O'Brien is a married salesman whom she inveigled a lift from. Ann is a penny arcade cashier, who has only kind words to say about her. Joanne Dru, now a society woman and formerly a prostitute who worked with Sylvia, tells Maharis how Sylvia financed her hospitalization when she was injured. Finally, he learns a sadistic wealthy client Lloyd Bochner was blackmailed by Sylvia; investing this money she obtained from him, she became wealthy enough to change her identity and start a new life. Now in love with her, Maharis tells Lawford he cannot find anything about her past and leaves. Baker, in turn, has fallen for Maharis and she tells Lawford all about her past, departing to be with Maharis.

NOTES: Sheree North was listed in the first casting of *Sylvia*, but stage commitments precluded her from appearing in the film. Joanne Dru took over the role.

THE OUTSIDER, 1967 (Universal)

Technicolor; Running time - 120 minutes
Written & Produced by Roy Huggins; Director: Michael Ritchie; Musical Supervisor: Stanley Wilson; Assistant.Director: Henry Kune; Director Photography: Bud Thackeray; Editor: Richard Belding; Music: Pete Rugolo; Color Coordinator: Robert Brower; Costumes: Grady Hunt; Sound: Frank H. Wilkinson; Set Decorations: John McCarthy and Claude Carpenter; Hair Stylist: Larry Germain; Make-up: Bud Westmore

CAST:

David Ross: Darren McGavin	Lieutenant Wagner: Ossie Davis
Collin Kenniston III: Sean Garrison	Mrs. Bishop: Audrey Totter
Peggy Leydon: Shirley Knight	Sergeant Delgado: Marlo Alcaide
Honora Dundas: Nancy Malone	Carol Dorfman: Anna Hagan
Marvin Bishop: Edmond O'Brien	Della Pike: Madame Spivy
Mrs. Kossek: Ann Sothern	Officer Dutton: Kent McCord
Ernest Grimes: Joseph Wiseman	

STORY: Darren McGavin is a private eye hired by Edmond O'Brien to find out if his mistress, Anna Hagan, is seeing someone else. He discovers that she is and when he tells O'Brien of this he meets his alcoholic wife, Audrey Totter. The other man is Sean Garrison, who has invented a new name and life for himself. When Hagan is murdered, McGavin is suspected, but eventually clears himself. Ann plays Garrison's mother, who tries to protect her son's new identity and discovers his girlfriend, Shirley Knight, has led her son into a major crime. Knight, secretary to O'Brien, is the mastermind of a blackmail scheme which leads also to the deaths of Garrison and O'Brien. O'Brien's demise is brought about by the act of his now insane wife, Totter, who shoots him.

CHUBASCO, 1968 (Warner Bros./Seven Arts)

Technicolor; Panavision; Running time - 99 minutes
Executive Producer: William Conrad; Associate Producer: James Lydon; Director/Screenplay: Allen H. Miner; Assistant Director: Fred Gammon; Photographers: Louis Jennings and Paul Ivano; Editor: John W. Holmes; Music: William Lava; Art Direction: Howard Hollander; Set: William L. Kuehl; Costumes: William Smith; Song: Gordon Jenkins & William Conrad

CAST:

Sebastian Marinho: Richard Egan
Chubasco: Christopher Jones
Bunny Marinho: Susan Strasberg
Angela: Ann Sothern
Laurindo: Simon Oakland
Theresa Marinho: Audrey Totter
Nick: Preston Foster
Matt: Peter Whitney

Judge North: Edward Binns
Benito: Joe De Santis
Frenchy: Norman Alden
Les: Stuart Moss
Juno: Ron Rich
Police Sergeant: Milton Frome
Mary: Toni Gerry

STORY: Ann is the owner of a bar with a neighboring brothel. Christopher Jones, in the title role, and Susan Strasberg are sweethearts, forbidden to see each other by her father, Richard Egan. Egan has bailed her out of jail, blaming Jones for her incarceration. Edward Binns, a sympathetic judge, finds Jones a job on a tuna fishing boat bound for Central America. Befriended by the skipper, Joe De Santis, he is able to meet and marry his sweetheart there. At a celebration, De Santis dies of a heart attack and Sothern, whose establishment hosted the event, agrees to look after Strasberg, when Jones gets work on another vessel. This turns out to be owned by Egan and, after much friction and fighting, the two protagonists finally become friends. When the boat puts into port, Egan is happy to see the newlyweds reunited.

NOTES: With a lot of stock footage of tuna netting, which perhaps some considered superfluous, the film's running time varied from country to country. Originally 99 minutes, it was cut to 98 minutes in England and 86 minutes in Australia.

THE GREAT MAN'S WHISKERS, 1969 (Universal, NBC)

Technicolor; Running time - 120 minutes
Producer: Adrian Scott; Director: Philip Leacock; Teleplay by John Paxton, from the play by Adrian Scott; Music: Earl Robinson and E. Y. Harburg; Photographer; John F. Warren; Editor: John Elias; Art Director: George C. Webb

CAST:

James E. Cooper: Dean Jones
Aunt Margaret Bancroft: Ann Sothern
Hagan: John McIver
Abraham Lincoln: Dennis Weaver
Katherine Witherby: Beth Brickell
Ballad Singer: Harve Presnell
Elizabeth Cooper: Cindy Eilbacher

Joseph Somerby: Richard Erdman
Ella: Isabell Sanford
Major Underwood: John Hillerman
Miss Albright: Maudie Prickett
Philbrick: Charles Lane
Pearl: Nicole Meggerson
Paddleford: Woodrow Chambliss
Whately: Alvin Hammer

STORY: Aunt Margaret (Ann) generally disapproves of her nephew Dean Jones and his motherless daughter, Cindy Eilbacher. This ten-year-old girl writes a letter to president Abraham Lincoln with advice that he should grow "whiskers." Dennis

Weaver, as President Lincoln, does grow a beard and visits the town where Cindy lives in order to meet her. This honor leads to music teacher Jones winning the town's and his aunt's respect, plus the love of Beth Brickell. The cheery finale has Ann, Cindy and others dancing in a circle.

NOTES: Considered an oddity, it was not aired on television until 1973. Nevertheless, there is a lot of appeal and old-world charm in John Paxton's teleplay, and the direction of Philip Peacock captures the period with real affection. Its onscreen title was *The Grate Man's Whiskurs*.

CONGRATULATIONS, IT'S A BOY!, 1971 (ABC)
Color; Running time - 90 minutes
Producer: Aaron Spelling; Director: William A. Graham; Teleplay by Stanley Z. Cherry; Photographer: Arch R. Dalzell; Editor: Art Seid; Music: Basil Poledouris and Richard Baskin; Art Director: Paul Sylos

CAST:
Johnny Gaines: Bill Bixby
Edye: Diane Baker
Al Gaines: Jack Albertson
Ethel Gaines: Ann Sothern
Rose: Jeff Donnell
Herb: Tom Bosley
Rhonda: Karen Jensen
B.J.: Darrell Larson
Riva: Judy Strangis
Ben Beigleman: Robert H. Harris

STORY: Ann is the matchmaking mother of Bill Bixby, a thirtyish and very swinging bachelor. The arrival of seventeen-year-old Darrell Larson disrupts Bixby's life, for the boy claims to be his illegitimate son. Diane Baker plays the quiet daughter of Tom Bosley and Jeff Donnell, whom Ann and husband Jack Albertson would welcome as a daughter-in-law. Diane is also genuinely in love with Bixby and he develops overdue maturity when he discovers his "son" is a more responsible adult than himself.

NOTES: In production, its working title was *So's Your Old Man*. Edmond O'Brien was the original choice to play Ann's husband, but ill health had him replaced by Jack Albertson.

A DEATH OF INNOCENCE, 1971 (CBS)
Color; Running time - 90 minutes
Producer: Mark Carliner; Director: Paul Wendkos; Teleplay by Joseph Stephano, based on the novel by Zelda Popkin; Photographer: Ben Colman; Editor: Gene Fowler, Jr.; Music: Morton Stevens; Art Direction: .Joseph R. Jennings; Production

Designer: Joseph R. Jennings; Assistant Director: D. Jack Stubbs; Costumes: Stephen Lodge and Betsy Cox; Set Decorator: James G. Cane

CAST:

Elizabeth Cameron: Shelley Winters
Marvin Hirsh: Arthur Kennedy
Buffie Cameron: Tisha Sterling
Annie La Cossitt: Ann Sothern
Charles Cameron: John Randolph
Alexander Weisberg: Harold Gould
Cara Fellman: Antoinette Bower
Helen McCloud: Peggy McCay

Joe La Cossitt: Tony Young
Jimmy Rekko: Richard Bright
Medical Examiner: Don Keefer
Judge Morahan: Regis J. Cordic
Mary Fingerhut: Doreen Long
Miss Santiago: Pilar Sevrat
Klein: Barney Phillips

STORY: Tisha Sterling and Tony Young are on trial for murdering an elderly woman. Ann plays Young's doting mother, with Shelley Winters and John Randolph as Tisha's parents. As the trial proceeds we learn that the innocent-faced Tisha is the more motivated of the two defendants. Both are found guilty.

NOTES: At the last minute, Ann replaced Kim Stanley, when a foot injury put the magnificent Miss Stanley out of action. Ann was thrilled to finally work with Arthur Kennedy, an actor she had long admired. Also, the fine recognition Tisha received for her work gave Ann great satisfaction. With some New York City location work, it was primarily filmed at CBS Studio Center, Studio City, California.

THE WEEKEND NUN, 1972 (ABC - Paramount)
Color; Running time - 90 minutes
Producers: Edward K. Milkis and Thomas J. Miller; Director: Jeannot Szwarc; Teleplay: Ken Trevey, inspired by the life of Joyce Duco; Photographer: Ronald W. Browne; Music: Charles Fox; Editor - Rita Roland; Art Director: William L. Campbell; Music Supervisor: Kenyon Hopkins; Title Design: Phil Norman; Supervising Sound Editor: William Andrews; Women's Wardrobe: Agnes Henry

CAST:

Sister Mary/Marjorie: Joanna Pettet
Chuck Jardine: Vic Morrow
Mother Bonaventure: Ann Sothern
Audree Prewitt: Kay Lenz
Sid Richardson: James Gregory
Bobby Sue Prewitt: Beverly Garland
Rock Seiden: Michael Clark
Bernetta: Tina Andrews
Priest: Judson Pratt

Sister Gratia: Barbara Werle
Connie: Lynn Borden
Mrs. Crowe: Marion Ross
Arlen Crowe: Stephen Rogers
Administrator: Ann Summers
Attendant: Larry Watson
Policeman: Ron Nyman
Brian Escalante: Anthony Rodriguez

STORY: Mother Bonaventure (Ann) is a sympathetic advisor to Joanna Pettet, who plays the title role. Working as a juvenile probation officer weekdays, she is a nun at night, living in the convent. One of her cases involves Kay Lenz and her mother Beverly Garland. When a criminal element, involved with her day job, starts to invade the convent, she realizes she cannot sustain two separate professions.

NOTES: The original title for this ABC-Paramount telefilm was *Matter of the Heart*. Choosing her character's name provoked memories of Ann reading the script of *Thunder on the Hill* (1951), shortly after she became ill. Universal had thought of her for the role of Sister Bonaventure, which was eventually played by Claudette Colbert.

THE KILLING KIND, 1974 (Media Trend)
Color; Running time - 95 minutes
Executive Producer: Leon Mirell; Associate Producer: Sal Grasso; Producer: George Edwards; Director: Curtis Harrington; Screenplay: Lony Crechales and George Edwards, based on a story by Crechales; Photographer: Mario Losi; Asst. Director: Jack Robinette; Music: Andrew Belling; Editor: Bryon Crouch; Music Editor: Don Ernst; Costumes: Tom Rasmussen; Hair Stylist: Jinx Lambo

CAST:

Thelma Lambert: Ann Sothern	Tina: Sue Bernard
Terry Lambert: John Savage	Louise's Father: Peter Brucco
Rhea Benson: Ruth Roman	Mrs. Orland: Marjorie Eaton
Louise: Luana Anders	Flo: Helen Winston
Lori: Cindy Williams	

STORY: Ann is a slatternly boarding house proprietor and photographer, whose son, John Savage, has just returned home from prison. He was the only innocent participant in a group of guys who had gang raped Sue Bernard. A new lodger, Cindy Williams, comes on to Savage, as does spinster neighbor Luana Anders. Ann loves her son, but is overprotective of him. When one of her pet cats is killed and later her son's lawyer, Ruth Roman, is murdered, Ann begins to grow suspicious. Bernard is also killed and later Williams comes to a rather gruesome demise in her bathroom. Realizing her son is homicidal, she nevertheless helps him dispose of Williams' body. In an earlier scene he loses control and almost chokes Ann. Still loving him, but not wanting him back in prison, in a very poignant scene, she poisons him with a mug of his favorite hot chocolate. Photographing him at the end, she then cradles him in her arms as approaching police sirens are heard.

GOLDEN NEEDLES, 1974 (Sequoia)
Movie Lab Color; Running time - 93 minutes
Producers: Fred Weintraub and Paul Heller; Director: Robert Clouse; Screenplay: S. Lee Pogostin and Sylvia Schneble; Editor: Michael Kahn; Photographer: Gilbert Hobbs; Music: Lalo Schifrin; Unit Production Manager: Marty Hornstein; Assistant to the Producers: Jeffrey Schechtman

CAST:

Dan: Joe Don Baker
Felicity: Elizabeth Ashley
Jeff: Jim Kelly
Winters: Burgess Meredith
Finzie: Ann Sothern
Lia Toa: Roy Chiao

Su Lin: Frances Fong
Kwan: Tony Lee
Lotus: Alice Fong
Claude: Clarence Barnes
Winters' Man: Pat Johnson
Bobby: Edgar Justice

STORY: Ann is the owner of a seedy-looking Hong Kong gambling den and is a friend of Joe Don Baker. Baker has been hired by Elizabeth Ashley to help her find a statuette, "The Golden Needles of Ecstacy." An aging millionaire, Burgess Meredith, is her client and he wants the statuette to restore his failing libido. Legend has it that if an acupuncturist inserts the seven needles into a male, he will obtain unending sexual prowess. The statuette is stolen by Baker and thugs torture Ann, hoping she'll divulge Baker's whereabouts. Baker and Ashley fall in love and, following much action and many pursuits, the pair deliver the statuette to the Chinese Government, forfeiting the money they had been offered by others.

CRAZY MAMA, 1975 (New World)

Metro Color; Running time - 82 minutes
Producer: Julie Corman; Director: Jonathan Demme; Screenplay: Robert Thom, based on a story by Francis Doel; Photographer: Bruce Logan; Editors: Allan Holzman & Lewis Teague; Art Director: Peter Jamison; Sets: Linda Spheeris; Costumes: Jac McKnelly; Stunts: Alan Gibbs; Music Coordinator: Marshall Leib; Old tunes plus additional music by "Snotty Scotty and the Hankies."

CAST:

Melba Stokes: Cloris Leachman
Jim Bob: Stuart Whitman
Sheba Stokes: Ann Sothern
Cheryl: Linda Purl
Albertson: Jim Backus
Shawn: Donny Most
Snake: Bryan Englund

Bertha: Merle Earle
Ella Mae: Sally Kirkland
Daniel: Clint Kimbrough
Wilbur Janeway: Dick Miller
Sheba (1932): Tisha Sterling
Melba (1932): Dinah Englund
Homer: Vince Barnett

STORY: Tisha Sterling plays Ann's character in a brief prologue sequence set in Arkansas, circa 1932. Flashing forward to the late 1950s Ann is now the mother of beautician Cloris Leachman, who in turn is mum to Linda Purl, an unmarried pregnant teenager. Ousted from their California beauty parlor, the trio, plus Linda's boyfriend, embark for Arkansas. In the prologue, Ann's husband was killed when he refused to leave his property because of unpaid mortgage installments. The travelers intend to reclaim this property, believing it to be rightfully theirs. When they arrive in Arkansas, they find a country club has been built on "their" land. Adding insult to injury, it has been named after Ann's husband's killer. Cloris, Ann, Stuart Whitman,

Linda and company disrupt a celebration at the club and in the ensuing gunplay Ann is shot and killed. The final scene has Cloris and the survivors opening a diner.

THE MANITOU, 1978 (Avco, Embassy)
CFI Color; Running time - 104 minutes
Producer/Director: William Girdler; Screenplay: Girdler, Jon Cedar and Tom Pope, based on the novel by Graham Masterton; Photographer: Michel Hugo; Editor: Bub Asman; Music: Lalo Schifrin; Set: Cheryl Kearney; Costumes: Michael Faeth & Agnes Lyon; Supervising Editor: Gene Ruggiero; Production Designer: Walter Scott Herndon

CAST:

Harry Erskine: Tony Curtis	Dr. Robert McEvoy: Paul Mantee
Singing Rock: Michael Ansara	Mrs Winconis: Jeanette Nolan
Karen Tandy: Susan Strasberg	Mrs. Hertz: . Lurene Tuttle
Amelia Crusoe: Stella Stevens	Floor Nurse: Ann Mante
Dr. Jock Hughes: Joe Cedar	MacArthur: Hugh Corcoran
Mrs. Karmann: Ann Sothern	Michael: Michael Laren
Dr. Ernest Snow: Burgess Meredith	Misquamacas: Joe Gieb

STORY: Ann plays the aunt of Susan Strasberg, who are both participants in a séance led by phony spiritualist Tony Curtis. Strasberg has the unenviable role of a woman who has a 400-year-old Indian, "The Manitou," growing on her spine. Michael Ansara is the modern-day Indian medicine man, who exorcizes "The Manitou" and saves the heroine's life.

THE LITTLE DRAGONS, 1980
(An Eastwind/Aurora Film Corporation Production)
Color; Running time - 90 minutes
Producers: Hannah Hempstead and Curtis Hanson; Executive Producers: Tony Bill and Robert Bremson; Director: Curtis Hanson; Screenplay: Harvey Applebaum, Louis Gattlee, Rudolph Borchert and Alan Ormsby; Photographer: Stephen Katz; Editor: Ronald Sinclair; Music: Ken Lauber; Art Director: Spencer Quinn

CAST:

J.J.: Charles Lane	Yancey: Joe Spinell
Angel: Ann Sothern	Carl: John Chandler
Zack: Chris Petersen	Sheriff: Clifford a Pellow
Woody: Pat Petersen	Lunsford: Stephen Young
Carol Forbinger: Sally Boyden	Karate Instructor: Pat Johnson
Dick Forbinger: Rick Lenz	Niles: Tony Bill
Ruth Forbinger: Sharon Weber	Deputy: Brad Gorman

STORY: Ann plays Angel, the mother of yokels John Chandler and Joe Spinell. They kidnap Sally Boyden, taking her to the shack where they live. Charles Lane plays the grandfather to Chris and Pat Petersen and together these three rescue Sally with the aid of a motorcycle gang and a group of karate exponents. Ann, in her final scene, is pictured unconscious, sitting in an outdoor privy, which has been exploded.

A LETTER TO THREE WIVES, 1985 (NBC/20th Century-Fox Television)
Color; Running time - 120 minutes
Executive Producer: Michael Filerman; Producer: Karen Moore; Supervising Producer: Robert P. Marcucci Co-producer: Terry Morse; Director: Larry E. Likann; Teleplay: Sally Robinson, based on the 1948 screenplay by Joseph L. Mankiewicz, based on *A Letter to Five Wives* by John Klempner and as adapted for the screen by Vera Caspary; Photographer: Laszlo George; Musical Supervisor: Lionel Newman; Music: Johnny Mandel; Art Direction: Richard Wilcox; Editor: Art Seid; Costume Supervisor: Erica Phillips; Executive Production Manager: Mark Evans; Make-up: Ann Brodie

CAST:

Lora Mae Holloway: Loni Anderson	Nicky Fletcher: Stephen Shellen
Rita Phipps: Michele Lee	Jenny: Nancy Warren
Deborah Bishop: Stephanie Zimbalist	Kate: Karen Austin
Porter Holloway: Ben Gazzara	Freddy: Hagan Beggs
Brad Bishop: Charles Frank	Captain: Richard Sargent
George Phipps: Michael Gross	Logan Phipps: Logan Connaughton
Ma Finney: Ann Sothern	Noah Phipps: Noah Connaughton
Sadie: Doris Roberts	Melissa: Louise Johann
Babe Finney: Whitney Kershaw	Carl: Campbell Lane
Frank Elkin: James Staley	Mickey: Shane Punt
Ted Polikoff: David Garrison	

STORY: Michele Lee and Michael Gross portray the roles Ann and Kirk Douglas enacted in the original 1949 movie, while Ann now plays the mother of Loni Anderson and Whitney Kershaw. The three wives, Stephanie Zimbalist is the third, receive word from a friend that she's run off with one of their husbands. Ben Gazzara is the errant spouse, but returns to his wife, Anderson, at the film's end.

NOTES: The telemovie was filmed entirely on location in Vancouver, British Columbia, Canada.

THE WHALES OF AUGUST, 1987 (Alive/Nelson Entertainment)
Color; Running time - 88 minutes
Executive Producer: Shep Gordon; Producers: Carolyn Pfeiffer and Mike Kaplan; Director: Lindsay Anderson; Screenplay: David Berry, based on his play; Photographer: Mike Fash; Editor: Nicolas Gaster; Music: Alan Price; Sound: Donald Summer; Production Design: Jocelyn Herbert; Set: Susie Hublitz; Art Directors: K.C. Fox and Bob Fox; Costumes: Rudy Dillon and Julie Weiss

CAST:

Libby Strong: Bette Davis
Sarah Webber: Lillian Gish
Mr. Maranov: Vincent Price
Tisha Doughty: Ann Sothern
Joshua Brackett: Harry Carey, Jr.
Mr. Beckwith: Frank Grimes

Old Randall: Frank Pitkin
Young Randall: Mike Bush
Young Libby: Margaret Ladd
Young Sarah: Mary Steenbergen
Young Tisha: Tisha Sterling

STORY: Ann plays a longtime friend to the blind Bette Davis and her sister Lillian Gish. Vincent Price is an impoverished Russian, looking for a home, who firstly flirts with Ann and then moves on to the more comfortably settled Lillian. The sisters quarrel about a window Lillian wants installed so that she can look for the whales on their annual visit. Bette is dead-set against this extravagance. Ann advises Lillian to sell the house and have Bette move in with her daughter. There is no dramatic resolution in this engaging, but slow-moving, study of aging. The sisters remain together at the conclusion, with Bette relenting in her decision on the installation of the window which Lillian wants so much.

INDEX